ANTIQUE TYPEWRITERS

& OFFICE COLLECTIBLES

Identification
&
Value Guide

Darryl Rehr

Best wishes
from
Your Cousin
The Author.

cb

COLLECTOR BOOKS
A Division of Schroeder Publishing Co., Inc.

The current values in this book should be used only as a guide. They are not intended to set prices, which vary from one section of the country to another. Auction prices as well as dealer prices vary greatly and are affected by condition as well as demand. Neither the Author nor the Publisher assumes responsibility for any losses that might be incurred as a result of consulting this guide.

Searching For A Publisher?

We are always looking for knowledgeable people considered to be experts within their fields. If you feel that there is a real need for a book on your collectible subject and have a large comprehensive collection, contact Collector Books.

Cover Design: Beth Summers
Book Design: Benjamin R. Faust

Additional copies of this book may be ordered from:

COLLECTOR BOOKS
P.O. Box 3009
Paducah, KY 42002-3009

or

Darryl Rehr
P.O. Box 641824
Los Angeles, CA 90064

@ $19.95. Add $2.00 for postage and handling.

Copyright © 1997 by Darryl Rehr

Printed in the U.S.A. by Image Graphics, Paducah, KY

Contents

About the Author

Author Darryl Rehr in October 1989, at the opening of the now-defunct National Office Equipment Historical Museum in Kansas City.

Darryl Rehr is a professional journalist who began collecting typewriters in 1984. More than a decade earlier, he purchased a 1911 Royal No. 5 and later, a 1908 Remington No. 10, not as collector's items, but for personal use. Those two early machines did more than just work well, they spurred an interest which has now become a passion.

Antique Typewriters and Office Collectibles is Rehr's first book-length work in the field, but he has written extensively on the subject for more than a decade. His first article appeared in the West-Coast-based publication *Antiques and Collectables* in 1986. Since then, Rehr has written for *Popular Mechanics, The Pittsburgh Press, Antique Trader Weekly, Pennsylvania Magazine, The Office Magazine, Business Electronics Dealer, Spokesman* (magazine of the National Office Machine Dealers Association) as well as dozens of regional and national antiques publications.

Since 1987, Rehr has been editor of *ETCetera*, the journal of the Early Typewriter Collectors Association. *ETCetera* is published quarterly and has become an important resource for collectors nationwide.

Acknowledgments

The author wishes to thank the following organizations, members of the collecting community, and other individuals who have shared their collections, their time, knowledge, and support, in the production of this book: Robert Aubert, Stefan Beck, Uwe Breker, Business Technology Associates, Anthony Casillo, Dennis Clark, Danmark Tekniske Museum, Richard Dickerson, Graham Forsdyke, Thomas Fürth, Thomas Fürtig, Ken Gladstone, Don Hoke, Thor & Gigi Konwin, Bill Kortsch, Thomas Kramer, Mr. & Mrs. David Linn, Linda Linn, Milwaukee Public Museum, Peter Muckermann, John Lundstrom, Bob Moran, Peter Muckermann, Gunter Pschibl, James Rauen, Mr. & Mrs. Aaron Rehr, Jay Respler, John Pace O'Shea, Tom Russo, Sr., Lou Schindler, Heinz Schropp, Alexander Sellers, Frank Smathers, Herb Smith, Lisa Stroup, Ron Wild, Larry Wilhelm, Bernard Williams.

The author himself photographed all machines shown from his own collection, the Milwaukee Public Museum and the Clark, Rauen, Russo, and Kortch collections. Photos of other machines were taken by the collectors themselves, unless otherwise specified.

Who Should Read This Book?

Antique Typewriters and Office Collectibles is intended to be an identification guide, offering a broad view of historical typewriters for anyone who is interested. Specifically, it tries to teach readers how to talk to typewriter collectors about the details of machines which may otherwise seem impossible to describe.

Those who should read this book include:

People who own old typewriters (and may want to sell them)
Using the pictorial guides, this book will allow you to properly identify what you have in terms that collectors can understand. Information in the appendices will show you how to describe a typewriter's condition to potential collector-buyers and how to ship the machine safely.

Dealers who occasionally have old typewriters
There are *thousands and thousands* of collectible typewriters in circulation. The vast majority of dealers who encounter them have no idea what to do with them. The numerous photos in this book will allow you to recognize good machines when they come to you, learn the differences among models, and distinguish those that merely "seem" valuable from those that actually *are* valuable. This book should remain as a handy reference on your shelf, intended to be quickly consulted when old typewriters are offered to you.

People who are curious about old typewriters
Anyone who has ever enjoyed pounding away on a classic machine can be forgiven for being fascinated with them. The incredible variety in historical typewriters is enough to amaze anyone, and this book gives you a wide-ranging look at many of the best. You get a quick history lesson, too.

Typewriter Collectors
The brief summary of typewriter history in this book does not attempt to comprehensively retell the typewriter's past, since that is already covered in other works. However, this is the first time such a large collection of historical photos has been seen in *color*. For that reason alone, this book has a place on every collector's shelf. The emphasis on differences among models will also be helpful to many collectors who want to fine tune their own knowledge of the field.

The Prices in this Book

The prices of old typewriters are highly variable, and often arbitrary. Although typewriter collecting is gaining in popularity, it does not attract the same numbers of people as more traditional antiques. Consistent market prices for typewriters, therefore, have yet to evolve. In other fields, such as stamps, coins, cameras, etc., the large number of collectors permits publication of catalogs with prices that collectors can, to some extent, depend upon. Determining typewriter prices, however, is still something of an art.

The prices in this book are those that a seller can reasonably expect an average typewriter collector to pay (factoring in the reality that many collectors will not want or can't afford a given machine at all). The prices shown are not the highest of retail or the lowest of wholesale and are intended only as a guide. Professional dealers who may specialize in typewriters, or have specific markets for them, do not need to consult these prices, because they already know what their customers will pay.

Rarity, Desirability, Condition

Typewriters are *no different* from any other class of collectibles in what determines price. The three factors are rarity, desirability, and condition.

Condition is critical to value. Good condition enhances the price of a typewriter, poor condition reduces it. Just as real estate agents always say, "Location, location, location," typewriter collectors will say "Condition, condition, condition."

The prices in this book are based on machines that measure at least *six* on a condition scale of *ten* (see Appendix A - Rating Typewriter Condition). A collector who agrees to buy a machine requiring restoration commits himself to a long tedious process, requiring weeks or months of work. Poor condition machines, therefore, may be valued at a *small fraction* of the value of good machines. That's how *important* condition is.

As for rarity and desirability, readers should understand that they are two different things. Certain very rare machines, for whatever reasons, simply don't have the "buzz" that others have among collectors. It's just this "buzz" that creates excitement and desirability. So, a machine that is very rare may not necessarily be very desirable, and therefore, two machines of equal rarity may not sell for equal prices.

Despite all these factors, the *real* value of an antique typewriter (or any collectible) is simply the price someone is willing to pay. At times, sellers will be surprised at how much someone will pay for one of these old pieces of "junk." At other times, fantasies of instant wealth will dissolve into disappointment when something that "looks so weird" turns out to be nothing more than an elaborate boat anchor.

Typewriters as an Investment

Modern interest in collecting typewriters began to gather steam in the early 1980s, going through a period of speculation and peaking about 1989. In many collecting fields, such peaks are often followed by crashes, which was the case for typewriters. Prices dropped rapidly after 1989, and by 1994, leveled off for mid-priced machines, but continued downward for the highest priced machines. Prospects for steady appreciation presently appear unlikely, making collectible typewriters an uncertain choice as an investment instrument for all but experienced experts.

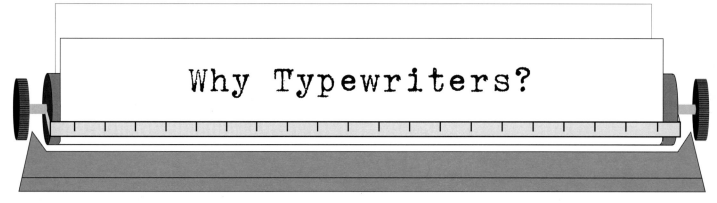

I, like many people, have some very special childhood memories of trips to the office with Dad. With business to do, he would put me in a corner with a few sheets of paper and an old typewriter, allowing me to clatter away to my heart's content. Only years later did a drill sergeant of a summer school typing teacher shout out the terse rhythm of "A! S! D! F!" as my classmates and I learned how to use the QWERTY keys to do our homework. Still, no matter how much the typewriter became an instrument of work, it always was something of a toy to me.

As I entered the professional world, and found myself actually writing for a living, the physical, tactile, muscular "clackety-clack" of manual machines allowed me to put a little bit of my *gut* on the page in a way that today's wimpy electronic word processors can't match. Early in my working life, I found myself in need of a machine for use at home. Being without much to spend, I settled on a Royal No. 5 found at a flea market for about $15. At the time, I didn't know it dated from 1911. All I knew was that it worked, it looked wonderful, and it made a miraculous noise.

The Royal on my desk nagged at my curiosity. Eventually, I did some library research and discovered that the typewriter, first introduced to the market place in 1874, had a history richer than I ever imagined. You'll read about it in the next chapter, but for now, you can imagine my surprise in learning about how many different typewriters were actually invented and how bizarre many of them were. Some of them looked nothing like typewriters at all!

Of course, I never imagined I'd ever be able to see any of those old gizmos outside of any museum (and in fact, most museums that have typewriter collections treat them poorly and don't display them). However, being a con-firmed flea market maniac, I was delighted to see some old machines turning up from time to time. So, I started to buy them.

When did I go from being merely "interested" to becoming a collector? I like to tell people that I became a typewriter collector not when I bought the *first* typewriter I didn't need, but when I bought the *second*. If you're looking for the definition of a typewriter collector, that's it.

Today, more than a decade later, I've found that hundreds of people nationwide share my interest. They are dealers in office equipment, writers, dentists, ad men, teachers, librarians, firefighters, biology professors, you name it! Few of them fill their homes with typewriters, but many display a dozen or two on a pair of convenient shelf units. Typewriter collecting, you see, need not take the huge amounts of space most people think.

While finding good old typewriters is not as easy as finding baseball cards, beer cans, radios, or other "pop" collectibles, good collectors manage to uncover them by keeping their eyes open at all times. That's why you may be surprised to find that a collector you happen to contact already has one of the same machines you'd like to sell. It's not *always* that way, though, and old typewriters should never be ignored, because you never know when what you have is just what a dedicated collector is looking for.

A Short History of Typewriters

For all practical purposes, typewriter history begins in the year 1868, when Christopher Latham Sholes got the idea for the machine that founded the typewriter industry. Working with a group of friends in a primitive Milwaukee machine shop, he created a writing machine which, five years later, was presented to the famous gunmakers E. Remington & Sons., of Ilion, New York.

The resulting machine was called the "Sholes & Glidden Type Writer," and it became the first in a long line of writing machines which later bore the Remington brand name. Carlos Glidden was an associate of Sholes who had an interest in the enterprise and as a result, got his name on the original machine.

Sholes & Glidden Typewriter.

Portrait of Christopher Latham Sholes, inventor of the typewriter. Sholes believed his invention was instrumental in emancipating the world's women by providing them the means to enter the office workplace (Herkimer County Historical Society).

Two entrepreneurs were most responsible for bringing the typewriter to production. James Densmore bought an interest from Sholes early in the process, and pushed the reluctant inventor to perfect the machine to make it marketable. George Washington Newton Yost, an accomplished salesman, helped make the pitch to Remington, persuading the company to sign on as the manufacturer. As the typewriter industry matured, the names of both Yost and Densmore would appear on later machines.

A number of writing machines had been invented before the Sholes & Glidden, but we have little to tell us if Sholes studied and was influenced by them. The first recorded patent for a writing machine is said to have been granted in England to Henry Mills in 1713. Without details about the device or surviving specimens, we aren't even sure it *was* a typewriter. According to typewriter historian Michael Adler, the first *documented* writing machine was made by the Italian nobleman Pellegrino Turri circa 1808. He made the device so a blind lady friend could correspond with him. The machine did not survive but some of the letters did. They are dated 1808 – 1809 and are the oldest known typewritten letters in existence. There are reports of another machine which may pre-date the Turri typewriter, but exact details have not yet surfaced.

Burt Typographer: *The first American Typewriter. (London Science Museum, photo by Bob Moran)*

The first *American* typewriter patent belongs to John Burt of Michigan for a crude machine of 1829 that he called the "Typographer." Other pre-Sholes typewriters of importance include machines invented by Italian Giusseppi Ravizza in 1855, Austrian Peter Mitterhoffer in 1864, and American Charles Thurber in 1843.

Although the Sholes & Glidden deserves credit for launching the typewriter industry, several earlier machines actually did go into production, even if those efforts were evolutionary dead-ends in typewriter history. In France during the 1850s, there was the Clavier Imprimeur invented by Pierre Foucauld. At the same time in Britain, the Hughes Typograph, invented by G.A. Hughes, was manufactured for use by the blind. In the U.S., inventor John Jones contracted with a Rochester, New York, company to make his Mechanical Typographer in 1853.

Mechanical Typographer: *Invented by John Jones. This beautifully decorated prototype was the personal property of the inventor. (Milwaukee Public Museum)*

The entire original production run is said to have been destroyed in a factory fire, but two examples do survive. One is the original prototype, but the other appears to have come from the factory. Perhaps the most-successful pre-Sholes machine to be manufactured was the 1870 "Skrivekugle" (Writing Ball) invented five years earlier by Malling Hansen, a Danish clergyman. The Skrivekugle is said to have had a wide distribution, and a number of examples still exist.

Still, despite all that went before, we mark the *essential* beginning of the typewriter with the first patents granted to Sholes in 1868, and the appearance of the Sholes & Glidden, which first came out of the Remington factory in 1874.

The machine sat on its own stand, with a treadle for the carriage return, and it was decorated with flower decals and gold trimmings. It was no coincidence that the typewriter looked a bit like sewing machines of the day. William Jenne, the Remington engineer who set up the typewriter factory, had been transferred from the firm's sewing machine division.

The Sholes & Glidden typed capitals only, using an "upstrike" design. The type-bars swung upward to the platen, forcing the user to lift the carriage to see the work. Machines of this upstrike format were the industry standard for the next quarter century. Because the typing was hidden from view, they became known as "blind writers."

The keyboard on the Sholes & Glidden was arranged in the QWERTY layout, which remains dominant today. Despite myths to the contrary, the QWERTY keyboard was *not* designed to slow down typists in order to prevent them from jamming the clumsy machine.

The problem was *inside* the machine, where two adjacent type-bars would clash if struck one right after the other. If you have trouble visualizing it, try wiggling your index and ring fingers. See how they rub together? The same thing happened with type-bars inside the developmental typewriter. So, we believe that Sholes arranged the type-bars on the inside so letters which occur frequently in pairs (such as "TH") were *not* adjacent, thus reducing the overall probability of type-bar clashes. When everything was hooked up to the keyboard, QWERTY was the resulting layout.

Skrivekugle (Writing Ball): Manufactured in Denmark beginning in 1870. An early enterprise which antedated the mainstream typewriter industry. (Danmarks Tekniske Museum, Denmark collection, photo: Jan Slot-Carlsen)

The Sholes & Glidden was not an immediate success. In fact, the machines caused their customers considerable trouble and were often returned for repairs. Additionally, potential buyers really didn't know what to make of a typewriter. At the time, the handwritten letter was standard for business correspondence, and there were few people who knew how to operate a typewriter.

It appears that Remington made a concerted effort to supply the work force with typists by training women to operate the machines. The "typist" of the time, however, was called a "typewriter," creating many an amusing situation when there was confusion between the *machine* and its *operator*. One joke of the time had a businessman writing a letter to his wife saying, "I'm sitting here with my typewriter on my lap..." Did he mean the machine... or the young lady who did his typing?

Until this time, there were few respectable occupations for middle-class women, and the business office was strictly an all-male environment. With the typewriter, though, women entered the white-

QWERTY keyboard as it appeared on an original Sholes & Glidden. (Milwaukee Public Museum)

Busy with the typewriter.

Early twentieth century postcard shows the double entendre created because "type-writer" referred both to the machine as well as its operator. (author's collection)

collar world. Today, the machine is seen as something of a ball-and-chain, locking women into low-status clerical jobs. At its beginnings, however, the typewriter was an instrument of female emancipation. An amusing (although corny) portrayal of the female office invasion was the subject of *The Shocking Miss Pilgrim,* a Hollywood film of 1947. Betty Grable played the "typewriter." If you're interested in this part of our social history, you'll get a kick out of this movie.

In 1878, Remington improved the typewriter, introducing its model No. 2. We should note that the machine at this point was marketed principally as the type writer with little reference to Sholes & Glidden or Remington. Only later did the Remington brand name actually appear on the machine. The No. 2 (see page 112) was a black open-framed machine typing both upper and lower cases. Here, finally, was a reliable, efficient, economical writing machine. Sales continued to be slow at first, but in a few years, they began to take off, and a decade after its introduction, the typewriter had gained wide acceptance in the business world.

Until 1880, Remington's typewriters had no competition. In that year, however, George Washington Newton Yost broke away from the Remington enterprise to offer the Caligraph Writing Machine (the term "typewriter" was not yet generic). The first Caligraph (see page 35) was a small, caps-only machine, but the second model gave the product its true identity. The Caligraph No. 2 was a double-case typewriter with a key for every character. On the Remington No. 2, you typed capitals by using the shift key, a novel development at the time. There were *no* shifts on the Caligraph, which instead had a massive "full-keyboard" (more popularly known as a "double-keyboard") with 76 keys, one for each capital, lowercase letter, numeral, and punctuation mark. For 30 years there would be a controversy over which was better, the shift-key or the full-keyboard. The shift-key's advantage was its utility with the 10-fingered touch-typing technique, and as a result, the full-keyboard eventually faded away.

The typewriter was a necessary tool in the burgeoning Industrial Revolution of the late nineteenth century. At the time, American companies were turning out manufactured goods at an incredible pace. However, while factory floors were highly mechanized, factory offices were not. They became bottlenecks of paperwork, all of which had to be laboriously prepared by hand. The typewriter was the means for bringing the laggard office up to the speed.

In 1880, only two typewriters existed on the market. A decade and a half later, there were hundreds. As buyers expressed a desire for writing machines, inventive ingenuity together with the entrepreneurial spirit coupled to bring all sorts of strange typewriters into being. One reason many of these machines took on such odd forms was that each inventor was looking for a way to produce a typewriter without infringing on his competitor's products.

Keyboards on these typewriters may have had anywhere from one to eight rows of keys, rows which usually were straight, but might have been curved or even circular. The type-bars on various models swung from below, behind, from the sides, or in front of the platen. If there were no type-bars, machines may have had type-wheels, type-cylinders, type-strips, or type-shuttles. Inking may have been by ribbon, ink-rollers, or ink pads.

The price of a typical office typewriter was $100 during this period, and that became a target for the competition. The market place was flooded with lower-priced models, some of which were downright cheap. For $1 to $15, almost anyone could buy what became known as an "index" machine — a little typewriter that had no keyboard at all. Instead, there was a pointer or dial for selecting letters and a separate lever for doing the actual printing. Some of these were little more than toys, others were obviously not.

This diversity of design aside, typewriters became largely standardized. The great majority of machines were office-sized blind-writers with either 4-row, shift-key keyboards or double-keyboards.

The standard would change as the typewriter headed for its next stage of development — *visible* writing. Despite industry assertions that good typists did not *need* to see their work, customers disagreed. The greatest success among the visible machines was the Underwood Typewriter (see page 132), introduced in 1895.

The Underwood was a typewriter with a 4-row, shift-key keyboard, but with type-bars striking from the front. This configuration allowed the user to see the work at all times with very few limitations. As the twentieth century began, Underwood came to dominate the typewriter industry, and all other major manufacturers ended up scrapping their blind-writers to produce visible machines. In fact, the 4-row, frontstrike machine became the *new* standard, and things stayed that way until 1961, when IBM introduced its famous single-element Selectric.

The Selectric brings to mind two other branches of typewriter history: that of single-element machines and that of electric typewriters. Beginning with single-elements, we go all the way back to 1879, when Lucien Crandall patented his typewriter based on a cylindrical type-element. The resulting Crandall Typewriter (see page 44) was first produced around 1884. Many other single-element machines found success in the early typewriter market.

As far as electric typewriters are concerned, there were many false starts. One important early failure was the Blickensderfer Electric of 1902 (see page 32). This was an electric version of an existing popular type-wheel machine, nearly 60 years before the IBM Selectric. Unlike the Selectric, in which the type-element moved along a stationary platen, the Blickensderfer Electric had a carriage moving past a stationary type-element. It did a pretty good job as a typewriter, but may have lacked the speed expected of an electric. It failed in the market place.

Remington introduced an electric type-bar machine in 1925, the forerunner to most modern electrics. Only 2,500 of these machines were made before contract problems scuttled the production. The patent owners then formed the Electromatic Typewriter Co. of Rochester, New York, to make their own machine. Electromatic was purchased by International Business Machines, then a manufacturer of time clocks, card sorters, and other office devices. IBM took the Electromatic and created the first great commercial success in electric typewriters. The company marketed the machine to government offices, where filling out multiple copies of forms was common, and the power of an electric to penetrate a stack of carbons was a boon. IBM's success was soon followed by other manufacturers, and electric type-bar machines became common.

When the Selectric came along, single-element typing quickly became the new state-of-the-art. The Selectric was an extremely complex machine, electro-mechanical in operation. The computer chip was not applied to the typewriter until 1977 when Exxon Corporation became the unlikely developer of QYX, the first *electronic* typewriter. Exxon's QYX used a daisy-wheel type element, which became standard among electronic machines. Curiously, the daisy-wheel dates back to 1890, when it was used on the Victor Typewriter (see page 134), a $15 index machine.

The typical modern typewriter is now an electronic daisy-wheel machine, usually embellished with a considerable array of computerized word-processing functions. In fact, many of the original writing tasks assigned to the typewriter are now done using computers and computer printers, with nothing that can be called a typewriter involved. In today's business world, actual typewriters are often relegated to occasional use only, perhaps just the typing of envelopes, labels, or pre-printed-forms, jobs which are inconvenient to do on laser printers.

Apart from the shrinking group of people who work on typewriters due to personal preference, the obsolescence of this machine is being delayed by its widespread use in the Third World. Established typewriter makers still find sizable markets for manual machines in developing countries, where electric service may be spotty or non-existent. So, the typewriter may have passed its prime, but it is not yet completely a thing of the past.

The Mechanisms of Typewriters

One of the factors critical to understanding old typewriters is understanding the different mechanisms designed into them. Read this section to understand how collectors classify the many kinds of typewriters that history has handed down to us.

Keyboard or Index?

Typewriters are generally divided up into two main classes: **keyboard** and **index** machines. The difference is simple. Keyboard typewriters have keyboards and index typewriters do not. Instead of keyboards, index machines use pointers or dials to select letters, which are printed (very slowly, of course) one at a time. Typewriter collectors like to describe the speed of index machines at about "a page a day."

Printing Mechanisms

Beyond the keyboard/index division, typewriters are described according to their printing mechanisms. Most typewriters have their printing letters on the end of rods called **type-bars** which swing to hit the platen in various ways. Otherwise, the printing mechanism may be some sort of **single-element.**

Type-Bar Typewriters

Type-bar machines represent the lion's share of typewriters, and they break down into a number of sub-classes depending on how the type-bars are oriented.

Upstrike: this is the classic mechanism introduced on the 1874 Sholes & Glidden, and standard on most typewriters until 1900. Type-bars swing up to the platen from underneath. The user has to lift the carriage to see the work. Also known as understrike or blind-writer (examples: Remington, Densmore).

Downstrike: type-bars standing up in the air, and swinging down to the platen. There are three variations:

Downstrike (front): type-bars arranged in front of the platen, swinging down and forward (examples: Franklin, Bar-Lock).

Downstrike (side): type-bars arranged in two groups, straddling the platen, and swinging down from the side. Sometimes called "side-strike" (example: Oliver).

Backstroke: type-bars arranged behind platen and swinging down from the rear (examples: Brooks, Fitch).

Thrust-action: type-bars usually arranged radially in a fan pattern in front of the platen. They slide forward along a plane toward the printing point (examples: Wellington, Ford).

Frontstrike: this is the format on 98% of all manual typewriters in existence (most of which are not collectors items). The type-bars are generally horizontal and swing forward to hit the platen from the front. On some fronstrike machines, the type-bars were not horizontal, but raised as much as 45 degrees. These are called *oblique* frontstrike machines. An alternative term is "semi-frontstrike." Frontstrike machines are also called visible typewriters, although the visible category also includes machines with downstrike, thrust-action, and grasshopper movements as well. The best known of the frontstrikes is the famous Underwood.

Grasshopper: odd format in which the type ends of the type-bars rest in ink pads and "hop" into place to contact the platen (examples: Williams, Maskelyne).

Plunger: types are on the forward cross-sections of rods, which strike the platen in the same direction as their axis. Often called "radial plunger" for machines such as the Skrivekugel, on which type-bars radiated from the printing point (examples: Skrivekugel, Edison).

Single-Element Typewriters

Many different types of single-elements were used on old typewriters. Wheel-shaped or cylindrical type-elements are usually called **type-wheels**. If the cylinder is elongated, the usual term is **type-sleeve**. A single-element in the shape of a curved strip is called a **type-shuttle** or a **swinging-sector** (that is, a sector of a circle). Many single-element keyboard machines work with a hammer at the rear striking the paper against the type-element. On others, the type-element strikes the paper directly.

Different Keyboards

Keyboards on early typewriters came in all shapes and sizes. Most common is the **4-row** keyboard, with three letter rows and one numerical row, using a shift key for capitals and punctuation (two characters per type-bar). Many other machines have **3-rows** for letters, with one shift key for capitals and a different shift key (usually labeled "figs") for numbers and punctuation (three characters per type-bar). Still other typewriters, may have as few as a single row of keys or as many as eight rows or more. Keyboards with six or more rows, offering a key for every character (that is, without shift keys) are usually called **double-keyboards.** Technically, a double-keyboard is one that duplicates the arrangement (usually QWERTY) for both upper and lower case letters. We distinguish this from a full-keyboard, in which the upper and lower case arrangements are different. Typically, lowercase letters are in the QWERTY arrangement, and the capitals are scattered on either side of the lowercase array. Double-keyboard, however is the common collector's term for either of these large keyboards.

Though most machines have keys arranged in straight rows, many do not. Keyboards may also be **curved** or **circular**. These oddities are certainly spectacular to the modern eye, even if some are fairly common to collectors.

Letter Layouts

There are also differences in how the letters are arranged on the keys. We're all familiar with the QWERTY format. It was present on the Sholes & Glidden, the first typewriter, and is still the standard keyboard today. No wonder it is also called the *Universal* keyboard.

There were many other layouts, however. The Blickensderfer Typewriter, for instance, is usually seen with a keyboard having the letters "DHIATENSOR" in the lowest row. The theory was to have the most common letters in the row closest to the user, and the company called it the *Scientific* keyboard. The 2-row, semi-circular keyboard featured on some Hammond Typewriters put the most-used letters under the right hand. Hammond dubbed its keyboard the *Ideal*, a name often mistakenly applied to the Blickensderfer and other non-standard layouts.

Inking: Ribbons, Rollers, or Pads

Ribbons have been used to ink the type on typewriters from the very beginning. Most machines prior to 1900 used rather large ribbons, usually about 1½" wide. Later, ½" became the standard ribbon width.

Other machines used **rollers** or **pads** to ink the type. Type-bar pad inkers (such as Yost and Williams) are particularly interesting because of the mechanical gymnastics needed to get the type-bar from pad to platen.

Index Machines

Though they make up the other major division among typewriters, **index** machines share some of the same characteristics. Most index machines print with single elements. They may have used type-wheels or swinging sectors as on some keyboard machines, but they are also found with type-elements that are unique to index machines. The Hall Typewriter, for instance, used a rectangular rubber plate. Many index typewriters used a straight solid rod or rubber strip, which slid back and forth as each letter was chosen. Such typewriters are called **linear** index machines.

The "index" on index typewriters refers to the chart used to select letters on the machine. It may be in the form of a straight line, a rectangular array, a curved strip, a circle, or even a simulated keyboard layout. As with other aspects of typewriter design, it seems that every possible alternative was attempted.

An index typewriter is generally described by either the shape of its index or type-element, whichever is more descriptive.

How to Describe a Machine to a Collector

Actually, if you correctly identify the name and model of a machine, knowledgeable collectors will know what you have with little further explanation. However, some people find machines with no names or those with obscure name-variants of familiar brands. If you can describe a machine in terms of its **keyboard (or index)** and **printing mechanism**, you will be well understood. An Underwood, for instance, is described as a "4-row, frontstrike," and a Blickensderfer is a "3-row, type-wheel." You'll get more of an idea of how this is done simply by reading the captions accompanying the photos in this book. Each machine is identified by name, followed by a shorthand description of its mechanism in parentheses.

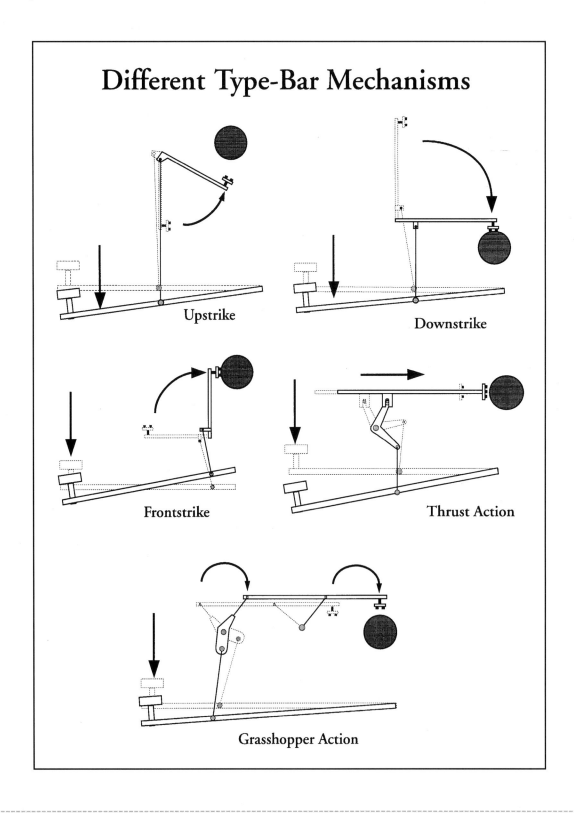

Different Type-Bar Mechanisms

Upstrike

Downstrike

Frontstrike

Thrust Action

Grasshopper Action

Different Single Elements

Type-Sleeve mechanism of
the Crandall Typewriter

Horizontal Type-Sleeve from
the Chicago Typewriter

Type-Wheel from the
Blickensderfer Typewriter

Type-Shuttle from the
Hammond Typewriter

Parts of a Typewriter

In the course of this book, references are made to certain parts of typewriters that may be unfamiliar to you. Just about everyone knows what a *keyboard* or a *carriage* is, but not all can point out the *paper table* or the *segment*.

Some of the important parts of typewriters are shown here in a number of illustrations. For more complete information, read the explanations below.

Carriage Return Lever — any arm, lever, or tab used to move or *return* the carriage to the beginning of a new line. The "return" key on computer keyboards owes its name to this typewriter function.

Feed Rollers — rollers which usually rest against the platen. The paper is fed through the feed rollers and the platen by friction between the two.

Index — on an index machine, the strip or chart from which you choose which letter you want to type.

Indicator — on an index machine, an arm, or pointer or similar device which points to (or "indicates") the letter to be printed.

Key — the button you press to type a character. Some people mistakenly use the word *keys* to refer to type-bars, but a key is little more than a button with a letter on it.

Key Lever — the long, metal (or wood) lever on which the key sits. It is generally attached to a type-bar link, usually a pull rod or its equivalent which actuates the type-bar.

Paper Bail — a rod with or without rollers, resting against the platen to hold the paper in place.

Paper Comb — a row of fingers cut into a thin strip of metal used to hold the paper against the platen. This device is most often seen on index machines.

Paper Fingers — usually curved metal strips mounted against the platen to hold the paper in place. These sometimes have small rollers built-in.

Paper Release — a lever on a typewriter which allows the paper to be pulled out quickly. Usually, it opens a gap between the feed rollers and the platen.

Paper Table — usually a flat or curved piece of sheet metal behind the platen. It helps to position the paper when you feed it into the machine and supports it afterward.

Platen — on most typewriters, this is the rubber cylinder resting under the paper as typing is done. Technically, it is any firm surface providing support behind the paper for printing. It can be a rubber cylinder, or a flat table, or even a tiny rubber cap on the end of a hammer.

Print Key — on an index machine, the key, or lever you must press for the machine to print after you've chosen your letter.

Scale — a ruler on a machine showing the numerical position of characters on a line.

Segment — usually a semi-circular metal block with slots to hold the type-bars at their pivot points.

Shift-lock Lever — on Remington upstrike machines, this is found on the left side, behind the keyboard. It is attached to a spring and flipping it shifts the carriage to one position or another. The shift-lock function on most other machines is a key or catch attached to the shift key.

Space key — on an index machine, the key or lever you press to get a space. Different in form (but not function) from the familiar space bar on most keyboard machines.

Type-basket — a term collectively applied to all of the type-bars on a given machine.

Type-bars — rods or bars with the actual printing types on their ends. The type-bars swing against the platen, hit the ribbon, and their impact creates the printed letter on the paper.

Type-bar Link — a connection between the key lever and the type-bar. When the key-lever is moved, it pulls on the type-bar link, which in turn, pulls on the type-bar to make it swing. The link can be a simple rod or something more complex.

Type-wheel — one variety of many single type elements used on machines which don't have type-bars.

Typewriter Parts

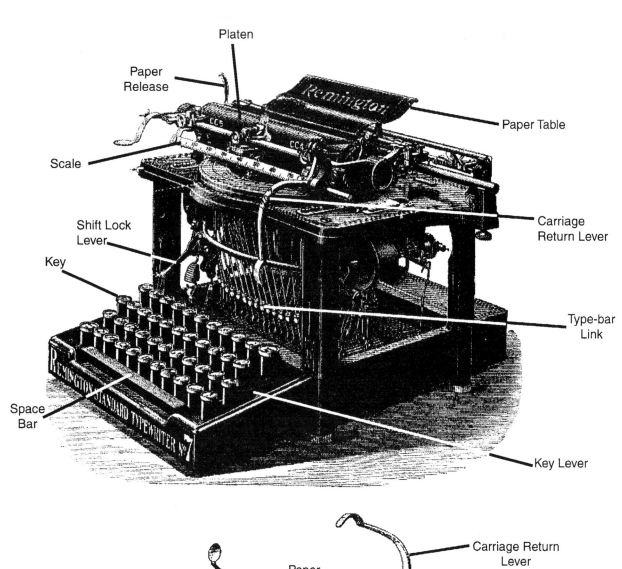

Platen

Paper Release

Paper Table

Scale

Shift Lock Lever

Carriage Return Lever

Key

Type-bar Link

Space Bar

Key Lever

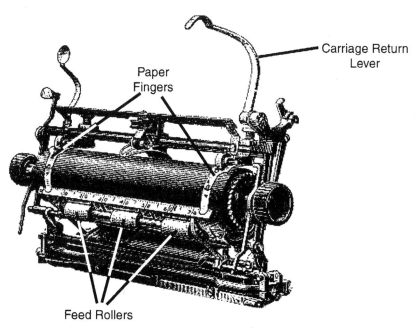

Carriage Return Lever

Paper Fingers

Feed Rollers

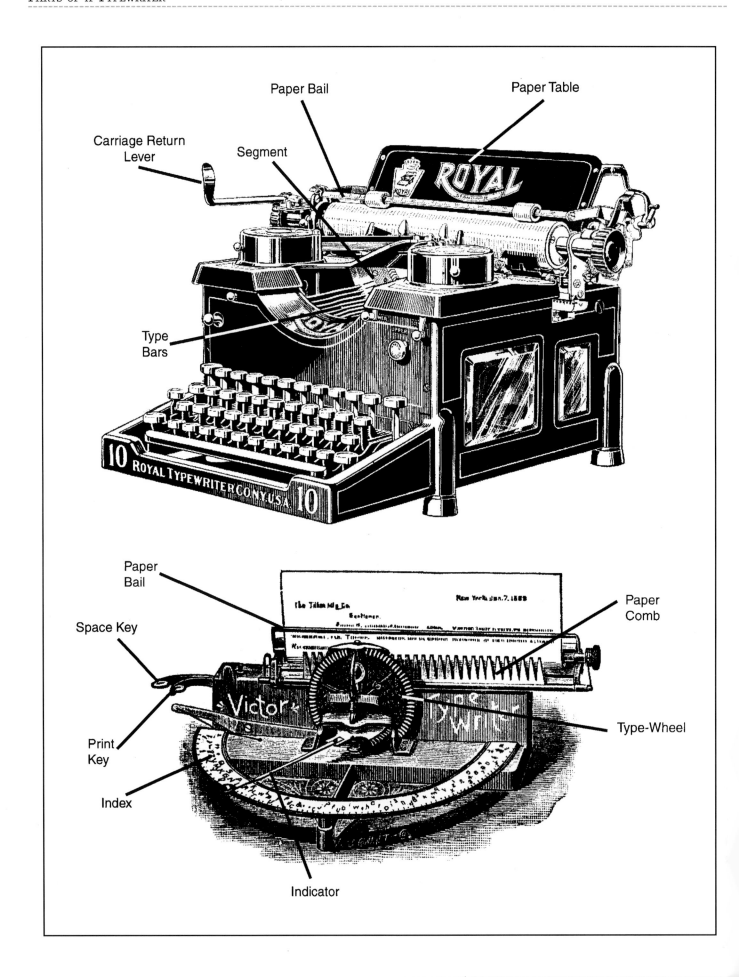

Paper Bail

Paper Table

Carriage Return Lever

Segment

ROYAL

Type Bars

Paper Bail

Paper Comb

Space Key

Type-Wheel

Print Key

Index

Indicator

Historical Typewriters:
Listings by Name

Historical typewriters of interest to collectors are listed here, alphabetically by name. Name-variants of the various makes are *italicized*. The accompanying photos illustrate the important models of each make, where photos were available. The owner or source of the machine in each photo (at the time the photo was taken) is shown in parentheses at the end of each caption. When available, the serial number is shown as well.

We should note that writing the history of something such as the typewriter is like shooting at a moving target. As soon as we think we've established one fact, new evidence surfaces to prove us wrong. The descriptions of the following machines represent the author's best efforts to pin down the pertinent details as accurately as possible, using documentary evidence as well as observations of machines themselves. A number of expert collectors have been consulted to confirm and correct the information presented. Still, there will be assertions here that will be conclusively disproven before the ink is dry on these pages.

Of particular concern is anything we might say in absolute terms. It's somewhat dangerous to contend that a certain machine *never* has a particular feature, or that another machine *always* has a specific characteristic. As soon as that's said, someone is bound to discover a machine that breaks the rule.

The scope of this section is fairly broad, but it doesn't include every typewriter ever made. Conventional 4-row, frontstrike machines, for instance, are not included unless they have certain importance in the story of the typewriter industry. This book also has an American slant, but many interesting foreign machines are listed as well. Brief notes on additional typewriters, not included in this section (and for which photos may have been unavailable), are listed in the annotated index.

Adler

Adler typewriters, made in Germany, have a long history, going back to 1898. At the time, the Adlerwerke company was in the business of building bicycles, but also saw great potential in the burgeoning typewriter market. So licenses were obtained from Wellington Parker Kidder to produce what is essentially a copy of his Wellington typewriter (see page 137).

The very first Adlers were labeled *Empire,* which was the name given to Wellington-design machines distributed outside the United States. These Adler *Empires* showed the Adler company as their maker and are desirable today. Many other models of this machine were made, the most familiar being the No. 7.

Later Adlers were developed independently of the Wellington/Empire enterprise, taking on their own particular form and style. Among them is the No. 8, which had an interchangeable type-basket to accomplish changes of typeface. Another Adler of special interest is the No. 11, a rather remarkable machine with six characters on each typebar. A double system of double-shifts allows typing from two separate typefaces on the same machine.

Other collectible Adler models include thrust-action machines with 4-row keyboards as well as 3- and 4-row portables (some called "Klein Adler") which were made well into the late 1940s. One 3-row portable was sold as the *Blick Universal* (relationship to Blickenderfer is unclear). Later models used conventional front-striking type-bars.

A machine called the *Protos* was made in 1922, a direct copy of the Adler No. 7. Machines under the *Protos* name also copied the Klein Adler portables. Another Adler imitator was 1923's *DWF.*

The company remained in business as Triumph-Adler through 1995, when it ceased production of typewriters.

Empire (made by Adler) $200.00
Adler No. 7, most other thrust-action models . . .$50.00
Adler 4-row portables, Klein Adler $50.00
Adler No. 8, removable type-basket $100.00
Adler No. 11, 3-row, 4 shifts $200.00

Adler No. 7 (3-row, thrust-action): The No. 7 is among the most common of the old thrust-action Adlers. Note the elaborate decal on the flat deck. "Adler" means "eagle" in German, and the company logo consists of an eagle perched on a bicycle wheel. That's because Adler made bicycles before it got into typewriters. An Adler No. 7 isn't very desirable unless the decals are in good shape. The company remained in business as Triumph-Adler through 1995, after which it was purchased by Olivetti.(Russo Collection, ser. 254809)

Adler No. 11 (3-row, thrust-action): The Adler No. 11 has an arrangement of four different shift keys, allowing the typing of six different characters from each type-bar. The arrangement permitted two different typefaces on the machine at the same time. (Fürtig Collection)

Klein Adler No. 2 (4-row, thrust-action): The Klein Adler No. 2 (1930s) is one of many later Adler models on which a 4-row keyboard is coupled to a thrust action. The characteristic fan shape is still in evidence, hinting at the layout of the type-bars within the machine. (Russo Collection, ser. 326803)

Allen

The Allen Typewriter got its name from Allentown, Pennsylvania, where it was manufactured beginning in 1918. It was the last machine created by Richard Uhlig, an inventor of many other typewriters.

Allen, 3-row (3-row, frontstrike): A fairly conventional 3-row machine. In American Typewriters, A Collector's Encyclopedia, *Paul Lippman wrote that the Allen came in two slightly different versions. One is the example shown, with the frame contour curved to match the type-basket. On the other, the frame is straight across. (Milwaukee Public Museum)*

The Allen appeared with both three and four rows of keys, and is said to be the first portable with a modern tab key. Besides the basic black, a nickel-plated version of the Allen has also been reported.

Allen (black) **$50.00**
Allen (nickel) **$150.00**

Allen, 4-row (4-row, frontstrike): Michael Adler, author of The Writing Machine, *wrote that the Allen's commercial failure was blamed on its 3-row keyboard. This photo shows that a 4-row machine was also attempted. (Milwaukee Public Museum)*

American

The American family of typewriters was a diverse little group of several appealing machines made by the American Typewriter Co. of New York.

The American keyboard machine (1901) had an odd, flat, rectangular deck dominating its unusual appearance. It was a 3-row upstrike machine in which key and type were at either ends of a single rod. The rod pivoted in the middle as the key was struck, sending the type end upward to the platen. The geometry of this system caused keys at the outer extremes of the keyboard to swivel to the side noticeably when struck. Collectors often say it feels like typing when you're drunk!

The American keyboard machine was made in a number of essentially similar models (Nos. 7 & 8 are most familiar). Reported name variants include *Congress, Eagle, Elgin, Fleet, Mercantile, Pullman,* and *Surety.* There were also foreign labels including *Armstrong* in England, *Herald* in France, *Europa* and *Favorite* in Germany.

The earlier American index machine (1893) was completely different from its keyboard cousin. It typed from a rubber strip mounted on a swinging sector, with inking by rollers. Two models were made. The No. 2 was slightly beefier than the No. 1, but was otherwise similar. The model numbers were not marked on the machine, making it difficult for the untrained eye to differentiate the two versions. The American index was sold in Britain as the *Globe.* Other examples are found marked with the name *Lyon Manutacturing Co., Toronto, Canada.* At least one specimen shows no name on the machine, but *Boston Crown* on a metal lid that fits over the base. Other name-variants reported are *American Globe, Champignon, New American,* and *Sterling.*

The American Typewriter Co. also produced several lightweight index machines, considered to be toys by many collectors. The American Visible Typewriter of 1901 (also sold as *Young American*) was a cheap sheet metal machine, printing via a rubber strip and with letter selection by an indicator passing over a false keyboard (which, in essence is a linear index). On most of these, pressing on this false keyboard did the printing, but on some models there was a lever on the left-hand side for that function.

American keyboard, any model **$100.00**
American index, any model **$100.00**
American Visible, any model **$125.00**

American No. 7 (3-row, upstrike): This typewriter is easily identified by its flat profile. On this particular example the paper table behind the platen has a decal reading "American No. 8," while on the frame, "No. 7" is indicated. Such incongruities are not uncommon among old typewriters. The factory could have run out of No. 7 paper tables during its final run and substituted a No. 8 from the bin awaiting production on the new machines. Or, a typewriter repair shop (or a collector) might have replaced a defective old paper table with a newer one. (Milwaukee Public Museum)

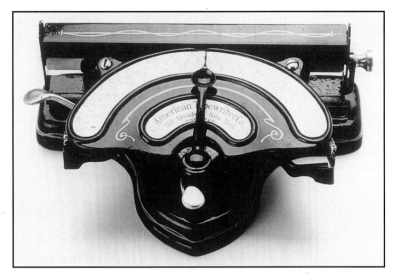

American index No. 1 (curved index): *A machine characterized by the broad curve of its letter index. The nickel-plated lever at the machine's left was pressed to print after each letter was selected. Illustrations in advertisements showed this machine marked as the "American $5 Typewriter." Later, the $5 was changed to $6. This specimen, however, shows only the name of its maker, "American Typewriter Co." (Konwin collection)*

American index No. 2 (curved index): *The second model of the American index was advertised as the No. 2, but not marked as such. This later version was slightly larger than its predecessor and is more commonly found. The number "583c" is seen stamped into most machines but cannot be considered a serial number. (Russo collection)*

American Visible, early (linear index): *A cheap, sheet-metal device which may have been intended to be a toy. This is apparently the earlier of two models, but we have no hard data to confirm the fact. "Early" and "late" designations here are educated guesses. Each letter was selected on the false keyboard with a pointer that moved from side to side. The nickel-plated lever at left made the machine print. (Rauen collection, ser. 5812)*

American Visible, late (linear index): *On this machine, you placed your finger in the thimble mounted on the indicator. When it arrived over the desired letter you pressed down, and the whole keyboard plate moved to do the printing. Note the sharp, angular lines at the front edge, as opposed to the curve on the other version. (Russo collection)*

American Standard
(see Jewett)

Anderson

The Anderson Shorthand Typewriter was an odd machine with an obvious purpose. At least five different models of this device were made from 1887 onwards in cities as diverse as Memphis, Tennessee; Boston, Massachusetts; and New York, New York. As with modern shorthand typewriters, many keys could be struck simultaneously, so that shorthand code for a complete word or syllable would be printed at a single stroke.

Anderson Shorthand Typewriter **$125.00**

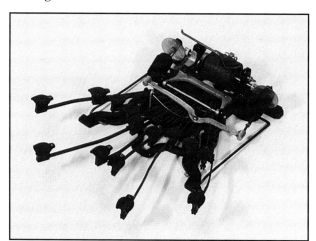

Anderson Shorthand Typewriter: *The forerunner of modern steno machines, this device typed several letters at a stroke to signify a whole word or syllable. The strange keyboard arrangement made use of every finger and even the heels of the hands. (Milwaukee Public Museum)*

Automatic

The Automatic Typewriter, made about 1881, was one of the most intriguing machines produced by the early typewriter industry in the U.S. It had an odd, flat design, typing caps only, with three rows of keys and a space bar placed above the top row rather than below the bottom row. Engraved on the space bar was the brand name "Automatic." The machine was made mostly of brass and had a jacket of wood surrounding the base.

The Automatic was an upstrike machine, inked with ink pads and with type-bars moving in a grasshopper action toward the platen. The machine employed "proportional" spacing, which allotted different widths to different letters (a "w" took more room than an "i," for instance). Its platen was faceted to offer a flat printing surface to the types, since the machine's makers apparently chose not to make (or purchase) type with the slightly curved typefaces to accommodate the circumference of a smooth cylindrical platen.

The Automatic was invented by a U.S. Army officer, Major E.M. Hamilton of Brooklyn, New York, and it is sometimes referred to as the *Hamilton Automatic.* Few of these machines were made, leaving even fewer survivors today.

Automatic . . . .**$1,000.00+**

Automatic (3-row, grasshopper upstrike): *Made mostly of brass, the Automatic is a small, flat machine of unusual design. Note the space bar located above the keys instead of below them. A wooden frame was provided to surround the machine, but it is absent in this specimen. (Dickerson collection, ser. 58).*

Bar-Lock

The Bar-Lock line of typewriters, invented by Charles Spiro of New York, included not only the Bar-Lock but also the later Columbia Bar-Lock and the still later Columbia. All of the machines had downstrike type-bars and were produced by the Columbia Typewriter Manufacturing Co. in New York.

The Bar-Lock name came from a unique alignment feature. There was a set of tiny vertical pins just in front of the printing point. In typing, each type-bar swung down, and was wedged (or "locked") between two of the pins ensuring a perfect printing position.

The most distinctive feature of the Bar-Lock machines was the shield which surrounded the type-bars. On the earliest machines (Nos. 1 – 3), the shield was iron, with small openings among the heavy ornaments. On Nos. 4 – 7, the fancy shield was made of copper, with large openings. Nos. 8 and later featured a plain copper shield, which was more functional than ornamental.

There has been quite a bit of confusion about the different models of Bar-Locks and related machines. Beyond the No. 1, all of the odd-numbered models apparently were simply wide-carriage versions of the even-numbered counterparts. For instance, an 1891 advertisement tells us the Bar-Lock No. 2 had a 9" carriage, and the No. 3 had a 14" carriage.

The most obvious differences between the No. 1 and No. 2 Bar-Locks were the details of their shields. The No. 1 had a large monogram of the letter "B" in the center, while the No. 2 had the name brand spelled out. It is reported that the No. 1 was sold in Europe only beginning in 1888. The man behind marketing the machine was W.J. Richardson of Britain, who had distributed the earlier Columbia index machine (see page 40) in his own country and on the continent. Richardson claimed he had considerable influence over the design of the Bar-Lock, insisting that Spiro include visible writing and no shift keys. American sales of Bar-Lock machines apparently began with the No. 2, which was widely advertised in late nineteenth century magazines.

Later models of the Bar-Lock were clearly marked. Models No. 4 and 6 bore model numbers embossed directly into the shield. Models 8 through 14 had name-plates mounted on the frame directly behind the keyboard.

Generally speaking, models earlier than No. 12 had double-keyboards, while 12 and later were 4-row machines with shift-keys for caps. There are exceptions, to be sure — at least one double-keyboard machine is marked as No. 19. To further complicate the situation, the machine was called simply "Bar-Lock" on all models prior to No. 8. The name then changed to "Columbia Bar-Lock" until the 4-row No. 12, when "Bar-Lock" was dropped, making the name "Columbia" (some are called "Columbia Standard"). The Bar-Lock downstrike machines were marketed as *Royal Bar-Lock* in England.

The Columbia Typewriter Manufacturing Co. eventually sold out its interests to a British firm, which set up shop in Nottingham as the Bar-Lock Typewriter Co. Under this banner, a new line of 4-row, frontstrike machines with the Bar-Lock name was made, with production continuing into the mid 1950s. Such machines have little collectible value. The Nottingham firm also produced the Bar-Let portable (1930), based on the German Mitex typewriter.

Most desirable among the downstrike Bar-Locks are the "fancy-front" machines. The double-keyboard "plain-front" machines are more common and have lesser value. The 4-row, plain machines are scarce but do not seem to have value proportional to their rarity. Wide carriage versions of all machines are quite rare, but their value is not necessarily much different than the corresponding short carriage machines.

Bar-Lock No. 1, iron fancy front with "B" $1,000.00
Bar-Lock No. 2 – 3, iron fancy front $600.00
Bar-Lock No. 4 – 7, copper fancy front $350.00
Columbia Bar-Lock No. 8 – 13, plain front $100.00
Columbia No. 12 – 14, 4-row $200.00
Bar-Let, black $35.00
Bar-Let, colors $50.00

Bar-Lock No. 1 (double-keyboard, downstrike): The Bar-Lock No. 1 is identified by its ornate type-bar shield made of iron. A large letter "B" is cast into the shield. (Williams collection, ser. 1559)

Bar-Lock No. 2 (double-keyboard, downstrike): The iron type-bar shield on this machine is even more densely ornate than the No. 1. Notice that there is no longer an initial "B," and the name is spelled out instead. (Williams collection, ser. 5188)

Bar-Lock No. 4 (double-keyboard, downstrike): The fancy shield on this model is made of soft copper. Large openings expose the type-bars behind the shield. (Milwaukee Public Museum)

Bar-Lock No. 6 (double-keyboard, downstrike): This model is practically indistinguishable from the No. 4. Fortunately, the model number is clearly marked at the lower right corner of the shield. (Dickerson collection, ser. 34396)

Columbia Bar-Lock No. 8 (double-keyboard, downstrike): Beginning with No. 8, Columbia was added to the Bar-Lock name, and the shield was simplified. It is probable that the shield on this specimen was polished bright by one of its previous owners. It was originally painted black with copper highlights. (Russo collection, ser. 47547)

Columbia Bar-Lock No. 10 (double-keyboard, down-strike): *This machine would be hard to tell from the earlier No. 8, but a small name plate, located on the frame behind the top row of keys, bears the model number, confirming that this is a No. 10. (Milwaukee Public Museum)*

Columbia Standard No. 14 (4-row, downstrike): *An obvious departure from earlier machines. Note the 4-row keyboard in place of the cumbersome double-keyboard. (Milwaukee Public Museum)*

Bar-Let No. 2 (3-row, frontstrike): *This little 3-row portable was available in black, red, blue, maroon, and green (shown). An earlier model had covered ribbon spools atop the machine's shell. On the No. 2, the spools are hidden within. (Williams collection)*

Bennett
(Junior)

The diminutive Bennett Typewriter of 1910 was was the smallest keyboard typewriter ever produced. A 3-row, type-wheel machine, it measured a mere 10" x 4" x 1" and slipped easily into any desk drawer. Most of these mediocre machines were probably forgotten there, a fact which may account for the relatively large number that have survived today.

This typewriter was the invention of Charles Bennett of New Jersey, and first appeared on the market as the Junior in 1907. Both the Junior and Bennett were essentially alike, except that the Junior was inked by rollers and the Bennett by a ribbon.

Bennett $60.00
Junior $100.00

Bennett, black (3-row, type-wheel): *The tiny Bennett typewriter was priced at $18 at a time when full-size machines cost $100. Even in 1910, though, you got what you paid for. The Bennett was not built for endurance and many do not function well today. Decals on black machines may be all gold or red bordered in gold as shown. (author's collection)*

Bennett, silver (3-row, type-wheel): *Collectors may show a slight preference for the silver version of this machine, which has decals in black and red. Otherwise, it is no different from the black version. The decal on the paper table is often in worn condition on Bennetts. (author's collection, ser. 33653)*

Junior (3-row, type-wheel, ink roller): *Predecessor to the Bennett, the Junior is nearly the same. Obvious differences are the lack of a paper table (the hinged metal flap behind the platen) and the use of an ink roller instead of a ribbon. Juniors always seem to appear in black. Apparently, no silver version was offered. (Milwaukee Public Museum)*

Bijou
(See Erika)

Bing

The Bing Typewriter dates from 1927 and was the product of Bingwerke, A.G., the famous toy maker of Germany. You would think then, that this was supposed to be sold as a toy typewriter, but we actually have little evidence to prove it, and collectors are divided on the issue. An instruction manual calls it "Bings Instructive Typewriter." But instructive for whom?

The Bing is a common 4-row, oblique frontstrike machine made entirely of sheet metal, excluding expensive castings of any kind. The Bing came in two models. No. 1 was inked by an ink pad, No. 2 by a ribbon. On the Bing No. 2, the row of text being typed was obscured by the ribbon, and the user had to press the lever on the left side to jog the carriage upward so the work could be examined.

Most Bings are black, although some were produced in white (or ivory) either under the Bing name or as the *Student* Typewriter. No Bing or variant is complete unless it has its tin base and cover.

Bing **$35.00**

Bing No. 1 (4-row, oblique frontstrike, ink pad): A German product of the late 1920s, made by a major toy manufacturer. Notice the absence of ribbon spools, and the ink pad placed in front of the printing point. (Milwaukee Public Museum)

Bing No. 2 (4-row, oblique frontstrike): The No. 2 model of the Bing has a small ribbon for inking and is usually clearly labeled as "No. 2." (Milwaukee Public Museum, no serial number)

Student (4-row, oblique frontstrike): The ivory colored Student typewriter, with its gold trim, is an interesting name-variant of the Bing No. 2. Notice the nickel-rimmed keys, different from the solid metal keys on the Bing machine. (author's collection, no serial number)

Blickensderfer

There are few old typewriters with as much charm and as much history as the Blickensderfer Typewriter. People never cease to be amazed when they see its little type-wheel spin into action at the press of a key, whirring into position before brushing past the ink roller on its way to deposit each letter upon the paper.

Invented by George C. Blickensderfer, it was introduced to the public in 1893 at the Columbian Exposition in Chicago. It created quite a stir at the time, and it's said that other major manufacturers dropped out of a planned typewriter competition when the Blickensderfer appeared.

Although company literature mentions Models 1, 2, and 3, apparently the first model actually manufactured for the public was the Blickensderfer No. 5, a small typewriter with a space bar that folded inward so the machine would fit inside its oak case. It was produced at the company factory in Stamford, Connecticut, but did not appear in substantial numbers until 1895. The original Blickensderfer factory still stands, by the way. It is currently vacant, but was recently occupied by Pitney-Bowes, the people who make postage meters.

The No. 5 and No. 7 Blicks (yes, they are called "Blick" for short) are the most common of these machines. The No. 7 of 1897, featured a wraparound space bar, and sat on a wooden base, which was usually accompanied by a bentwood cover. A heavier version of the No. 7 was offered after 1900. It is identified by the four screws holding the top casting to the machine's base. Earlier machines have only two screws for that purpose.

Hundreds of different Blickensderfer-type elements were available in every imaginable type style and language. Extra type elements, in fact, are often found with surviving Blicks today.

Most Blickensderfers are found with what the company called its Scientific keyboard. The most often-used letters (DHIATENSOR) were placed on the bottom row, closest to the user. The company did offer the Universal (QWERTY) keyboard upon request, but strongly advised against it.

Blickensderfer models were not necessarily released in numerical order. Machines postdating the Nos. 5 & 7 include the Blickensderfer No. 6 (c. 1906), an aluminum clone of the No. 5 (although you will occasionally see an aluminum No. 5 as well, since the company offered all models in aluminum if requested). The Featherweight Blick was another aluminum machine, very similar to the No. 6, but with a backspace key. The No. 8 (1908) featured a wraparound frame similar to larger typewriters and offered a tabulator system. In 1916, the No. 9 succeeded the No. 8, but was very similar with only subtle differences. Interim machines included names such as the Home Blick, Service Blick, World Blick, and others, made for mail order or other special markets. In France, the Blickensderfer was sold under the *Dactyle* name. At least two dozen Blickensderfer variations are known.

The dazzling star of the Blickensderfer lineup is the Blickensderfer Electric, which first appeared around 1902, but died a quick death. Another attempt at marketing the machine in 1906 was also unsuccessful. The Blick Electric essentially did everything that the IBM Selectric did more than 50 years later; everything except succeed in the market place, that is. Very few of these machines survived, and if you find one, *don't* plug it in. The insulation may fail and damage the motor. It's thought that most Blickensderfer Electrics ran on DC current, but at least one example has an AC motor.

Other oddball Blicks include the Blick Oriental (1908), a special-purpose machine with a carriage geared to move left to right, typing languages such as Hebrew and Arabic. The Noco-Blick (1910) was made to type music, and featured a special mechanism for moving the type-element up and down relative to the lines on the musical staff. Blickensderfer also apparently offered typewriters to produce secret codes, probably for military use. The *Niagara* was an index machine made by Blickensderfer (see page 96).

Two type-bar typewriters also bear the Blick name. The Blick Ninety (later sold as the *Roberts Ninety*) was a 3-row, frontstrike portable made after George C. Blickensderfer died in 1919. The Blick-Bar was a conventional, office-size 4-row frontstrike machine made by the Blickensderfer Co. briefly in 1913, before it was withdrawn from the market. Neither of these type-bar machines were inventions of Blickensderfer himself, but were made under license from other patent holders.

No collection should be without at least one Blickensderfer. The different versions are clearly labeled by model number or name, so identifying them is easy. Fortunately, most models are very common making them accessible to anyone who wishes to own one.

Blick No. 5, 7. . . . .$65.00
Blick 6, Featherweight, others $75.00
Blick 8, 9 . . . .$100.00
Blick Oriental $150.00
Noco-Blick . . . .$1,000.00+
Blickensderfer Electric . . . .$3,000.00+
Blick Ninety $100.00
Blick-Bar $100.00

Blickensderfer No. 5, early (3-row, type-wheel): The early versions of this common machine, as shown, have the name painted on the frame. Still earlier Blick No. 5's show other differences, including keytops that are not round but are 16-sided polygons. The wooden cylinder at left is actually a screw-top box for storing an extra type-element. (Type Writer Times)

Blickensderfer No. 5 (3-row, type-wheel): The machine shown is typical of those most often found: black paint, metal nameplate, DHIATENSOR keyboard. (author's collection, ser. 4426)

Blickensderfer No. 5 with case: Most Blickensderfer No. 5's come in their original oak cases, often with extra type-wheels inside. Absence of the case makes the machine less desirable. (author's collection)

Blickensderfer No. 6 (3-row, type-wheel): Although other Blickensderfer models were offered in aluminum as an option, the Blickensderfer No. 6 was issued exclusively in the lightweight metal. Note the copper name plate. (author's collection)

Featherweight Blick (3-row, type-wheel)*: Another Blickensderfer model offered only in aluminum. Very similar to the No. 6, the Featherweight's ink roller was fitted to an arched arm, which folded to the side so the machine could fit in its case. There is a variation, however, without the folding arm and nearly identical to the No. 6. A key to identification is the Featherweight's backspace key, not to mention its nameplate. (Russo collection, ser. 176514)*

Blickensderfer No. 7 (3-row, type-wheel)*: A more-substantial version of the basic Blick design. It featured an elevated scale and a wraparound space bar. Note the paint wear on the space bar of this specimen. This is typical of Blick 7's. The machine was made to be mounted on an oak base, without which no Blickensderfer No. 7 is complete. Each machine also had a bentwood cover. Notice the single mounting screw securing each side of the top casting to the base, indicating a pre-1900 date. Even earlier versions of the No. 7 have short tabs to advance each line instead of the longer carriage-return lever shown on this model. (Russo collection, ser. 74845)*

Blickensderfer No. 7, aluminum (3-row, type-wheel)*: For $10 extra, Blickensderfer offered any of its regular line machines in aluminum. The aluminum versions probably date from after about 1908 – 1910, when the aluminum No. 6 was introduced. The top casting attaches to the machine base with two screws at each side, characteristic of No. 7's after 1900. (Russo collection, ser. 145645)*

Blickensderfer No. 8 (3-row, type-wheel)*: The successor machine to the No. 7. Though totally unnecessary, the machine was given a wraparound frame, probably to make it look more like conventional typewriters. Many examples of this machine include a 7-position tabulator, operated using removable stops on the elevated scale above the print head. Some No. 8's, however, may have no tabulator, or a simpler version. Note this specimen features the QWERTY keyboard, offered only upon request. (author's collection, ser. 137637)*

Blickensderfer No. 9 (3-row, type-wheel): *Essentially similar to the No. 8 but without the elevated scale, and with a folding ink roll arm. (Russo collection, ser. 184581)*

Blickensderfer Electric (3-row, type-wheel): *A rare and revolutionary machine, using electric power with the Blickensderfer type-wheel design. This specimen features Blickensderfer's DHIATENSOR keyboard, surrounded by a rounded frame. Other known specimens have QWERTY keyboards, with square frames. (Milwaukee Public Museum, ser. 93351)*

Blick Bar (4-row, frontstrike): *Blickensderfer's brief experiment with conventional typewriters. It did not succeed well in the market place. (Milwaukee Public Museum)*

Blick Ninety (3-row, frontstrike): *A rather ordinary type-bar machine, it had one unusual feature. The entire basket of type-bars was removable, making a change of typeface easy — something you would expect of a company which made its reputation on machines having interchangeable type wheels. The decal on the left end of the paper table illustrates the type-basket feature. (Milwaukee Public Museum)*

Boston

The Boston Typewriter of 1888 was apparently based on a design patented in 1886 by D.R. Kempster of that city. The Boston was an index machine on which you selected letters using a knob passing over an arc-shaped index. A type-wheel did the printing.

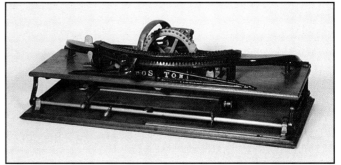

Although a number of Bostons have surfaced in recent years, they remain very desirable.

Boston . . . .$1,000.00+

Boston (curved index): The photo makes the Boston appear deceptively small. When most collectors see one for the first time, they are surprised to learn the actual machine is nearly 2 feet wide. (Milwaukee Public Museum)

Brooks

The Brooks Typewriter of 1895, is one of the desirable class of machines that used a backstroke mechanism. Its type-bars stood erect at the back of the machine and swung down to the platen with each stroke of a key. If you think about it for a moment, you'll realize that any such typewriter posed a big problem: *Where did you put the paper?* In the case of the Brooks, each sheet was rolled up into a paper basket in *front* of the platen, and fed into a paper basket *behind* the platen. The backstroke strategy was designed to make the work visible to the user, but only a line or two could be seen before they disappeared.

The Brooks Typewriter was the invention of Byron A. Brooks, a prolific typewriter inventor also credited with designing the familiar shift key, which first appeared on Remington No. 2 typewriters, and, of course, remains with us today.

Some models of this machine were sold as the *Eclipse.* Any model is highly sought-after.

Brooks . . . .$1,000.00+

Brooks (4-row, backstroke): Notice the off-center placement of the decal on the front of this specimen. Quality control may have been shoddy at the Brooks factory. This odd backstroke machine did not last long. (Milwaukee Public Museum)

Burnett

The Burnett Typewriter was a 4-row, oblique frontstrike machine dating from 1908. It was produced by the Burnett Typewriter Co. of Chicago, and marketed by Sears & Roebuck with little success.

The Burnett, with a few cosmetic changes, was essentially the same machine as the Triumph Visible, which had an equally unsuccessful life a year earlier.

Burnett $800.00

Burnett (oblique frontstrike): The radically angled type-bars in this machine represent a configuration known as "oblique frontstrike." It was thought this gave the user improved visibility. (Milwaukee Public Museum)

Burns

This rare double-keyboard machine was made in 1894 – 95 by the Burns Typewriter Co. of Buffalo, New York. Patented in 1889 by Frank Burns, it embodied a number of innovative features, among them one of the first backspace keys in the typewriter industry (although this is not seen on all known specimens).

The Burns was characterized by its ornate side panels made of copper, echoing the decoration of the vastly more popular and successful Smith Premier No. 1. Perhaps the Burns was too similar to its competitor, since it achieved no success in the market place.

Burns **$1,000.00**

Burns No. 1 (double-keyboard, upstrike): *The "No. 1" designation on this machine was wishful thinking on the part of its maker. Very few of these were made, and there was never a "No.2." (Milwaukee Public Museum)*

Burroughs

Burroughs is a name mostly associated with adding machines rather than typewriters. In the 1920s however, the company marketed its Burroughs Moon-Hopkins, a remarkable combination typewriter and calculator.

This monstrous machine originally consisted of a caps-only (double-case was offered later) upstrike typewriter, with a huge, glass-sided calculating machine mounted on the back. Later sold as the *Burroughs General Accounting Machine*, it is obvious that this device was intended as a do-it-all for any office needing to do billing or use figures in its correspondence.

The calculating module of the machine could be equipped with multiple registers, so that numbers could be calculated and stored for later use — a kind of primitive memory akin to today's computers. The Burroughs Moon-Hopkins was one of a very few direct multiplying machines, meaning it did not multiply by doing successive additions as on most calculators of the time. It also automated a number of other tasks, including rounding off fractions of pennies to the next highest whole cent.

The Burroughs machine was successor to the earlier Moon-Hopkins apparently produced by the Moon-Hopkins Billing Machine Co., which was founded in St. Louis in 1911. Burroughs acquired rights to the machine in 1921.

Burroughs also made a conventional 4-row, frontstrike typewriter in 1931. A 1932 electric version of the same machine, however, is of more interest to collectors. The Burroughs Electric is a big, heavy typewriter on which the motor powers the carriage return only. Perhaps since Burroughs' market was geared to accounting needs, for which wide spreadsheets required wide carriages, it made sense to power this heavy and cumbersome part of its typewriter.

Burroughs Moon-Hopkins (typewriter/calculator): *A large combination machine. Note the keyboard divided up into two parts. The upper four rows operated the typewriter, the lower two rows operated the calculator. (Milwaukee Public Museum)*

Burroughs Moon-Hopkins . . . .$1,000.00+
Burroughs Electric $50.00
Burroughs, 4-row, frontstrike $10.00

Burroughs Electric (4-row, frontstrike): Only the carriage was electrically powered in this conventional machine. The large nickel-plated key at bottom right operated the carriage return. (Russo collection, ser. A 350491)

Caligraph

The Caligraph was the second typewriter to appear on the American market and the first of the big double-keyboard machines. It was produced by the American Writing Machine Co. of New York, under the leadership of George Washington Newton Yost. Yost defected from Remington after helping it to launch the typewriter industry with production of the Sholes & Glidden. In fact, the Caligraph was made under many of the same basic patents as that machine. So, in a way, we can say the Caligraph was the invention of Christopher L. Sholes, just as the Sholes & Glidden was.

The Caligraph's appearance was dominated by the flat, sloping deck in front of the keyboard. It also differed from other machines by having two space bars at either side of the machine instead of one at the bottom of the keyboard.

The Caligraph No. 1 first appeared on the market in 1880, and was a rather small, caps-only machine which continued in production at least as late at 1896, concurrently with the later models. The No. 1 remains rare today. Quite common are the models 2, 3, and 4, all double-case machines with the giant keyboards. The makers of the Caligraph believed it simpler to offer a "key for every character" rather than the shift key featured on double-case machines from Remington. The shift key was seen as confusing, and many people agreed, since double-keyboards were offered on many machines well into the twentieth century. Only the widespread acceptance of touch typing, which taught the typist not to look at the keyboard, caused double-keyboards to die out.

Early models of the Caligraph featured platens with flat facets for good contact with the type. Later models had smooth, round platens, which were used once the manufacturers learned to grind subtle curves into type for contact

with typewriter platens. Most Caligraphs featured an elaborate decal on the front deck, clearly showing the model number. This decal is often damaged or missing. In that case, you can identify the models in other ways. No. 2 had 72 keys, No. 3 had 78 keys. No. 4 also had 78 keys but also had a knob at left for rotating the platen. Caligraphs may have had any of three different kinds of keytops: flat keys covered with glass and nickel key rims, cups with celluloid inserts, or composite (solid). Keyboards are often sore points for Caligraphs, and a good keyboard will make a machine more attractive to the collector.

The Caligraph seems light for its size, since its construction lacked heavy castings. It was very popular in its day, and many examples still survive. A twin to the machine was made in Germany under the name *Frister & Rossman.*

Caligraph No. 1 . . . .$1,000.00+
Caligraph Nos. 2, 3, 4 . . . .$100.00

Caligraph No. 1 (6-row, upstrike, caps-only): Alone among Caligraphs, the No. 1 is a small caps-only machine with 48 keys. Many are found without the red decal on the front deck, leading some to believe none was ever present on a No. 1. It was suspected that decal panels cut down from No. 2's were installed on this and other specimens, but examination of the decal here shows it to be smaller than that on a No. 2, with no evidence of tampering. The advertising record also shows the machine with the decal. (Milwaukee Public Museum)

Caligraph No. 2 (double-keyboard, upstrike): The double-keyboard Caligraph is a large, but lightweight machine. Notice the faceted platen on this one, which also has cup keys with celluloid inserts. (Dickerson collection, ser. 34693)

Caligraph No. 3 (double-keyboard, upstrike): Nearly identical to the No. 2, the Caligraph No. 3 differs only in the number of keys. This particular model has solid keytops. A much earlier single-case machine with 54 keys was also called a No. 3, but is very rare. (Rauen collection, ser. 6125)

Caligraph No. 4 (double-keyboard, upstrike): With the same number of keys, it would be nearly impossible to tell a Caligraph No. 4 from a No. 3 if it weren't for the model number on the decal. The distinguishing detail is the thick nub at the left side of the platen. That's a knob for twirling the cylinder, something earlier Caligraphs did not have. (Russo collection, ser. 9843)

Carissima

Despite its Italian name, this charming machine came to us from Germany. It was an index machine, with characters on a type-wheel manipulated with a knob running along a linear index. The most engaging thing about this machine is its Bakelite housing and lid. The Carissima, made in 1934, is also sometimes seen under another name, *The Bee,* which was sold in England.

Carissima $200.00

Carissima (linear index): This petite linear index machine was small enough to fit inside a desk drawer. Its Bakelite housing made it very light as well. It weighed only 4 pounds. Due to the brittle nature of Bakelite, the cover or housing of the machine is often cracked. (author's collection)

Cash

The Cash was a downstrike machine patented in 1887 by Arthur W. Cash of Hartford, Connecticut. Various sources say he marketed the machine himself originally, until another concern took over in 1896, adding "Typograph" to the name.

The Cash printed on a flat platen riding underneath the whole type assembly. In many ways, it looks like book typewriters, which had the same kind of downstrike type-bars.

The frame on the machine was made in two different styles. One is curved at the front, the other is not.

The Cash was not very practical, and it is a rarity among collectors today.

Cash . . . .**$1,000.00+**

Cash (4-row, downstrike, flat platen): A large machine designed to type on a flat platen below the type-bars. The platen was covered with leather. (Milwaukee Public Museum)

Century 10

The Century 10 appears to have been the last line of typewriters that began with the Caligraph in 1880. The Caligraph's name was eventually changed to New Century Caligraph, and from that we get Century.

Different sources date this machine at 1914 or 1919. It hardly seems important. The Century 10 was a conventional frontstrike type-bar machine with a 3-row keyboard. It made little impact on the market, and is not sought after by collectors today.

Century 10 . . . .**$50.00**

Century 10 (3-row, frontstrike): This small, 3-row machine was made by the same company that made the double-keyboard Caligraph. Notice the decal on the front reading: "American Writing Machine Co." (Milwaukee Public Museum)

Chicago

The Chicago Typewriter, introduced around 1899, was an ingenious little 3-row machine with a design that's hard to believe until you see it in action. Its printing end was an elongated type-sleeve which both rotated and moved from side to side as the keys were pressed. At the same time, a hammer swung forward with each stroke, hitting the paper from behind, striking it against the type-sleeve with the ribbon in between. The hammer was mounted on a long arm, which slid into the frame when not in use so the machine could fit inside its case.

The Chicago came in two basic configurations. One was simply called The Chicago, and the other was the Chicago No. 3, each quite different in appearance. You would think there was also a No. 2, but no examples are known.

The Chicago was made with some variation in its trim. Some models bore only the words "The Chicago," while others were trimmed with a bit of fancy scrollwork and included patent dates and numbers. A plain Chicago is less desirable than one with scrolls but only marginally so.

The Chicago was the direct descendant of the Munson typewriter (see page 93). In fact, models 2 and 3 of the Munson were practically identical to the Chicago. Those familiar with early Sears Catalogs might have seen a listing for the *Draper* typewriter, which was simply a Chicago sold under another name. The Chicago was sold under a long list of alternate names: *American No. 10, Baltimore, Competitor, Conover, Galesburg, Yale,* and more. One model, the *Mitzpah,* was designed with a reverse carriage for typing Hebrew.

Chicago (and name-variants) $150.00
Chicago No. 3 . . . .$400.00

Chicago, scrolls (3-row, type-sleeve): *Apparently the earliest of the Chicagos, this machine features fancy scrollwork bracketing the brand name. (author's collection, ser. 23250)*

Chicago, plain (3-row, type-sleeve): *The absence of scrollwork and a lone pinstripe around the edge of the Chicago's front plate apparently signifies a later machine. (Russo collection, ser. 72835)*

Chicago No. 3 (3-row, type-sleeve): *The rarest of the Chicago models, it is easy to identify, having a prominent logo, flat-decked shape, and narrow ribbon spools. Unlike other Chicagos, it also features a backspace key, and one key labeled "key release" which is called a margin release on other machines. (Milwaukee Public Museum)*

Conover (3-row, type-wheel): *One of many name-variants of the Chicago. Ornamentation is similar to the Chicago with scrolls. The name of the firm Hubbard, Spencer, Bartlett & Co. is stenciled on the cover plate, possibly the machine's retailer. (Milwaukee Public Museum)*

Coffman

The Coffman Typewriter was one among many little machines marketed as typewriters, but which were nothing more than cheap novelties with little practical use. Introduced around 1902, this linear index machine was first sold as a pocket typewriter. The original model had no platen, but typed directly on a flat piece of paper. A second model included a cylindrical platen.

The Coffman used a linear rubber type strip, which rolled past two ink rollers as the user moved it back and forth. Though it was inconsequential in its time, the Coffman is a highly desirable collector's item today.

Coffman $1,000.00

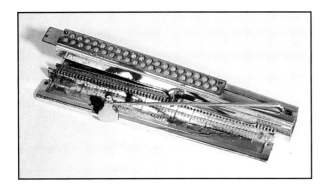

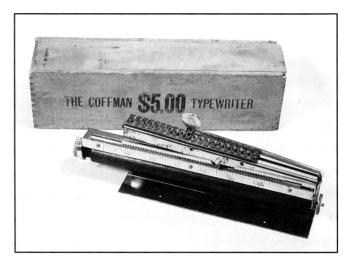

Coffman, flat (linear index): A tiny machine which typed directly on flat paper. It was made to fit in your pocket, if your pocket was big enough! (Russo Collection, no serial number)

Coffman, platen (linear index): A second version of the Coffman, this with a cylindrical platen. The top of the paper was inserted into a slit rolling up around the platen and into the machine as each line was typed. Shown with its original wooden box. (Kortsch collection, no serial number)

Columbia
Columbia Bar-Lock
(see Bar-Lock)

Columbia Index

The little 1885 machine with its nameplate from The Columbia Typewriter Co. is known by collectors as the "Columbia index," to distinguish it from the Columbia Bar-Lock and later Columbia keyboard machines made by the same company (see Bar-Lock, page 25). The index machine, obviously, was totally different.

This Columbia was a circular index typewriter, printing from a type-wheel mounted perpendicular to the platen. It was a very pretty and well made device and was one of the few early machines to use proportional spacing. That is, each letter takes up the space proportional to its width. An "i," as we've said, will take up less space than the much wider "w." This is how books are printed, of course, but almost all typewriters use monospace lettering, in which all letters are of equal width.

There were three models of the Columbia index. The first typed upper-case only. The second made use of two type-wheels to add upper/lower case capability. The user moved the handle in or out to shift. The third model printed upper and lower cases using a single, larger type wheel, and it bore an engraved nameplate. This is the version most often found, but any model of this machine is a desirable collector's item.

Columbia index $1,000.00

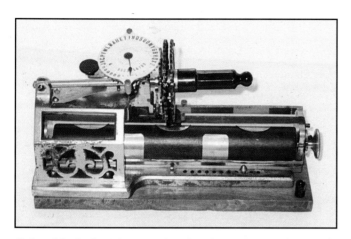

Columbia index No. 1a (circular index): *The earliest versions of the Columbia index featured small type-wheels and indicators with only one point. This example, dubbed "No. 1a" by collectors, is a double-case machine using two different type-wheels for that purpose. The single-case model ("No. 1") looks the same but has only one type-wheel. Note the ornamental frame. (Williams collection, ser. 369)*

Columbia index No. 2 (circular index): *The more common version of the Columbia index is this one. It is a double-case machine, and features a single type-wheel large enough to accomodate all the necessary characters. The indicator is an arrow with two heads. One head of the arrow for capitals, the other for lowercase. An ornamenal nameplate is mounted at lower left. (Rauen collection, ser. 1046)*

Commercial Visible

The Commercial Visible, a three-row typewriter of 1898, was one of the most attractive of the type-wheel machines. Collectors often describe it as "wasp-waisted," referring to the odd narrowing of the frame in the center. The design was the work of Richard Uhlig, inventor of many typewriters and typewriter features.

This machine operated using a hammer at rear, striking the paper against the type-wheel with the ribbon in between. The rear striking hammer was used on a number of other machines, most notably the Hammond and the Chicago/Munson family. Another interesting feature of this machine is a clip atop the left ribbon spool cover meant to hold a pen or pencil for drawing straight lines on the paper.

Most surviving examples of the Commercial Visible are model No. 6. It is not clear why, because there apparently were never any models 1 through 5. Two examples of a "Model A" version have been reported, however.

In a 1924 trade journal, Alexander M. Fiske, head of the company that produced the machine wrote that it was originally made around 1898 as the *Fountain*, to be sold by the Siegel-Cooper department store of New York City. Only 200 – 300 machines were made. A contemporary illustration of the *Fountain* shows it with a scalloped space bar, in contrast to the long, straight one found on Commercial Visibles.

Fiske also wrote that two years later, the company name was changed to the Visible Typewriter Co., and a completely retooled machine was offered beginning 1901. About 3,000 were sold in all. Serial numbers observed on these machines seem to run much higher than 3,000, but this could be deceptive. A collector familiar with Commercial Visibles tells us all serial numbers he has seen fall within the 22,000 – 25,000 range. The company may well have been trying to give an inflated impression of its production.

Variations to be seen in Commercial Visibles include color of the keytops. Most are black, but some are white. The paint on virtually all machines is black with gold trim, but at least one known machine is white with gold trim. The Commercial Visible is often missing the covers for its ribbon spools, and no machine is complete without them.

Commercial Visible, black $350.00
Commercial Visible, white $650.00
Fountain $500.00

Fountain (3-row, type-wheel): The earliest product in the Commercial Visible line. Notice the small, scalloped space bar. In addition, the harp serving as the guide for key levers is open at the top, and the frame at the front has no cutout for the space bar as on later models. The wooden roller behind the type element is a feed roller. A rubber tip on the rear-striking hammer is the true platen. The decal behind the keyboard reads "Commercial Typewriter," but the name "Fountain" does not appear on the machine. (Clark collection, ser. 223)

Commercial Visible No. 6, white (3-row, type-wheel): Not only is the paint white, but so are the key tops. This specimen shows some of the things that can be wrong with a Commercial Visible. Note the chipped paint and missing decal above the keys, also the missing left ribbon cover. Despite the defects, its rarity makes this machine very desirable. (Clark collection, ser. 23380)

Commercial Visible No. 6 (3-row, type-wheel): Compare this to the Fountain and notice the different space bar shape, the frame cutout at front for the space bar, the different key lever harp, and the rubber feed roller. The decal behind the keyboard reads "Commercial Visible Typewriter." Condition of the decals on any Commercial Visible is important to the machine's value. (Dickerson collection, ser. 22208)

Corona

A whole book could well be written on the Corona Typewriter, its history and impact on the typewriter industry. The makers of this revolutionary machine have been in business longer than anyone else in the field. The modern Smith-Corona company (which emerged from a 2-year bankruptcy in 1997) traces its roots directly back to the Corona Typewriter Co. which began as the Standard Typewriter Co. in 1907. The Smith family, Corona's later merger partners, entered the typewriter industry in 1889.

The first Corona was built in 1912. It was a compact machine made so that its carriage folded forward over the keys for portability. The Corona was actually the third model of a line of typewriters originally called "Standard Folding" (see page 129). For this reason, the term "Corona 3" is often generically applied to this machine. Otherwise, it is generally called a "folding Corona."

The folding Corona was produced until 1940 and was one of the most popular portables ever made. The machines came in a number of minor variations. The earliest models had "Standard Folding Typewriter" in parentheses below the large "Corona" decal on the frame above the keys. For the first decade, these machines had only one set of shift keys on the left side of the keyboard (one for figures, one for caps — a standard configuration for 3-row machines). During the 1920s, the frame was widened to accommodate two sets of shift keys, one on each side of the keyboard. Most 3-row Coronas are black except for the Corona "Special" models, painted in a variety of colors (red, blue, green, and others). There are other variations as well, but they are simply too numerous to mention. One name variation that should be noted is *Coronet*, a label under which the machine was sold in England.

In 1926, the Corona Typewriter Co. merged with L.C. Smith & Bros., a prominent maker of office-sized machines. This was the beginning of the famous Smith-Corona firm. Before the merger, the first of many 4-row, frontstrike Coronas was introduced. These outsold the 3-row folding model, which was eventually offered at deep discounts to its original $50 price.

About 700,000 folding Coronas were produced, and for this reason, many still survive today. In fact, this machine is usually one of the very first that any beginning typewriter collector will acquire. A 3-row Corona should have its original case to be considered complete. They are often found with accessories such as an oiler and cleaning brush, in addition to the original owner's manual. A scarce accessory is a folding tripod typewriter stand.

A particular detail about the Corona creates fits for people trying to make one work today. The ribbon follows an "S" path on the machine, feeding off the front of the left ribbon spool and onto the back of the right spool. If you thread the ribbon off the same side of each spool, it won't advance properly, and you might conclude your little clunker just doesn't work!

Four-row Coronas (even those in bright colors) hold little interest for most collectors, but there are a few exceptions. One is the 1932 "Sterling" model, some of which were made with coverings of solid sterling silver. It's not known whether these were offered to the public, or were intended as presentation pieces to company salesmen or executives.

Another 4-row Corona of interest is one with an "animal" keyboard. These were introduced for one season only in 1931, and were made to teach children to type. Animals on the keys corresponded to rings the children wore showing which keys were to be typed with each finger. The animal keyboard machines are quite scarce. The accompanying rings are even scarcer.

Corona, Corona Special (3-row, folding, black) $30.00
Corona, folding, with tripod stand $100.00
Corona Special (colors excluding black) $50.00
Corona (4-row) $10.00
Corona Sterling (sterling silver covering) ..$1,000.00
Corona (4-row, animal keyboard) $100.00

Corona, folding (3-row, frontstrike): The classic folding Corona in basic black. Note the number "3" at each side of the lower front frame edge. This is the model number and leads many collectors to call any such machine a "Corona 3." Note the shift keys at keyboard left only. Later models had shift keys on both sides. (author's collection, ser. 422453)

Corona (folded position): The carriage on the folding Corona flips down over the keyboard, reducing the machine's bulk for portability. (author's collection)

Corona/tripod stand: *The collapsible tripod stand allowed the folding Corona to be set up and used anywhere. The tripod is a scarce and desirable accessory today. (author's collection)*

Corona Specials in colors: *Coronas were offered in various colors during the late 1920s through the 1930s. Note the wider frame to accommodate shift keys on both sides. Coronas in color are more desirable than those in black. (Russo collection, red ser. SX618664, blue ser. BX664930, green ser. BX628046, black/gold ser. GX651543)*

Folding Corona, white: *A rare color variation, this machine was painted white at the dealer level. This typewriter was purchased at the Alhambra Typewriter Shop near Los Angeles. The dealer was able to repaint the frame, according to the customer's wishes, and apply standard Corona decals over the new color. (author's collection, ser. 289244)*

Sterling Silver Corona: *It's not just silver plated. The covering of this machine is solid sterling silver and bears the mark of Gorham Silver to prove it. Issued in 1932 (Silver Anniversary of the Corona Typewriter Co.), it may have been an award or presentation model. Corona used the "Sterling" model name on many machines, none of which should be confused with the sterling silver one. (author's collection, ser. 1013917 S)*

Animal Keyboard Corona: *Made in 1931 only, this machine had pictures of little animals on the keys. It was an unsuccessful attempt at marketing a machine to teach children how to type. With the Great Depression deepening at the time, there was hardly a market for a luxury such as this. (author's collection, ser. A1C 32729)*

Animal Keyboard Corona (keyboard detail): *A different animal was chosen to correspond to each of the fingers on the child's hand. The little typist wore a set of rings matching the animals on the keyboard. (author's collection)*

Crandall

The Crandall Typewriter is considered by collectors to be one of the most spectacularly beautiful machines ever produced. Beauty, however, is in the eye of the beholder, and this machine will appeal mostly to those who appreciate the heavily-ornate Victorian style of decoration seen on this machine. The black paint of most models is densely covered with gold leaves, lines, and curlicues, together with inlays made from mother-of-pearl overpainted to resemble roses in bloom.

Introduced about 1884 (and patented in 1879), this machine was among the earliest of the single-element keyboard machines. It was the design of Lucien Crandall, a prominent typewriter inventor.

The elaborately decorated New Model Crandall is the model most often seen. Earlier models were a bit more modest, decorated in gold over the black undercoat (with no mother-of-pearl). They also had square, nickel-rimmed keys as opposed to solid black keys seen on the New Model.

Later models, the No. 3 (Universal Crandall) and No. 4 were essentially similar. They had 3-row keyboards in the familiar QWERTY arrangement, with no decoration other than some modest pinstripes over plain black. One improvement offered on the No. 4 was a pair of buttons to change the position of a bichrome ribbon. The same machine was sold under the name Crandall Visible in the Sears & Roebuck Catalog of 1906. The price was $24.50 (the original Crandall retailed for $75.00), and it included a 10-year guarantee.

Crandall (any model) $1,000.00

Crandall, early (2-row, curved-keyboard, type-sleeve): *The early versions of the Crandall are characterized by square, nickel-rimmed keys and a round space key. Note also the platen of white rubber. The ornate gold decoration on this specimen has faded with age. (author's collection, ser. 1323)*

Crandall New Model (2-row, curved-keyboard, type-sleeve): This is the version of the Crandall usually found. Decoration is more elaborate than the earlier model, with mother-of-pearl as an important accent. Other important differences are the shape of the escutcheon and the solid black keys. (Dickerson collection, ser. 3806)

Universal Crandall No. 3 (3-row, type-sleeve): The same type-sleeve mechanism as the earlier models, but with a 3-row QWERTY keyboard and little ornamentation. (Milwaukee Public Museum)

Crary

The Crary Typewriter of 1892 was certainly among the more bizarre products of early typewriter industry. It consisted of a large keyboard/type-bar assembly which rode on rails over the paper as the typing proceeded.

The Crary was dominated by its large circular keyboard. The type-bars stood vertically within the circle and swung down to hit the paper below.

The Crary's basic design, though functional, was fairly impractical and the machine had a short life on the typewriter market.

Crary . . . .$1,000.00+

Crary (circular-keyboard, downstrike): The circular keyboard is a rarity among typewriters. This also happens to be a double-keyboard, with no shift and a key for every character. (Milwaukee Public Museum)

Crown

The Crown Typewriter of 1888 is an attractive and well-built index machine developed by Byron Brooks, an inventor with many typewriter credits. The Crown operated using a pointer moving along a linear strip. The type-wheel was geared to the pointer and rotated to the appropriate letter before the whole assembly was pushed down to print.

There were two varieties of the Crown Typewriter. The earlier of the two had a square metal frame at front, the later was only slightly different, with a rounded front. Either one is a desirable machine.

It's interesting that this machine's maker, the National Meter Co. of Brooklyn, New York, also manufactured a duplicator called the Broderick Copyograph. Patented in 1888, it seems probable the device was intended to accompany the Crown Typewriter. A.B. Dick, maker of the Edison Mimeograph duplicator tried the same thing in reverse, offering the Edison Mimeograph Typewriter to accompany its duplicator (see page 53).

The name "Crown" can be a source of confusion, because there were at least two other machines with the same name. One, dating from 1887, had a circular keyboard somewhat like the Crary, and is exceedingly rare. The other is a name-variant of the National portable of 1916 (see page 95) and has only modest value.

Crown $1,000.00

Crown, round front (linear index): Compare the lower front edge of this machine with the earlier square front model (below). Notice the rounded shape of the frame. The change may have been made to add strength to the small machine. This model also has a wooden feed roller, strikingly different from the nickel roller on the earlier machine. Other subtle differences include position of the bell. (Milwaukee Public Museum)

Crown, square front (linear index): Notice the straight, square shape of the frame at the lower front edge. This is how the earlier of the two models is identified. (Casillo collection)

Darling

The Darling Typewriter was made around 1910 by Robert Ingersoll & Bros. of New York. The firm made a number of small, cheap typewriters, several under the Darling name, and at least one other very bizarre machine called the Ingersoll (see page 79).

On the Darling, you chose your letters, one by one, using a circular index. A number of different models are said to have been made. One was just a round printing assembly attached to a rod that held the paper, another was a similar contraption that clamped to a tabletop, and the third was a fully self-contained unit complete with a base and platen.

Darling $500.00

Darling (circular index): *This is the most elaborate of three models made under this brand name. Note the leather cover with the brand name "Darling" embossed. (Clark collection, ser. 795)*

Daugherty

The Daugherty Typewriter was essentially the first modern typewriter to be placed on the market. By "modern" typewriter, we mean one with the 4-row, frontstrike format. Think about it: if you look at virtually 98% of all manual (and most electric) machines made before 1960, they will share this same configuration — four rows of keys and front striking type-bars.

The Daugherty was introduced in 1893, the invention of James Daugherty of Kittanning, Pennsylvania. The strange, elongated profile of the machine gives it a personality unlike other 4-row frontstrikes. This "odd-duck" image may have contributed to its eventual failure, along with the long, awkward type-bars that limited its efficiency. For this reason, the vastly more successful Underwood, introduced in 1895, usually gets credit for being the first modern typewriter.

Most Daugherty machines are designated Daugherty Visible, although some earlier examples bear no name other than Daugherty. After the original Daugherty enterprise failed, the company was reorganized to produce a very similar machine under the name *"Pittsburg Visible"* (see page 107).

Daugherty $350.00

Daugherty (4-row, frontstrike): *Most 4-row, frontstrike machines have little value. The Daugherty is an exception, not only because it was the first, but also because of its strange, elongated profile. (Dickerson collection, ser. 2032)*

Daugherty Visible (4-row, frontstrike): *Slightly later version of the Daugherty, with the name "Visible" added. The 4-row, frontstrike design was created to make the work visible to the eye, and thus the name. (author's collection, ser. 4135)*

Dayton

The Dayton typewriter was a 4-row, frontstrike portable which is quite rare, but likely to be overlooked. It dates from 1924, apparently the product of the Dayton Portable Typewriter Co. of Dayton, Ohio. It was to have been a bargain-priced product, featuring only 559 parts. The Dayton is seen in two colors: black or battleship gray.

Dayton $75.00

Dayton (4-row, fronstrike): Though most collectors would tend to ignore it, the Dayton has an appealing profile. This specimen is in battleship gray. A note which came with this machine claimed it was produced by a subsidiary of the National Cash Register Co., of Dayton, Ohio. The author has not been able to confirm this fact. (author's collection, ser. 2407/102)

Densmore

The Densmore Typewriter (1891) was created by a group of people headed by Amos and Emmett Densmore, brothers of James Densmore, the entrepreneur most responsible for bringing the Sholes & Glidden to market in 1874 as the founding machine of the typewriter industry. The Densmore was very popular in its day, due to its dependable, efficient design.

Densmore typewriters all have the same basic configuration, differing only in details. They were promoted for having ball bearing type-bars, and they are distinctive in appearance, each with a "crown" of type-bar mountings encircling the top of the machine.

Identifying different models of the earliest Densmores may be confusing. Some machines were marked "No.1," but others were not. Those without clear "No.1" labels may be called "pre-No. 1's" by collectors. We'll call the earliest models "1a." They were usually distinguished by little circular rings midway up the type-bar links (the rods connecting the type-bars to the key levers) and a metal nameplate on the upper front edge of the machine. A second version ("1b") had no such rings, and the name "Densmore" was in paint. Finally, there were the company-designated No. 1 ("1c") and No. 2, which were clearly labeled with their model numbers. These two machines were virtually identical. The only difference was some additional keyboard characters on the No. 2, which was made concurrently with the No. 1 for the European market.

Later Densmores were usually clearly marked with model numbers. Models No. 4, 5, and 6 featured type-bar mounts more widely spaced than earlier models, enhancing the crown effect on these attractive machines.

Densmore No. 1, 2 . . . .$200.00
Densmore (other models) $100.00

Densmore No. 1a (4-row, upstrike): The main features identifying the 1a are the rings in the type-bar connectors and the metal nameplate at the top/front. However, at least one specimen is known with a painted Densmore logo in place of the metal nameplate. (Rauen collection, ser. 2201)

Densmore No. 1b (4-row, upstrike): *There are many subtle differences between this machine and the 1a. Not so subtle, however, is the absence of type-bar connector rings and metal nameplate. (Rauen Collection, ser. 6867)*

Densmore No. 1c (4-row, upstrike): *The third, and apparently final version of the Densmore No. 1. The machine is clearly labeled with a model number. A very similar No. 2 (also clearly labeled) was marketed overseas. (Dickerson Collection, ser. 9457)*

Densmore No. 4 (4-row, upstrike): *Proudly displaying its model number, the No. 4 differs from earlier models in decals and appearance of type-bar bearings. It has 39 keys. (Dickerson Collection, ser. 11074)*

Densmore No. 5 (4-row, upstrike): *Aside from the large "No. 5" on the front, the only difference between this model and the No. 4 is the number of keys. The No. 5 has 43. (Russo collection, ser. 27966)*

Densmore No. 6 (4-row, upstrike): *It is unclear whether the row of tabulator keys on this No. 6 was a standard feature for the model number, or an option. In any case, the No. 6 is clearly identified by its logo. (Milwaukee Public Museum)*

Dollar

The Dollar typewriter of 1891 is one of many different very cheap machines turned out by manufacturers interested in... well, a quick dollar.

This machine consisted of little more than a wooden base with ruler markings, a simple type-wheel embedded with rubber type, an ink roller, and a few cheap tin strips made to ratchet the whole thing into some sort of writing function.

As you may have guessed, this sold for $1.00. It was probably worth only half that much.

There were a number of other machines, not identical to the Dollar, but certainly created with the same kind of market in mind. Among them, the *Eureka*, *Yankee*, and the *Wilson Dollar* typewriter.

Dollar, Eureka, Yankee, Wilson Dollar **$100.00**

Wilson Dollar Typewriter (type-wheel index): *Similar to the Dollar, the Wilson Dollar Typewriter has its type-wheel oriented in a different direction. This specimen is designated "No. 1." We have no indication that there was also a No. 2. (Clark collection, no serial number)*

Dollar (type-wheel index): *Typewriters don't come much cheaper and simpler than this. With a careful hand and steady attention, it might even have produced decent looking work. (Rauen collection, no serial number)*

Yankee Typewriter (circular index): *A type-wheel cover on this cheap machine doubles as the index. Similar in concept to the Dollar. (Clark collection, no serial number)*

Duplex

The Duplex Typewriter of 1894 appears at first glance to be similar to many large, double-keyboard machines, but it had an important difference. This machine's double-keyboard may be better described as a *dual*-keyboard, because it was designed to type two letters at a time on a "double center."

The makers of the Duplex believed you could effectively double your typing speed by pressing two keys at once. Unfortunately, the brain work required to divide up all the words into two-letter chunks probably drove most Duplex users insane before they could get anywhere with this odd device.

There was some variety among Duplex machines. The *Dennis* Duplex (named for inventor A.S. Dennis) used a pad for inking. The Duplex used a ribbon. There was also a Duplex No. 2 "single center," which was a conventional double-keyboard upstrike machine. The Duplex also included a feature for shading letters for emphasis.

The company eventually regrouped and offered successive models under the name Jewett (see page 81).

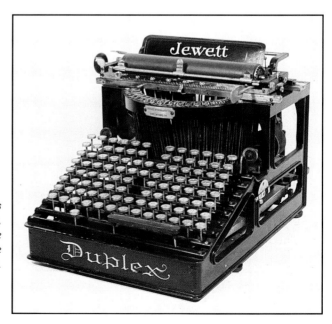

Duplex (double center, upstrike): *The massive keyboard is actually two keyboards, designed to be operated together, printing two letters at each stroke. The name "Jewett" on the paper table is a curiosity. It may have been added when the machine was in the shop for repair. (Dickerson collection, ser. 1025)*

Duplex or Dennis Duplex, double center .$500.00
Duplex No. 2, single center $150.00

Duplex No. 2 (double-keyboard, upstrike): A more conventional upstrike machine. The No. 2 may have replaced the double center Duplex when it proved to be impractical, or it may have been offered concurrently with the original. This single center model is virtually identical to the first model of the Jewett typewriter. (Dickerson collection, ser. 526)

Eagle

There is not much information available to us on this machine, which apparently was introduced around 1905. It was similar in format to the Keystone, using a 3-row keyboard to control a swinging-sector type-element. A rear-striking hammer brought the type into contact with the ribbon and paper.

The Eagle was also sold as the *Defi* a rather intriguing sort of name. Is it pronounced "Deffy" or "Dee-fie," as in "I *Defi* you to type on me!" I Defi you to *find* me is more like it, because this is a very scarce machine. The first model of a machine called the Sterling (see page 130) is enough like the Eagle to lead us to believe there was some connection between the two.

Eagle, Defi $800.00

Defi (3-row, swinging-sector): Notice the slender hammer at top/rear, poised to strike the paper against the type element. The rear hammer was a frequently-used feature in early typewriter design. The very similar Sterling (see page 130) included a frame around the keyboard, which is left open on the Defi. (Milwaukee Public Museum, ser. 5052)

Edelmann

The Edelmann Typewriter (1897) was a German index machine rather well made considering its simple design.

The type-wheel was geared to a handle at front, which is moved back and forth along a curved letter index. It's interesting that the index is often made of porcelain with baked-in characters. This made it very durable, and while the index strips of its contemporary machines are often in decay, many of those found on Edelmanns look near-new.

Edelmann $200.00

Edelmann (curved index): This type-wheel machine was a high-quality product of 1897 from Germany. The same basic idea resurfaced years later in cheap, sheet metal machines such as the Gundka and MW. (Milwaukee Public Museum)

Edison Mimeograph Typewriter

The 1892 Edison Mimeograph Typewriter was an unusual and intriguing machine with a famous name.

The Edison had no keyboard, so it was certainly an index machine (although one machine is reported with a keyboard for the blind). Its type was located on the ends of little rods (often called "plungers"), which were pushed upward toward the platen by the action of a lever and a hammer. Letter selection was made by rotating the circular index at the base of the machine.

Despite its name, the Edison was not invented by Thomas Edison. Instead, it was the design of A.B. Dick, the man who put the first mimeograph duplicator on the market in 1887.

Dick was originally a lumber merchant who needed an easy way to make copies of his inventory lists, which changed daily. He invented a duplicator, only to find later that his friend, Thomas Edison, already had patents on the same idea. This story, from A.B. Dick Company literature, may exaggerate Dick's friendship with Edison prior to their business relationship. Edison's name, however, had star quality, and there is no question that Dick made use of it by selling his machine as the "Edison Mimeograph."

Dick then decided to market a typewriter designed to produce better mimeograph stencils, and so invented the Edison Mimeograph Typewriter. It was a bad idea, a bad typewriter, and it was pushed off the market by typewriter dealers on whom Dick depended to distribute the mimeograph. Such rejects, however make excellent collector's items.

There were three models of the Edison Mimeograph Typewriter. They differed mainly in their number of characters: No. 1 (78 char.), No. 2 (86 char.), No. 3 (90 char.).

Edison Mimeograph Typewriter ....$1,000.00+

Edison No. 1 (circular index): A large disk underneath the machine was rotated to bring the correct letter to the printing point. A little cup was provided for the user's fingertip, one of the few conveniences on a machine that must have been very difficult and slow to use. (Milwaukee Public Museum)

Edland

The Edland Typewriter was a circular index machine patented in 1891 by Joe L. Edland. The cheap little typewriter was made in New York by the Liberty Manufacturing Co., and the name appeared prominently around the center of the type-selector disk.

At least two different models of this machine were made. One had a printed letter index. The other had embossed letters on the index. Also reported was a third model which used a small type-wheel (similar to the Blickensderfer) geared to the index handle.

A recently discovered sales flyer tells us that the first Edland machines were shipped from the factory on September 20, 1892. Seldom do we have such an exact date for the debut of an antique machine. The company claimed to be making machines at no profit, with hopes of making money only after increasing volume. Considering the relative rarity of the Edland today, it's likely that profitability remained elusive, even with the attractive selling price of $5 ($6 west of the Mississippi).

There's an interesting story about Edland typewriters. In the 1960s or thereabouts, somebody apparently discovered a whole stash of the embossed index machines, one of those wonderful "new-old-stock" finds. Each machine was wrapped in newspaper, just as they probably came from the shipper. At one point, it had been thought that these were the only survivors, but the appearance of printed-index Edlands shows us that is not the case.

Edland (any model) $500.00

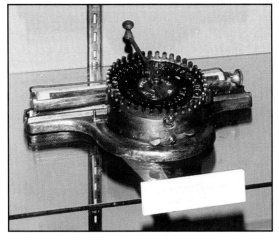

Edland, embossed index (circular index): *This version of the Edland Typewriter features a letter index that is embossed instead of printed. Notice the attractive gold color of the base. This is the machine apparently discovered in quantity during the 1960s. (Clark collection, no serial number)*

Edland, printed index (circular index): *The index on this machine is printed on paper rather than embossed. It is unclear which version of the two Edlands is earlier. The printed index may have come later, introduced as an economy measure. The base on this machine appears darker than the other version, but we do not know if this was original or the result of age. (Clark collection, no serial number)*

Electromatic

The importance of the Electromatic Typewriter stems largely from its role in launching IBM into the typewriter business, beginning the subsequent wide ranging success of electric typewriters. However, the story of the machine itself is fascinating on its own merits.

The Electromatic's roots go back to 1914, when James Smathers, of Kansas City, Missouri, received the key patents for the power roller system designed for typewriters. The patent called for a power-roller in constant motion. Depression of a key put a drive shoe in contact with the roller, which drove the type-bar toward the platen. The concept would become standard for electric typewriters in the future. At the time, however, Smathers envisioned power-roller typewriters in a "writing factory," with each machine driven by a belt from an overhead shaft connected to a central power supply.

According to his son Frank, Smathers sold his patent rights to the North East Electric Co. of Rochester, New York, about 1924. N.E. Electric was in the business of selling electric motors. It hoped the Smathers patents would help it forge a relationship with a typewriter company, so that it could make electric motors for electric typewriters.

The company approached Remington and secured a contract for 2,500 machines. N.E. Electric manufactured the motor together with a power-roller base, and all Remington had to do was attach its machines (modified from the Remington No. 12).

Contrary to the conventional wisdom, the Remington Electric of 1925 apparently was not a failure. The 2,500 machines made under the N.E. Electric contract were sold as fast as they came out of the factory. Remington wanted its partner to keep making machines, claiming they could sell as many as N.E. Electric could produce. N.E. Electric, however, insisted on a firm contract for a firm number of machines.

Unfortunately, Remington at the time was in the midst of the merger talks which would change it into Remington-Rand. The negotiations created a power vacuum for the powered typewriter, and there was no one to approve the contract that N.E. Electric wanted. As a result, the Remington Electric went out of production after 2,500 units, instead of creating a revolutionary new segment of the typewriter industry.

North East Electric then took matters into its own hands, producing a new electric typewriter named the Electromatic, which debuted around 1929. Along the way, N.E. Electric was purchased by General Motors and turned into the automaker's Delco division. The Electromatic Typewriter Co., apparently, emerged from the purchase as an independent concern. James Smathers headed a company formed to administer the still-active patents.

In 1933, the Electromatic Typewriter Co. was purchased by a company which specialized in time clocks and punch-card sorters: International Business Machines. IBM sold the Electromatic as its Model 01. Model 04 was later added to the line. It featured proportional spacing.

The Electromatic was a heavy, paper-pounding machine built like a tank. They are still frequently found today, and very often are still in working condition. Despite their rich history, collectors do not seek them out, since they are very large and difficult to display or store.

Electromatic **$50.00**

Electromatic, IBM (4-row, fronstrike, electric): Electromatic machines made before the 1933 IBM purchase are labeled simply "Electromatic." Those made by IBM will bear either the company logo, the word "International" or some other indication that IBM was involved. On this specimen, the company name is on the front panel. (Frank Smathers collection)

Elliott-Fisher
Elliott-Hatch

A book typewriter is designed to write not on single piece of paper wrapped around a round platen. Instead, it is made to type into an open, bound book, on a flat surface. The Elliott-Fisher and Elliott-Hatch Typewriters were such machines, and they found wide applications in business during the early part of the twentieth century.

The Elliott-Fisher machine was the result of a merger between two firms, the Elliott & Hatch Book Typewriter Co. and the Fisher Book Typewriter Co. Each made similar machines prior to their union in 1903, though it seems none of the Fisher machines may be extant. The Underwood Typewriter Co. eventually purchased Elliott-Fisher, creating the Underwood Elliott Fisher Co., a designation seen on many of these machines.

The Elliott typewriters consisted of a keyboard/type-bar/ribbon unit which rode on rails above the surface of the book. As each letter was typed, the entire machine moved one notch to the right along the support rails. Some models of these typewriters also included adding machines, giving them full bookkeeping functions.

As unusual as they are, Elliott-Fisher and related machines tend to be in the "white elephant" class for many collectors. Their size makes them somewhat unmanageable for display, and after all, few people need typed copy in bound books anymore.

Elliott-Fisher $150.00
Elliott-Hatch $150.00

Elliott-Fisher (4-row, downstrike, book typewriter): Widely used in offices during the first part of the twentieth century, the Elliott-Fisher was made to write on the pages of bound books. Later acquired by Underwood, many models of this machine include that famous name. (Milwaukee Public Museum)

Elliott-Hatch (4-row, downstrike, book typewriter): One of the predecessors to the Elliott-Fisher. This machine is fitted with eight tabulator keys, a valuable feature when typing is done in columnar accounting books. (Milwaukee Public Museum)

Emerson

The Emerson Typewriter of 1907 was one of many inventions by the well-known typewriter designer Richard Uhlig. This particular machine had an odd frontstrike action unlike any other. The type-bars did not swing up to the platen as on other frontstrikes. Instead, they were mounted on vertical rods and pivoted to the printing point from either side of the machine.

Virtually all known Emersons are designated "No. 3" and were made at a factory in Woodstock, Illinois. This was the facility set up when the Emerson business was apparently purchased by Alvah Roebuck (of Sears & Roebuck) in

1910. Prior to that time, trade literature tells us the Emerson was made first in Kittery, Maine, with a sales office in Boston. An existing advertising picture shows a machine with a decal listing the Boston location. This however, would be a scarce variation since other Emersons generally show the Woodstock site.

After production ceased, the remaining inventory was evidently purchased by an entrepreneur named Harry A. Smith, who sold the machine as the *Smith* typewriter. Another possible name-variant is *Roebuck*.

Emerson $150.00

Emerson (3-row, pivot frontstrike): Because of its unique pivoting action, the type-bars of this machine are arrayed in two banks on either side of the center. Just as a door swings on its hinge, the type-bars swing toward the printing point with each stroke. (Milwaukee Public Museum)

Empire
(see Wellington)

English

The English Typewriter was an odd machine with an appearance similar to the more familiar Hammond No. 1. Unlike the Hammond, which was a type-shuttle machine, the English was a downstrike, with type-bars swinging down from the front. The paper, after typing, rolled up into a drum behind the platen. The promoters thought this feature a good idea, so nosy onlookers could not read what was being written.

This rare typewriter was patented in 1890, sold in England and never exported to the U.S. It is the sort of thing one might find among the remaining possessions of some transatlantic traveler from the nineteenth century, or perhaps, in a container load of antiques shipped from England by people with little knowledge of typewriters!

English . . . .$1,000.00+

English (curved-keyboard, downstrike): This is said to have been the first type-bar machine invented in Britain. Subsequent inventors did much better, as the English was a failure. (Typewriter Times)

Erika

The Erika Typewriter (1910) was a diminutive 3-row portable with a folding carriage, similar to the Corona. Both the Corona and Erika were evolutions of the Standard Folding Typewriter.

The Erika was produced by Seidel & Naumann of Dresden, Germany, which issued the folding machines in models No. 1 through No. 4. Name variants include *Bijou, Gloria, Daro, Seidel & Naumann, S&N*. Like its American cousin, the Corona, the 3-row Erikas were eventually succeeded by non-folding 4-row models. Only the folding models generate much interest among collectors today.

A similar machine, called the *Perkeo* was developed as succesor to the *Albus*, an Austrian twin to the Standard Folding.

Erika (3-row) $50.00

Erika, folding (3-row, frontstrike): *A European relative of the folding Corona, the carriage folds forward over the keys for portability. (Milwaukee Public Museum)*

Bijou, folding (3-row, frontstrike): *A simple name-variant of the Erika folding machine, made by the same company. This specimen was sold in England and bears the decal of the seller at left behind the keys. (Milwaukee Public Museum)*

Famos

The Famos Typewriter was made in Germany and first offered for sale in 1910. This odd machine was a striking sight, with its large type-wheel and index mounted perpendicular to the platen. Stranger still was the way the paper was handled. Each sheet was attached to the platen, which rotated for letter spacing and moved horizontally for line spacing — just the opposite of nearly all other typewriters.

One name-variant is *Victoria*, marketed in France.

Famos $500.00

Famos (circular index): *Perhaps this typewriter should have been called the Infamous, because it was deliberately designed to punch holes in the paper. To advance to each successive letter, the platen rotated (instead of moving horizontally). To accomplish this, the machine had a little pin, which punctured the paper as it gripped the platen for rotation. The resulting document would have been well ventilated, if nothing else. (Forsdyke collection)*

Fay-Sho / Fay-Sholes
(see Rem-Sho)

Fitch

The Fitch Typewriter of 1888 is one of the handful of machines using downstrike type-bars in the backstroke configuration. While other backstroke typewriters had their type-bars standing erect at the rear, the Fitch had them poised in an angled position over the platen. On this machine, a V-shaped bracket guided each type-bar on its journey to the printing point. The actual types on the type-bars were made of hardened rubber (vulcanite) and were more fragile than those on all-metal type-bars. Inking was by an ink roller. As with other backstroke machines, paper was held in cylindrical paper baskets both in front of and behind the platen.

The Fitch was invented by Eugene Fitch of Des Moines, Iowa, and originally manufactured in Brooklyn, New York, but with little success. Another try was made in London, England, and so there are two slightly different versions of the Fitch. Each is marked accordingly.

Fitch . . . .$1,000.00+

Fitch, American (3-row, backstroke): The earlier of two versions, this machine features a front paper basket of formed metal rods, together with a curved plate decorated with patent numbers. Note the space key in the center of the bottom row: it looks just like all the other keys. (Dickerson collection, ser. 424)

Fitch, British (3-row, backstroke): Essentially the same machine as the American version, but a number of details are different. Most obvious is the front paper basket made of flat metal strips formed into near-complete circles. A short space bar is placed below the bottom row of keys. (Russo collection, ser. 3293)

Ford

The Ford Typewriter of 1895 has nothing whatever to do with Ford automobiles, which trace their roots back to the same era. The Ford Typewriter, named for its inventor E.A. Ford, was a thrust-action typewriter with an unusual open-weave covering, giving it a distinctive appearance.

Most Fords were produced with a standard cast-iron frame, but the Ford Typewriter Co. of New York was among the first to offer its product with an aluminum frame as well. Aluminum was an exotic material at the time, and its use in typewriters was considerably high-tech. In fact, even the iron-base machines had many aluminum parts, including the carriage, which was made of the lightweight metal for better speed. Surviving examples of this machine are often missing a removable plate which covered the printing ends of the type-bars as well as the three metal feed rollers which held rubber bands pressing against the platen to transport paper through the machine.

The Ford Typewriter was also sold in France as the *Hurtu* and in Germany as the *Knoch*. Despite the advanced use of aluminum, the machine was a market place failure, making it a desirable collector's item today.

Ford . . . .$1,000.00+

Ford, aluminum (3-row, thrust action): The entire frame of this machine was cast in aluminum, giving it a distinctive light appearance (as well as weight) when compared to its iron-framed sibling. This example is missing its type-bar cover plate, otherwise located just behind the basket-weave front. (Dickerson collection, ser. 72)

Ford, iron (3-row, thrust action): Exactly the same machine, except for the frame material. The iron Ford had to be painted black to prevent rust, a detail unnecessary on the aluminum-frame model. Both machines sport the open-weave front panel decorated in alternating stripes of black and copper, a very popular motif on all mechanical objects of the time. Look closely and you'll see a gap running the entire length between the platen and the carriage. This is evidence of missing feed rollers, common on Fords found today. (Clark collection, ser. 879)

Fox

The original Fox Typewriter appeared in 1898, made by the Fox Typewriter Co. of Grand Rapids, Michigan. It was a 4-row, upstrike machine, the standard configuration for the day. Fox machines had an unusually snappy feel and some even included levers to adjust their escapements for extra speed.

The upstrike models usually seen are No. 3 and 4, although models numbered 1 through 10 have been reported. In 1908, visible frontstrike models were introduced. Fox Typewriters No. 23 and 24 are both frontstrikes. In most cases, the difference among similar model numbers was in the number of keys. Fox visible machines were also sold under the name *Rapid Typewriter*, not to be confused with the rare, early thrust action machine of the same name made in Dayton, Ohio.

Other Fox machines include the intriguing 3-row, frontstrike Fox Portable of 1917 (sometimes called the *Baby Fox*). Models No. 1 and 2 of this machine were similar, and had a folding feature different from the familiar Corona. The carriage on the Fox Portable, instead of folding forward over the keyboard, collapsed down behind the machine. Litigation with Corona over patent infringement forced Fox to take this machine off the market, replacing it with the Fox Sterling, a conventional 3-row, frontstrike portable without the folding feature.

Fox Typewriters have a particular charm for their decorative decals. On many is the company logo with a realistic picture of a fox's head on a gold Maltese Cross background. On others, there is the company logo with an image of the Fox visible machine. Condition of these decals is a key element in the value of any Fox typewriter.

Fox (upstrikes) $100.00
Fox (frontstrikes) $50.00
Fox Portable No. 1, 2, Baby Fox $150.00
Fox Sterling $150.00

Fox No. 4 (4-row, upstrike): The basic appearance of all Fox upstrikes is the same. Model number is clearly indicated on a decal placed on the frame behind the top row of keys. Note the attractive decal of the fox's head on the paper table behind the platen roller. (author's collection)

Fox Visible (4-row, frontstrike): Even in switching to the conventional 4-row, frontstrike format, the Fox retained its attractive decoration and handsome appearance. (Milwaukee Public Museum)

Fox Portable No. 1 (3-row, frontstrike, folding): Somewhat similar to the folding Corona, this machine was designed with a collapsible carriage, for greater portability. The machine is identified as the No. 1 by a large, clear decal at right. Carriage in this photo is shown in the "up" position, ready for use. (Dickerson collection, ser. 211)

Fox Portable No. 1: Photo shows the carriage in the "down" position, allowing the machine to fit into its slender case.

Fox Portable No. 2 (3-row, frontstrike, folding): Nearly identical to the No. 1, the Fox Portable No. 2 is identified by its different decals. Note the Fox Type-writer logo at machine right. Also, if you look very care-fully between the shafts of the Q and W keys and the I and O keys, you will see the numeral "2," indicating the model number. (author's collection)

Fox Sterling (3-row, frontstrike): In eliminating the folding feature, Fox also squared off its machine, resulting in a chunkier appearance. The attractive decals, however, remain. (Dickerson collection, ser. S12887)

Franklin

To the modern eye, the Franklin Typewriter is one of the most radically different typewriters of all. Its curved, nearly semi-circular keyboard and solid shield covering erect type-bars give this machine a profile that immediately draws everyone's interest. It was a popular machine in its time, and many specimens survive today.

Introduced about 1891, the Franklin was the first major typewriter created by Wellington Parker Kidder, the Boston inventor later responsible for many other machines. The Franklin's type-bars were unusual in that they were linked to the keys by gears, a novel idea used in some later machines, but first tried by Kidder in this machine.

All Franklins are similar, but their naming, numbering, and identification have proven troublesome. The different models are mostly identified by the name decorating the front of the machine. In 1987, collector Richard Dickerson cataloged the different machines as follows (in order of manufacture):

Type I: "THE FRANKLIN" in sans-serif capitals on a gold swash.
Type II: "The Franklin" in Old-English lettering, upper and lowercase.
Type III: "New Franklin" in plain Roman letters, upper and lowercase. Some of these have plain black paper tables which may have pin-striped borders (**IIIa**), others have paper tables decorated with a shield showing a picture of the typewriter and the slogan "Perfection the Aim of Invention" (**IIIb**).
Type IV: "Franklin" in flowing script letters. In this type, machines have model numbers. No. 7 had 40 keys. No. 8 had 42 keys. Some in this group (**IVa**) have paper tables with shields like the IIIb's, others (**IVb**) have shields with portraits of Ben Franklin.
Type V: "Franklin" in flowing script letters. Ribbon spools hidden below the machine as opposed to spools on a bracket over the printing point on all earlier models. Machines in this group also had model numbers: No. 9 had 40 keys, No. 10 had 42 keys.

In a number of sources, the very first version of Franklin is said to have had only two rows of keys, however existence of this model has yet to be confirmed.

Most Franklins come with a wooden baseboard, and if the base is missing, the machine should be considered incomplete. As with most other machines, presence of the original tin cover is also always desirable.

Franklin (Type I) $500.00
Franklin (all other models) $250.00

Franklin, Type I (3-row, curved-keyboard, down-strike): The earliest Franklin. It is distinguished from others by the decal on the front. (Clark collection, ser. 49)

Franklin, Type II (3-row, curved-keyboard, downstrike): The second model of this machine has its name displayed in Old English lettering. Note also the brass manufacturer's plate below the keys. (Dickerson collection, ser. 2280)

New Franklin, Type IIIa (3-row, curved-keyboard, down-strike): This model may have been "New," but newer only than the machines that preceded it. At least three models came later. The brass plate behind the keys has been replaced by decals. (Dickerson collection, ser. 7746)

Franklin No. 7, Type IVa (3-row, curved-keyboard, downstrike): The "Franklin" name in script is the most common decoration seen on this long line of machines. Note the clearly visible ribbon system mounted behind the type-bar shield. A similar ribbon mechanism appears on all Franklins to this point. (Dickerson collection, ser. 10089)

Franklin No. 10, Type V (3-row, curved-keyboard, downstrike): On the last Franklin models, the earlier awkward ribbon system was replaced with the spools below the frame and out of sight. Visible in this view is the paper table decal featuring the portrait of Benjamin Franklin. Type V Franklins may be either No. 9 or No. 10. (Dickerson collection, ser. 19168)

Garbell

The Garbell Typewriter, invented by Max Garbel and introduced in 1919, was a lightweight, flat portable with thrust-action type-bars actuated through a gear linkage to the keys. It was a rather attractive little machine, very flat in profile and only four inches high. There are references in trade literature to different models, but No. 3 is the most likely to be found, and there appears to be little difference, if any, among models.

Garbell $200.00

Garbell No.3 (3-row, thrust-action): The Garbell has the fan-shaped housing characteristic of most thrust-action machines, which have type-bars arranged radially out from the printing point. This lightweight machine probably never worked very well, and had a short life in the market place. (Milwaukee Public Museum)

Gardner

The Gardner Typewriter, said to have been manufactured as early as 1890, was a rather bizarre product of the British typewriter industry. Its 14-keys were arranged in a cluster.

The Gardner's operating principle called for a "chording" technique, with the user pressing a number of different keys at once for each letter. The same principle is used today by some one-handed keyboards made for computers.

The Gardner was also sold in Germany as the *Victoria*, with trade literature also mentioning a French model sold as the *Victorieuse*.

Gardner $1,000.00

Gardner (cluster-keyboard, type-sleeve): The 14 keys on the Gardner's keyboard are arranged in a cluster, and the user often had to press several at once to get the desired character. (Williams collection, no serial number)

Geniatus

This lightweight index machine was a German product dating from about 1928. Cheaply made of sheet metal, it printed by means of a loose rubber belt attached to a swinging sector. The rubber was hardened to give the type enough body to print through a ribbon. This hardened rubber made it necessary to score the strip into segments to make it flexible. The Geniatus is one of several inexpensive novelty machines made in Germany during the late 20s. Others include the *Bing* (see page 28) and *Gundka* (see page 66).

Geniatus $50.00

Geniatus (curved index): The lightweight construction of this German machine is not much better than that of a toy. It was probably intended, however, for adults. (Kramer collection)

Gourland

The Gourland was a somewhat conventional 4-row portable of the early 1920s. It had the odd feature of a hinged carriage, which could be lifted up — highly unusual for a visible machine. While the hinged carriage was necessary for viewing the work on early upstrike machines, on the Gourland it was there to provide access to the tab stops. At least one source says the Gourland was sold as the *Alexander*, which is a very similar, though not identical machine. A machine called the *Wright Speedwriter* has also been called a twin of the Gourland, although it too is similar but not identical. The Gourland is not at all common, but few collectors will go out of their way to acquire one.

Gourland $50.00

Gourland (4-row, frontstrike): This machine was made about 1920 – 25 and is a fairly ordinary portable. The carriage lifts up to allow access to tab stops. (Milwaukee Public Museum)

Granville Automatic

The Granville Automatic was a thrust-action typewriter invented by Bernard Granville, of Dayton, Ohio. It was manufactured in 1896 by the Granville Manufacturing Co. of that city, with later production in Providence, Rhode Island, by the Mossberg & Granville Manufacturing Co. The machine was an outgrowth of an earlier machine called the Rapid (see page 109), which had the same basic type-bar action.

The Granville Automatic was deemed "automatic" because most of the functions, including carriage return, could be performed from the keyboard. Trade literature tells us the machine failed in the U.S. and later was equally unsuccessful in England.

Granville Automatic $500.00

Granville Automatic (4-row, thrust-action): This big machine included large keys to handle functions such as the carriage return from the keyboard, thus earning the designation "automatic." The maker's name and location ("Mossberg & Granville Manufacturing Co., Providence, R.I.") is embossed on the front panel of this specimen. (Russo Collection, ser. 5964)

Graphic

This German machine of 1895 was a close cousin to the Hall Typewriter (see page 67), which debuted more than a decade earlier in the U.S. Given a choice between the two, however, any collector would take the Graphic. It was very attractive with deep red paint accented with the name surrounded by vines and leaves in gold. In addition, the Graphic is quite rare, while the Hall is quite common.

One other item of interest concerning the Graphic is the fact that its original manufacturer, C.F. Kindermann & Co. of Berlin, remained in business well into the twentieth century, making photographic enlargers and other darkroom equipment.

A very similar machine called the *Kneist* was offered in 1893. Another similar machine was the *Eureka* of 1898, on which the index handle was mounted at the top of the printing assembly, instead of the bottom.

Graphic, Kneist, Eureka $1,000.00

Graphic (rectangular index): The index and type plate of the Graphic is only roughly rectangular. It is slightly curved as well, setting it apart from the very similar Hall Typewriter. (Milwaukee Public Museum)

Gundka

"Gundka" was just one name for this cheap, little index machine made in Germany during the 1920s. This typewriter resembled the earlier Edelmann in form, but hardly in quality. While the Edelmann was made of heavy castings and came with a fancy bentwood cover, the Gundka was built from inexpensive sheet metal, with a tin cover.

The Gundka was made under a multitude names, including *G&K, Frolio, Scripta, Write-Easy, MW,* and more. More than 80,000 of these machines were manufactured, making the large number that survive today no surprise.

Gundka (and name variants) $50.00

Gundka (type-wheel index): A bit deceptive in appearance, the attractive little Gundka looks more substantial than it really is. Constructed of cheap sheet metal, this machine is little more than a toy. (Milwaukee Public Museum)

MW (type-wheel index): One of many, many name variants of the Gundka Typewriter, and perhaps the one most often found in the U.S. The tin cover on most MW's is painted with a wood-grained green. The initials "MW" hint that this might have been marketed by Montgomery Ward, but this fact has not been confirmed. (author's collection)

Hall

The Hall was the first index machine to be placed onto the market following the launch of the world typewriter industry by Remington in the 1870s. Patented in 1881, the Hall was originally sold at a price of $40, a low cost alternative to the $100 Remington. At a time when few people knew how to type, it didn't seem important that the user of a Hall had to pick out letters one-by-one at a snail's pace.

The Hall worked using a rectangular rubber type plate located within the square metal printing mechanism positioned directly over the paper. Underneath was a hole through which the selected letter contacted the paper. As the indicator handle was pressed to print, the entire type plate contacted the ink pad, with the exception of the letter being printed through the hole. Repeated strokes kept all of the letters sufficiently inked. The paper remained stationary.

Each machine was built into its case, which was usually made of black walnut. An attractive brass nameplate was displayed on the exterior, and locking hardware was included. No machine is considered complete without its case.

Halls traditionally have been divided up into two varieties. The first has simply been called the *Hall*, the second, the *Improved Hall* (many collectors refer to these as Nos. 1 and 2). A closer examination, however, reveals three distinct varieties of this machine. Since they did not have official model numbers, we'll refer to them in chronological order as the: *New York* Hall, *Salem* Hall, and *Boston* Hall.

The earliest Halls were made in New York. They had nickel-plated printing assemblies, 72-character type plates, and pinch levers for carriage return. Engraved into the printing assembly was the brand name, with New York indicated as the place of manufacture. The handle plate on the outer case of this earliest model read "Hall Typewriter Co., New York, U.S.A."

The second model (Salem Hall) was designated by the company as the "Improved Hall, Model of 1887." This machine had a black printing assembly, with an oval nameplate of brass showing Salem, Massachusetts, as the place of manufacture. It also had a press lever for carriage return and printed 82 characters. It's interesting how Hall claimed 82 characters using a type plate of 9-by-9 characters. The comma was located in the middle of the bottom row. The index handle, which fit into a single hole for each other character, had a choice of two offset holes for the comma, which could thus be printed in two different positions. One hole gave you the comma, the other gave you the apostrophe.

The third model (Boston Hall) was nearly identical to the Improved Model of 1887 except for two important cosmetic details. These later machines had rectangular nameplates, indicating Boston as the place of manufacture, and most of the handle plates on the outer cases were engraved with "The Improved Hall Typewriter." In addition, the Boston Hall's nameplate usually indicated the National Typewriter Co. as its maker instead of the Hall Typewriter Co. shown on earlier models. Some examples of the Boston Hall had a bracket at the bottom of the printing assembly which functioned as a space bar. There was also variation in the letter layout, with some specimens showing a 72-character type plate (8 columns by 9 rows) with a grid of raised lines on the top plate of the printing assembly. It has been suggested the grid might have been an aid to blind typists, but we have no documentation to confirm it.

Other variations in Halls include the case materials. Besides the standard walnut, Hall cases were also offered in rosewood, mahogany, leather, or plush for an additional $10. Cases other than walnut or mahogany are scarce.

We do have a general idea of dates for the different Halls. The Hall Typewriter Co. began doing business in Salem on June 1, 1885, giving us a dividing date between New York and Salem Halls. The company was no longer in the Salem city directory for 1889 – 1890, giving us a date to divide Salem and Boston Halls. The Hall was heavily advertised during its production, but ads in the major national magazines dropped out around 1894. There have been reports that production continued until the late 1890s.

The Hall was imitated widely. Other makes which used the same (or very similar) design include the Morris, made in the U.S., as well as a number of German machines: Eureka, Fortuna, Graphic, and Kneist.

The Hall was obviously a very popular machine. Thousands were manufactured, and it seems a substantial number have survived. The Hall's unusual design is very appealing, and collectors can be grateful these odd devices are so accessible.

Hall (New York) $200.00
Hall (Salem, Boston) $175.00
Hall (any model with case
    other than walnut or mahogany) ...$200.00

Hall, New York (rectangular index): The earliest model of the Hall, featuring a nickel-plated printing assembly. The bell is mounted on the inside of the frame at right. (Russo Collection, ser. 2004)

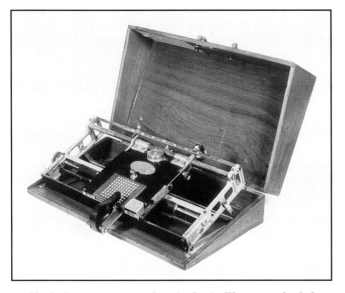

Hall, Salem (rectangular index): The second of three major Hall variations. On this model, the printing assembly is black, with an oval brass nameplate. The bell is mounted on the upper rail. (author's collection, ser. 6689)

Hall, Boston (rectangular index): The latest of the Hall variations, showing a rectangular nameplate. This example also has the space bar at the bottom of the printing assembly as well as the raised grid on the letter index. (Russo collection, ser. 12897)

Hammond

The Hammond Typewriter, invented by James B. Hammond and introduced in the early 1880s, is one of the most fascinating writing machines ever produced. Its design was so durable that it remained in production until nearly 1980, perhaps the most successful typewriter concept of all time.

The Hammond printed using a type-shuttle: a curved strip of hardened rubber that slid from side to side into position as each letter was selected from the keyboard. A spring-loaded hammer swung from behind, striking the paper against the type-shuttle with the ribbon in between. The reason for the spring-loaded hammer was to give each letter a uniform impression, rather than relying upon a constant touch by the typist. When paper was loaded into the machine, it was rolled up into a cylindrical paper basket and then fed out line-by-line as typing progressed.

Hammond type-shuttles were available in hundreds of different typefaces and for every language you can imagine. The Hammond exploited the interchangeability of typefaces more fully than any other single element typewriter until the arrival of IBM's Selectric in 1961.

The Hammond Typewriter Company produced so many different models and variations that identifying them can be a problem. If you know which details to examine, though, your job can be much easier.

The Hammond No. 1 was a very attractive machine, with the mechanism entirely jacketed in wood. Its thick ebony keys were arranged in two semi-circular rows and arranged in what was called the "Ideal" keyboard. For some reason, early typewriter trade journals erroneously applied the term "Ideal" to many other non-standard keyboards (especially the Blickensderfer) and some collectors continue the tradition. It is, nonetheless, incorrect. "Ideal" applies to the Hammond alone.

There are a few other details about the Hammond No. 1 that are important to note. This model did not have a single-piece type-shuttle as seen on later models. Instead, the element is made of two halves, which pivot from a center point. The central "turret" on the No. 1 was covered with an olive-colored celluloid sheet, etched with the Hammond brand name. This piece is so frequently missing that some collectors believe not all machines included it. The author believes a Hammond No. 1 without this piece is incomplete. Some (but not all) examples of the No. 1 also have a small metal nameplate on the horizontal deck of the machine, just behind the keyboard. Some others have a curved cutout, probably intended as a grip for lifting the machine out of its wooden jacket.

The Hammond Typewriter Company responded to the demand for the standard, straight-row, QWERTY keyboard and eventually offered its No. 1 model with that configuration. The No. 1 "Universal" did not have the wooden covering seen on the No. 1 Ideal, and the exposed mechanism makes it look like many later models. The key to identifying it is the two-piece type element.

Hammond also introduced a transitional model which collectors call the "1b." This was a curved-keyboard machine, with the two-piece type-element, but without the wooden covering seen on earlier No. 1's. The "1b" is quickly identified by its thick ebony keys. Some are also reported with nickel-rimmed keys of a different style than later models.

The Hammond No. 2 was introduced in 1895. The wooden covering seen on the No. 1 was completely gone. More important, the two-piece type-element was replaced with the single-piece, curved type-shuttle which would remain a feature of all future Hammonds. The shuttle was mounted in a thick metal ring called the "anvil," which provided the heavy support needed for the strike of the hammer. Hammond frequently referred to its "shuttle and anvil" system in advertisements of the time. The Hammond No. 2 was offered with either the curved Ideal keyboard or the 3-row Universal keyboard. Some models also included a celluloid card or strip with the Hammond logo just above the keyboard. This served as a platform for keyboard charts supplied with alternative type-shuttles.

The similarity of the No. 2 to some later models creates confusion in telling them all apart. The key to identifying a No. 2 is the large metal tab at the front of the turret in the middle of the machine. This tab was used to push the ribbon down out of the way so the user could see the line currently being typed. On earlier models the current line was hidden until the paper was fed out of the machine.

Most Hammonds were equipped with two shift keys, one for capitals, the other for figures. This accommodated the standard shuttle, which had three rows of type. A few models throughout the years were offered with three shifts to operate special 4-row shuttles which included special mathematical or scientific symbols.

All Hammonds also included an "impression strip," a flat rubber band hooked onto the carriage and placed between the hammer and the type. This served the same function as the rubber used on round platens of other machines and was critical to a getting a good type impression. The impression strip is almost always missing on surviving Hammonds, but occasionally you will find one intact.

Hammond also made machines with model numbers 3 through 8. These were all based on the No. 2 but offered with wider carriages or other special features. The specifics are as follows:

No. 3: 11⅓" carriage
No. 4: regular 8½" carriage, 9 characters per inch
No: 5: Ideal keyboard only, triple-shift, 4-row Greek shuttle
No. 6: 16" carriage
No. 7: 20" carriage
No. 8: 30" carriage

The author knows of no documentation for any Hammond models 9, 10, or 11.

The Hammond No. 12, introduced in 1905, was the next major improvement in the line. In appearance, it was very similar to the No. 2. Its main difference was the absence of the big metal tab on the front of the turret. Instead, you will notice a thick wire bracket, nearly a full-circle in shape, attached to the ribbon holder. This bracket was part of what's called the ribbon "vibrator," which moved the ribbon upward to meet the hammer for each letter typed. At rest, the ribbon was down out of the way, so that the user could see the typing. By 1905, you see, the visible typewriter was becoming the standard, and customers demanded nothing less than full visibility. Most Hammond 12s included the celluloid strip or card behind the keyboard, with a logo identifying the machine as a No. 12. As with other Hammonds, this machine was offered with either the Ideal or Universal keyboard.

The Hammond Multiplex, first marketed in 1913 continued the evolution of this fine typewriter line. The machine was dubbed "Multiplex" because it was designed to carry two type-shuttles at one time. The anvil ring at the top of the turret was configured with a knob allowing the user to switch between the two shuttles with one quick turn. Thus, a Roman typeface and an italic typeface could be kept on the machine, making a change between the two quick and easy. The Multiplex also used a metal drawband to power the carriage return. Earlier models used a more expensive rack-and-pinion system.

The first Hammond Multiplex machines were similar in appearance to the No. 12, with an exposed mechanism and the celluloid strip above the keys. Around 1916, Hammond improved the machine by adding a metal covering to enclose the works. The Multiplex was offered with either Ideal or Universal keyboards. Other variations included multiple-pitch, aluminum frames, and triple or quadruple shifts. Some Multiplexes were painted military green for use by the Army in World War I.

In 1923, the Folding Multiplex was introduced. This portable featured a keyboard which folded upward for portability, possibly inspired by the folding Corona. The Folding Hammond is also seen labeled "Model 26."

The future of the Hammond changed around 1927 when new management took over the company. According to typewriter historian Paul Lippman, James B. Hammond died in 1913 and willed his patents to New York's Metropolitan Museum of Art. A Frederick Hepburn Co. bought the patents and changed the name of the machine to *Varityper*, but eventually went bankrupt. Business machine salesman Frank B. Coxhead led a group of investors to buy the company in 1933 and continue producing Varitypers. Under this banner, the machine evolved into a cold typesetting device, made to produce masters for printing by photo-offset. The Varityper was electrified and updated into the 1970s, when it was finally taken off the market in favor of photographic and electronic typesetting systems. Still, the basic mechanism of a Varityper from the 1970s was the same in concept as the original Hammond.

That original Hammond, incidentally, has traditionally been dated at 1880 – 81 in existing historical literature. However, researchers in Indiana have recently uncovered a letter written by Hoosier scholar Charles Peirce specifically mentioning his "new" Hammond Typewriter — *number 85*. The letter is dated 1884, making that year more likely for the market introduction of this historic machine.

Considering all the variations, it would be possible to build a rich collection based on Hammond Typewriters alone. Fortunately, Hammonds today are very common, making them available to any collector who wants to own one.

Hammond No. 1 (curved or straight) $250.00
Hammond No. 1b (curved-keyboard) $200.00
Hammond No. 2, 3, 12 (curved-keyboard) $150.00
Hammond No. 2, 3, 12 (straight-keyboard) $75.00
Hammond No. 4 (curved-keyboard, triple-shift) $150.00
Hammond No. 5-8 (straight keyboard) $175.00
Hammond No. 5-8 (curved keyboard) $200.00
Hammond Multiplex (curved keyboard) $100.00
Hammond Multiplex (straight keyboard) $60.00
Hammond Folding (or Model 26) $75.00
Varityper (any) $50.00

Hammond No. 1 (curved-keyboard, type-shuttle): *The beautiful first model of the Hammond Typewriter. On this example, the center turret has its celluloid cover intact, and a nameplate is in place on the deck. Ribbon spools are made of hard rubber, and they accommodate a narrow ribbon, only 5⁄16" wide (7⁄16" on some other specimens). The case material on this machine is mahogany. It also is seen in oak. (Dickerson collection, ser. 3898)*

Hammond No. 1 (detail): *Overhead view of the type-shuttle on the Hammond No. 1. Notice how it is divided into two fan-shaped lobes. On later models, the type-shuttle was a single curved strip. (Dickerson collection)*

Hammond No. 1b (curved-keyboard, type-shuttle): *Mechanically, this machine is nearly identical to the original Hammond No. 1. However, there is no wooden jacket, and works are visible to the user. (Dickerson collection, ser. 21135).*

Hammond No. 2, straight (3-row, type-shuttle): *This specimen includes the celluloid nameplate above the keyboard. Not all No. 2's came with this piece. (author's collection)*

Hammond No. 2, straight (detail): *The finger tab on the No. 2 is pressed to move the type-shuttle out of the way so the user can view the line being typed. This tab is a key feature for distinguishing No.2 machines and their variants from other models. (author's collection)*

Hammond No. 2, curved (curved-keyboard, type-shuttle): *All Hammond models were available with either the straight (Universal) keyboard or the curved (Ideal) keyboard as shown here. On this example, the curved celluloid nameplate behind the keys is black. It is also seen in ivory. Note the worn spot on the finger tab showing where the user of this machine constantly touched it to see the work. The serial number, "Remod 9996" indicates that this machine was rebuilt from an old No. 1. (author's collection, ser. Remod 9996)*

Hammond No. 12, straight (3-row, type-shuttle): *To the untrained eye, the Hammond No. 2 and No. 12 are very much alike. An informed collector will notice, however, that there is no finger tab atop the turret on this machine. (author's collection)*

Hammond No. 12 (detail): *The telltale feature identifying a Hammond No. 12 is this curved bracket on top of the turret. The bracket automatically raises the ribbon for each stroke, and then immediately drops it out of the way, so typing is completely visible. The little loop at front lets the user raise the ribbon manually for replacement or adjustment. (author's collection)*

Hammond Multiplex, open, straight (3-row, type-shuttle): *The earlier version of the Hammond Multiplex, with open works similar to the No. 2 and No. 12. The machine is clearly identified as a "Multiplex" on the celluloid nameplate. A twirl of the knob atop the turret at its center lets the user switch between one of two type-shuttles always carried on the machine. (Rauen collection, Ser. 180880)*

Hammond Multiplex, open, curved (curved keyboard, type-shuttle): *The curved or Ideal keyboard was available on all Hammond models up to and including the Multiplex. This open machine is identified as a Multiplex on the black nameplate behind the keyboard. Otherwise, it looks much like a No. 12. (Wild collection)*

Hammond Multiplex, closed, straight (3-row, type-shuttle): *The later version of the Multiplex, with sheet metal covering over the works. Informally called "closed" by collectors, who term the earlier machine "open." The designation "Multiplex" is clearly seen on the cover plates. (Rauen collection, Ser. 190274)*

Hammond Folding (3-row, type-shuttle, folding): *All Folding Hammonds are Multiplexes. This inventive design put all the features of the standard machine into a package that was considerably more portable. (author's collection, ser. F243172G2)*

Hammond Folding (folded position): The keyboard on the Folding Hammond flipped up upon release of catches on each side. For carrying, a boxy lid slipped down and fastened to the base. (author's collection)

Hammonia

The Hammonia Typewriter, of 1882, is notable as the first typewriter ever made in Germany. Looking much like a paper cutter, the caps-only machine had its type on the edge of a thin metal bar with a handle on the end. The user moved the bar in or out to select the letter and pushed down to print. The paper did not move for letter spacing. Instead, the whole printing mechanism moved left to right as the typing proceeded.

The Hammonia was sold mostly in Europe by the German firm Guhl & Harbeck, but some machines were exported to North America.

Hammonia . . . .**$1,000.00+**

Hammonia (linear index): The Hammonia of Germany is certainly one of the more unlikely looking machines of typewriter history. At a casual glance it might seem more suitable for cutting paper or slicing bread. (Milwaukee Public Museum)

Harris Visible

The Harris Visible, introduced in 1911, was a rather conventional frontstrike typewriter with a 3-row keyboard. This machine was at one time marketed through the Sears & Roebuck catalog. It was also sold as the *Rex, Rex Visible, Autocrat,* and *Reporter's Special.* Some models had numerical designations, but differences among them were minor.

Harris Visible (and name variants) **$50.00**

Harris Visible No. 4 (3-row, frontstrike): There are few differences among Harris Visibles and their variants. This model No. 4 has a ribbon color lever at right, which is not seen on some earlier models. The Harris is relatively unimportant to typewriter history. (Milwaukee Public Museum)

Hartford

The Hartford Typewriter was made in three different models. The first was a double-keyboard, upstrike machine, introduced in 1894. No. 2 was another double-keyboard machine, but we have little documentation to tell us how it differed from the first model. The third model, offered concurrently with the No. 2 beginning about 1901, was called the "Shift-Key" Hartford (some are marked "No. 3"), which was a 4-row upstrike. The makers apparently offered the two different keyboards to accommodate consumer preferences of the time. The only feature which distinguished these machines from others of their day was the spring-loaded carriage, which flipped up at the touch of a lever to reveal the work. Trade literature says the machine was renamed *Cleveland* when the factory was moved to that Ohio city from Hartford, Connecticut.

Hartford (any model) **$200.00**

Hartford, double-case (double-keyboard, upstrike): One of many double-keyboard machines made in the mid 1890s. It sold for $50, which, according to one trade magazine, may not have left enough profit for its makers to stay in business. (Milwaukee Public Museum)

Hartford, shift-key (4-row, upstrike): The 4-row version of the Hartford Typewriter, with a shift key for capitals. Some examples have no model designation, others are labeled "No. 3." (Milwaukee Public Museum)

Helios

The Helios Typewriter was an intriguing German product introduced to market in 1908. It used a very different keyboard with only two rows of keys instead of the three usually found on type-wheel machines. To accommodate all the letters, numerals, and punctuation needed for typing, each key handled four different characters, selected by using one (or none) of three different shift keys.

Around 1914, the Helios was improved and marketed as the *Helios-Klimax* and was also sold under the name *Ultima*. Other name-variants reported are *Bamberger* and *Portable Extra*.

Helios **$300.00**
Helios-Klimax & name variants **$250.00**

Helios (2-row, type-wheel): With only 21 keys arranged in two rows, some fancy fingerwork and three shift keys were required to type anything on the Helios. Note the type-wheel, which has four rows of characters. (author's collection, ser. 3226)

Herrington

The Herrington was a simple index machine using a circular type-wheel mounted with its diameter perpendicular to the platen. It was patented by G.H. Herrington and D.G. Millison in 1884, and made by McClees, Millison and Co. in Chicago. The machine was marked "Herrington Simplex" and was similar in design to the Dollar typewriter, but better made. A British machine known as the *Simplex* seems to be nearly identical to the Herrington.

Herrington **\$250.00**

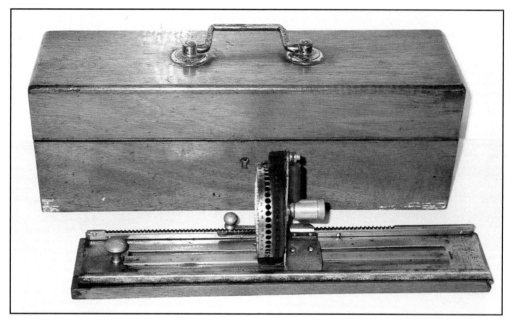

Simplex (circular index): *British machine matching the Herrington, which was made in the U.S.A. This specimen is made of silver-colored metal and is marked "Universal Simplex." A Herrington in the Clark collection is made of gold-colored metal, but we do not know if these differences are seen on all such examples of each machine. (Williams collection)*

Horton

The Horton Typewriter, patented in 1883, was manufactured in Toronto, Canada. It was one of the very earliest of the frontstrike design. Indeed, it has been credited as the first visible type-bar machine. Its ribbon path was perpendicular to the platen, obscuring the center of the typed line. Early models feature a long extension of the base at the rear of the machine (the reverse of what is seen on the Caligraph). Very few were made, and it is a most desirable collectors item today.

Horton . . . .**\$1,000.00+**

Horton (double-keyboard, oblique frontstrike): *The open frame and angular structure give the Horton an appearance somewhat like a skyscraper under construction. The bulky mountings for the large number of type-bars were accommodated by placing them in three parallel arcs. Space bars are located at each side as on the Caligraph. This is the later version of the machine, without the extended base at rear. (Clark collection, no serial number)*

IBM
(see Electromatic & Index entry)

Ideal

The Ideal Typewriter was patented by two Americans in 1897, but it was manufactured in Germany by Seidel & Naumann of Dresden (makers of bicycles and sewing machines, as well as the Erika Typewriter). This was a 4-row, oblique-frontstrike machine noted for its distinctive open metalwork frame with the logo molded-in.

In this case, quite a bit of quality went along with the pretty exterior. The type-bars were U-shaped in cross section, giving them exceptional rigidity with light weight. The carriage return lever was located at the left side of the keyboard rather than on the carriage itself. The shift keys offered a very light touch, since they shifted both the type-bars and carriage together, the two meeting at a midpoint (virtually all other machines shifted either the carriage or the type-bars, but not both). Also of note was the tabulator, a lever at bottom in the front.

Later development of the Ideal eventually turned it into a plain-looking 4-row, frontstrike machine without the ornamental metalwork. The machines of interest to collectors are those with the ornamental frame, said to be designated Models A1 through A4. Models A1 and A2 had logos and decals done in a lettering style that is older looking and fancier than the subsequent A3 and A4. As with so many other machines, however, the apparent model designations can be confusing. For instance, a machine labeled "Ideal A" was displayed a few years ago. It resembled the later machines, A3 and A4.

Ideal (with ornamental frame) ...$65.00

Ideal A4 (4-row, oblique frontstrike): The thick logo painted gold and molded into the side of the machine gives it eye appeal. A number of mechanical innovations makes it special as well. Note that even the ribbon spools on this model bear the machine's logo. (Milwaukee Public Museum)

Imperial

The Imperial Typewriter Co., of Great Britain, produced a long line of typewriters, most of which are conventional machines of little interest to collectors. What will attract collectors, however, are the earliest products of this company: Models A, B, C, and D.

The Imperial A (1908) and B (1915) were essentially similar, with 3-row, curved keyboards and vertical type-bars striking down from the front. A lightweight Model C was also offered, with an aluminum frame.

Besides the curved keyboard, there were additional details that added to the charm of these machines. First, a press on the shift keys moved the entire keyboard unit forward or back to accommodate typing of alternate characters. Second, the entire keyboard/type-bar assembly was a single unit, made to detach from the machine by releasing a few simple levers. This allowed for easy interchange of different typefaces, and it also permitted easy cleaning inside the machine.

The Imperial D (1919) was similar to the A, B, and C, but it had a 3-row, straight keyboard instead of the curved, with an aluminum frame standard. It otherwise shared the basic features of the earlier models. The Model D was also called the *Imperial Portable* and is said to have been sold under the *Imperial Junior* name as well. These portables are usually found in green, although they were made in black as well.

A German copy of the Imperial B was sold as the *Faktotum, Forte-Type,* and *Leframa.* In France, the same machine was called the *Typo.*

Imperials were all sold in great numbers, and many still survive today.

Imperial (curved keyboard) $175.00
Imperial (straight keyboard) $125.00

Imperial B (3-row, curved-keyboard, downstrike):
This British machine is very appealing, not only to look
at but to type on as well. The downstrike mechanism and
the curved keyboard make it something of a cousin to the
earlier Franklin Typewriter from the U.S. (author's col-
lection)

Imperial Portable (3-row, downstrike): Essentially
similar to the earlier Imperial, but with a straight instead
of a curved keyboard. Also known as the Imperial D.
(author's collection)

Index Visible

This strange rarity was known to collectors only through old trade ads until 1995 when a specimen was finally uncovered.

The Index Visible was an index machine that looked something like a keyboard machine. The user was intended to put his finger in a loop at the end of a braided cord. On pulling the cord, and placing the finger on the appropriate "key," the type-wheel spun into the correct place. All the keys in each row were mounted on a single support bar, so when one key was pressed for printing, the whole row went down with it. The cord action is somewhat similar to the Saturn Typewriter from Switzerland (see page 121)

Index Visible (type-wheel, pull-cord index): A very unusual
machine with a keyboard typewriter appearance, but with an index
typewriter function. The leather loop at right fit around the user's fin-
ger as each letter was selected from the "keyboard." (Clark collection,
ser. 116)

Index Visible ....$1,000.00+

Ingersoll

The Ingersoll Typewriter is surely one of the cheapest, most improbable, and least practical designs ever offered in writing machines.

Placed on a thin base of sheet metal, two wooden pegs supported a stiff coiled wire on which the rubber types slid, each letter mounted on a small wooden block (type-slug). The base sat atop the paper, which lay flat on the table. The user was expected to select letters, one-by-one, press them onto one of two ink pads (one red, one black) and then press them down to the paper to print.

The same machine was also sold as the *Domestic Typewriter*, and possibly under the name *Nason* as well. The closest date we have for the Ingersoll comes from its appearance in an 1886 office supply catalog, where it was priced at $2.25.

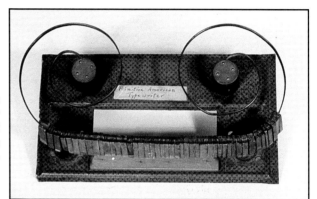

Late, apparently, the Ingersoll sold for $1.00. Even at that price, it cost too much!

Ingersoll $500.00

Ingersoll (type-slug index): Each letter on the Ingersoll was mounted on a wooden slug and was moved into place as needed for printing. Another version of the Ingersoll has a wooden base, but this specimen has a thin sheet metal base. The label "Primitive American Typewriter" was applied by the collector who originally found the machine. (Clark collection, no serial number)

International

The International Typewriter, patented in 1889, was invented by Lucien Crandall, designer of many typewriters, including a famous one bearing his own name. The International is interesting for the two different models offered.

One model was a double-keyboard upstrike machine with the upper and lower halves of the keyboard separated by a bar on the frame. The machine also featured attractive ornamental cutouts in its sides.

The other model of the International had a 4-row keyboard, using a shift-key to print capitals. There was a big difference, however, between the International and other shift-key machines. With others, each type-bar carried two or three characters (depending on the number of shift keys), and the carriage or type-basket shifted in position to bring the proper type to the printing point. On the International there was a separate type-bar for each character, so that each key controlled two type-bars. When the shift key was pressed, the entire circle of type-bars shifted one position to the side, bringing the proper type-bar into place.

There is some disagreement in the historical literature over which model was first, the single- or double-keyboard. Some sources, however, say the earliest machines had a ribbon that ran front to back, and there are early advertising cuts showing the single-keyboard machine with that configuration. This supports the idea that the 4-row model was introduced first.

Neither International made much impact in the market place. Today, therefore, each is a desirable collector's piece.

International (either model) . . . .$1,000.00+

International double-keyboard (double-keyboard, upstrike): The cloud-shaped cutouts on the side frame of this machine gives it a distinctive look. The keyboard is separated into two different banks, with a dividing partition in between. (Milwaukee Public Museum)

International single-keyboard (4-row, upstrike): A close look at the type-bar rods behind the keyboard shows a very crowded arrangement. That's because every key controlled two type-bars, each with only a single letter. Note the unusual square shape of the keys on this machine. (Milwaukee Public Museum)

International No. 5
(see New American No. 5)

Jackson

The Jackson Typewriter, like a number of others in this book, is one that is not adequately described in the typical collector's shorthand. Although this machine could be called a 4-row, frontstrike, it was hardly typical of that format. With types resting in an ink pad, the type-bars made each letter's printing surface do a somersault on its way to the platen. Each type-bar resembled an elongated pantograph, with the scissors action accomplishing the mechanical gymnastics.

The Jackson was invented in 1895 by Andrew W. Steiger of Bridgeport, Connecticut, and it was manufactured in Boston, Massachusetts.

Jackson . . . .$1,000.00+

Jackson (4-row, frontstrike, ink pad): The type-bars are broadly fanned out in front of the printing point on this machine to make room for the complex linkages. At rest, each type-head is in contact with an ink pad. (Clark collection, ser. 723)

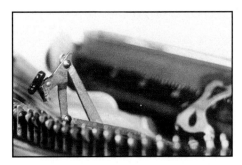

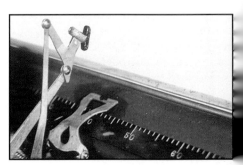

Jackson action: This close-up shows the type-bar at the beginning of its journey to the platen. The type head is beginning its somersault...

...in midstream, the scissors action of the type-bar linkage is most apparent...

...at the end of the stroke, the type-bar is ready to strike the platen. The type-head has now rotated completely into the correct position. (Clark collection)

Jewett

As mentioned earlier in this book, the Jewett was an evolution of the Duplex Typewriter. The Jewett, produced in Des Moines, Iowa, was an attractive double-keyboard, upstrike machine, apparently first sold as the "*American Standard*." However, trademark litigation with Remington (which called its machines "Remington Standard") forced the name change to Jewett. This *American Standard* should not be confused with a 3-row, upstrike machine of the same name designed by Lucien Crandall, but apparently never produced.

The Duplex No. 2, the *American Standard*, and Jewett No. 1 are all apparently identical. They are distinguished by their lightweight, open-sided frames and the small space bar located at the bottom right of the keyboard. Later models of the Jewett had larger space bars, centered at the bottom of the keyboard.

The company which produced these machines went through a number of name changes. Beginning as the Duplex Typewriter Co., it then became the Duplex-Jewett Typewriter Co. and finally, the Jewett Typewriter Co. George Jewett, a lumber merchant of Des Moines, Iowa, was the chief financial backer and became the moving force behind the business. He literally traveled the world to market his machine, and the Jewett is said to have been the first typewriter used by the Russian government in the Kremlin, as well as the first machine used by the Vatican and by Kaiser Wilhelm of Germany.

Dates for the Jewett have been reported as early as 1892. The *American Standard* version of the machine was advertised as early as 1894, concurrently, it seems, with the Duplex. The brand name "Jewett" was not used in ads until 1898, and the machine illustrated in the ads appears to be the No. 2. It remains unclear just when the original Jewett made its debut.

Numbered models of the Jewett apparently went as high as No. 11. The Jewett No. 1 bore no model number, but later models did. Otherwise they'd be difficult to identify, since the differences among them are subtle. Early trade literature also mentions front-striking models of this machine. The Jewett was also assembled in Germany and sold under the name *Germania* and *Germania-Jewett*. Important to the value of any Jewett is the condition of the large gold decals prominently seen on this machine.

Jewett (any model) $125.00
American Standard $250.00

American Standard (double-keyboard, upstrike): *Apparently identical to the Jewett No. 1 and Duplex No. 2. The nameplate at the top/front of the machine indicates the Duplex Typewriter Co. as the manufacturer. Note the open-sided frame and short space bar offset to the right of the machine, an identifying characteristic of the Jewett No. 1 and its lookalikes. (Milwaukee Public Museum)*

Jewett No. 2 (double-keyboard, upstrike): *The prominent "No. 2" on the frame of this machine makes it easy to identify, as is the case with subsequent Jewett models. The only Jewett not showing a model number is the No. 1. Note the larger, centered space bar and the maker's name: "Duplex-Jewett Typewriter Co." (author's collection)*

Junior
(see Bennett)

Kanzler

The remarkable Kanzler Typewriter was a German machine, introduced in that country in 1903. It was a massive device, with an unusual type-bar mechanism. Thrust-action is seen on other machines, but not quite in the way it was used on the Kanzler. Each type-bar on this typewriter carried the characters for four keys — eight characters in all when considering the shift. An ingenious set of linkages raised or lowered each type-bar to the appropriate position as it moved forward to strike the platen on each key stroke.

There were four models of the Kanzler. The first is much smaller than the others and very scarce. The others are very large, and the differences among them are slight. This machine apparently was popular in its time, and there are many survivors.

Kanzler No. 1 . . . .$750.00
Kanzler No. 2-4 . . . .$250.00

Kanzler No. 3 (4-row, thrust-action, curved keyboard): This German typewriter presents a massive, bulky appearance, with a distinctively curved keyboard. A curious feature is its "cascading" keys. When any key is pressed, it carries down with it all of the others in its vertical row. The two large knobs at the bottom of the keyboard are the shift keys. (Dickerson collection, ser. 3284)

Keaton Music Typewriter

The Keaton Music Typewriter is one of the more modern machines that attracts today's collectors' eyes. Invented in 1936, this machine was marketed mostly in the early 1950s.

The Keaton's keyboard formed a near-complete circle and was manipulated up and down along tracks to print on a piece of staff paper mounted on the flat platen below. These machines were rather slow to operate and were not used as much by musicians as by small music publishers, who found them ideal for producing sheet music masters for small-run printing.

The Keaton Music Typewriter came in a large carrying case without which no machine should be considered complete.

Keaton Music Typewriter $300.00

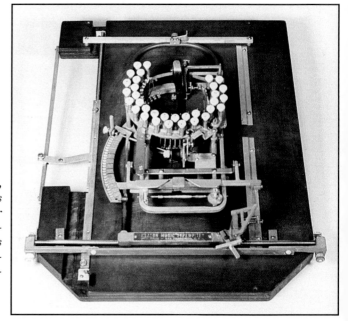

Keaton Music Typewriter (circular keyboard, downstrike): The downstrike mechanism of this machine is similar to the much earlier Crary Typewriter (see page 45). However, here it is adapted to music writing. A lever along the curved track seen at the machine's left moves the printing point up or down for correct positioning on the musical staff. (Milwaukee Public Museum)

Keystone

The Keystone Typewriter of 1899, made in Harrisburg, Pennsylvania, was a lightweight, single-element machine using a swinging sector type-shuttle and a rear-strike hammer. It was rather cheaply made and had little market impact.

The poor quality metal used in the Keystone's carriage poses problems for modern collectors. Owners of Keystones are warned that oil of any kind can damage this important component. As it is, many Keystones are found with carriages that are already broken.

There were two models of the Keystone. On one, the key linkages were uncovered. The other had a cover plate bearing an attractive keystone logo.

Keystone **$300.00**

Keystone, open (3-row, type-shuttle): This machine is characterized by its open works and attractive nickel-plated trim. If you look carefully, you can see the keystone-shaped nameplate mounted on the base to the left of the machine, as well as the name in gold at front. Some examples are reported with copper stripe decoration. (Russo collection, ser. 1007)

Keystone, covered (3-row, type-shuttle): The other model of this typewriter features a cover plate with a red and gold keystone-shaped logo. It is assumed that this machine is a later model than the open version. (Dickerson collection, ser. 4085)

Kosmopolit

Rather large as index machines go, 1888's Kosmopolit was the second typewriter product of the German firm Guhl & Harbeck, which also produced the Hammonia, Germany's first writing machine (see page 74). A careful observer will note that the Kosmopolit and Hammonia apparently shared the same base casting, although the mechanism was different on each.

The Kosmopolit was operated by swinging a handle from a pivot point. Unlike its prececessor, it typed both upper and lower case letters. Guhl & Harbeck did export their products to North America, so although this rare machine is more likely to be found in Europe, it may be possible to find it on this side of the Atlantic as well. The machine is also said to have been marketed in England as the *Cosmopolitan*.

Kosmopolit . . . .**$1,000.00+**

Kosmopolit (swinging sector index): This is a heavyweight compared to other index machines. It is characterized by its large swinging arm and massive alignment comb. As with its cousin, the Hammonia, the printing assembly moved left to right while the paper remained still. (Milwaukee Public Museum)

Lambert

There are few machines that appeal to typewriters collectors in just the same way as the Lambert. This ingenious device dating from 1902 was truly a one-of-a-kind design. Although it appears to be an index machine at first glance, it was in actuality a keyboard typewriter. Unlike other keyboards, however, this one was circular in shape with all of its keys attached to a solid surface. The type element was a section of a sphere. When any key was pressed, the type element pivoted into place via a ball-and-socket joint. Inking was by an ink pad, and the paper feed was unusual in that the top of the sheet was clamped into the roller and fed into the machine as each line was advanced.

Lambert, embossed (circular keyboard): Model numbers for Lamberts are confusing. Those with the logo embossed into the base are apparently either No. 1 or No. 2, but it's unclear which is which. (author's collection, ser. 4449)

The Lambert was one of many inventions produced by Frank Lambert, a French immigrant to the United States, who took 17 years to perfect the design. Lambert's voice, incidentally, is on the oldest playable recording in existence: the drum of a mechanism for a prototype "talking clock" Lambert designed (with the approval of Thomas Edison) in 1878.

Lambert typewriters were made both in the United States and Europe. The machine's manufacturer in England was the Gramophone and Typewriter Co., which also produced phonographs and originated the famous "Master's Voice" trademark.

There has always been some confusion in the model designations of Lamberts. Basically, there were two varieties: those with the name decoratively embossed in the base and those with a plain gold-stenciled name on the base. Until recently, many collectors called embossed Lamberts "No. 1" and stenciled Lamberts "No. 2." An instruction manual for the Lambert No. 3, however, reveals that the stenciled version officially bore that model number. It's unclear, however, what distinguished Models 1 and 2, each with embossed bases.

Researcher Peter Muckermann points out another difference to be noted, that of carriage width. Embossed-base machines had 10¼" carriages. No. 3 had a 11½" carriage, and a name-variant called the *Butler* had a 12¾" carriage.

Many Lamberts come with a very attractive wooden case. The case on the earlier models was curved and most bore a wonderful logo featuring the planet Saturn. Later cases were angular, without the logo.

Muckermann estimates a total of 30,000 Lamberts were manufactured in the first decade of the twentieth century. Besides the *Butler*, another known name-variant is *Garden City*, which was featured in a 1902 Sears & Roebuck catalog. With several hundred Lamberts in the hands of collectors today, they are far from rare, but their charm is undeniable, and they remain a collector's favorite.

Lambert Case: This is the oak case which accompanies the embossed Lambert shown above. Note the Saturn logo with the machine's name on the rings. (author's collection)

Lambert $250.00

Lambert No. 3 (circular keyboard): The plain stenciled name on the base identifies a Lambert as Model No. 3. It also has a slightly wider carriage (11½") than the embossed model (10¼"). (Milwaukee Public Museum)

Lasar

The Lasar Typewriter was an oddity patented in the late 1880s and apparently driven off the market soon after it appeared. The caps-only machine had vertical type-bars, swinging down to the platen from the front. It featured a distinctive nickel-plated band surrounding the type-bar mounts and had unusual oval-shaped keytops. The carriage return lever extended out from the right side, giving the machine a bulkier appearance than it might otherwise have had.

The U.S. Patent Office granted inventor Godfrey Lasar 17 patents on his machine between the years 1886 and 1889. Even so, it appears that Lasar's patents infringed on many others, and it's believed that was the reason for the machine's failure.

The Lasar was made by the Lasar Typewriter Co., of St. Louis, Missouri, but very few seem to have been made. Only one example is currently known.

Lasar . . . .$1,000.00+

Lasar (4-row, downstrike, caps-only): The Lasar's strange appearance is accentuated by the prominent nickel-plated band across the type-bars, and the broad arc of the carriage return lever. (Casillo collection, ser. 21)

Liliput

The Liliput was a circular index machine introduced in Germany around 1907. Though similar in concept to some very cheap machines (such as the Simplex), it was better made and much more substantial.

Liliput $1,000.00

Liliput (circular index): The round index wheel, with its periphery of holes (presumably for alignment), give the Lilput its characteristic profile. Apparently marketed for children, its construction was better than that of a cheap toy. (Williams collection)

Manhattan

As a virtual copy of the Remington No. 2, the Manhattan Typewriter of 1898 is an interesting example of marketing during the early years of the typewriter industry. The Remington No. 2 was introduced in 1878 and eventually enjoyed immense success. The Manhattan was made using expired patents from the Remington, its backers evidently feeling that such a tried and true machine could still find some buyers, despite the improved models that had then come to market.

The Manhattan apparently found some sort of niche, albeit a small one. It is indeed very much like the Remington No. 2, though there are some minor differences. Differing models of the Manhattan were generally designated by letter rather than number. Model "A" had 38 keys, model "B" had 42 keys. Some numbered models have also been reported.

Collectors today are unlikely to go wild over a Manhattan. It is much more important to any collection to have a Remington No. 2. A Manhattan would be strictly a bonus, desired only by those with space to store it.

Manhattan $75.00

Manhattan "A" (4-row, upstrike): A machine designed to emulate the famous Remington No. 2. There are differences, however. Among them are the shift-lock mechanism and inclusion of platen knobs. (Milwaukee Public Museum)

Maskelyne

This bizarre British machine had much in common with the distinctive and more successful Williams Typewriter (see page 138). Each of these machines used "grasshopper" movements, their type-bars resting in ink pads and then "hopping" forward to meet the platen. On the Maskelyne, however, all of the type-bars were arrayed in front of the carriage, while the Williams placed them both in front and behind. The Maskelyne also included the sophisticated refinement of proportional spacing, allowing differing widths for different letters.

There were three models of the Maskelyne. The first two, apparently, were very similar. The third, known as the *Maskelyne Victoria* had a different type-bar configuration. On this machine, the type-head faced upward, resting against the downward facing ink pad. On striking a key, the type-head did a somersault on its way to the platen (somewhat akin to the Jackson, see page 80).

The Maskelyne dates from 1899, and is said to have been the invention of John Nevil Maskelyne, a famous British magician of the era. Maskelyne's machine, despite its magical qualities, had a short life, without success in the market place. Consequently, it is a rarity today.

Maskelyne . . . .$1,000.00+

Maskelyne (3-row, grasshopper movement): The fan-shaped array of type-bars on this machine hints at their method of movement: a grasshopper-style hop to the platen. (Milwaukee Public Museum)

Maskelyne (with cover): When not being used, the Maskelyne was provided with an attractive cover, which fit over the type-bars and platen. This machine is usually illustrated with the cover removed, so many collectors do not realize this part exists. (Milwaukee Public Museum)

Masspro

The Masspro, of 1932, is an example of an uncommon machine which has little value due to the indifference of most collectors. It was developed by George Rose, son of inventor Frank Rose, who designed the Standard Folding Typewriter, predecessor to the wildly successful Corona. The Masspro looks much like the folding Corona, except that it does not fold.

According to author Paul Lippman, the Masspro did not succeed, because during the early Depression years other more advanced typewriters were being offered even more cheaply than the $25.50 Rose was charging. Lippman wrote that the Masspro was sold in Europe when it failed to make a dent in the U.S. market, and most specimens have keys for European languages.

Masspro $50.00

Masspro (3-row, frontstrike): Cut from the same mold as the Folding Corona, the Masspro is an obscure typewriter. This example appears to have an American keyboard. Most others, we are told, have European keyboards. (Milwaukee Public Museum)

McCool

The McCool Typewriter was one of the also-rans of typewriter history. The invention of William McCool, it was produced by the Acme-Keystone Manufacturing Co. at Beaver Falls, Pennsylvania. Dating the machine is a problem. It was apparently invented in 1903, but the patent wasn't granted until 1910. A contemporary advertisement indicates the machine was being sold in 1909.

The McCool was similar to the Commercial Visible, using a type-wheel, with pressure applied by a rear striking hammer. This machine was made to sell for $25 at a time when standard office machines were priced at $100. The "No. 2" may have been the only model ever offered.

As an unsuccessful product in its time, the McCool today is a desirable item, seldom seen along the collector's trail.

McCool $850.00

McCool No. 2 (3-row, type-wheel): The large name and model number on the front of this machine's frame makes identification a snap. Look carefully behind the type-wheel and you'll see the black rubber impression strip similar to that used on the Hammond. The "patents pending" indication dates this specimen before 1910. (Milwaukee Public Museum)

McLoughlin

Collectors of toys will recognize the McLoughlin Bros. name, which here applies to a typewriter that may or may not have been intended for the juvenile market. Dating from as early as 1884, the McLoughlin was an unsophisticated type-wheel machine using a circular index. Some examples of this typewriter are found with an alphabetically-arranged index, others have their letters arranged for more efficient typing.

McLoughlin $500.00

McLoughlin (type-wheel index): This machine was made by a toy manufacturer, but it does not have the lightweight feel of most toy typewriters. A crude machine by any measure. (Rauen collection, no serial number)

Merritt

The Merritt Typewriter of 1890 was originally made by the Merritt Manufacturing Co. in Springfield, Masssachusetts, and later by the Lyon Manufacturing Co. of New York City. It is as charming an index machine as you can find. Its brand name was decoratively cast into its frame on most examples, and its mechanism was unique among linear index machines.

The business end of this machine was a sliding rack which held a complete font of printer's type. As the handle was moved back and forth, each type came to the printing point. The handle was then depressed, and the type was pushed up through a guide hole to the paper which rode on the platen above. As with other blind machines, you had to raise the carriage to see your work. A set of two rollers inked the typefaces as they moved back and forth in the course of the work.

Certain early Merritts had plain frames with no name cast into the face. Some models had a key at the rear which placed a pointer to show where the next character would be typed on the page. Most Merritts came with a wooden cover which fit onto the wooden base, although some had more elaborate cases. A sheet of instructions was generally pasted inside the wooden cover.

The number "1234" was stamped into the right rear corner of the Merritt's base. We're not sure why. In the left rear corner of most machines, you'll find a serial number. Early models had serial numbers on the side of the base.

The Merritt originally sold for $15, and appears to have been quite successful considering the many that survive today.

Merritt $200.00

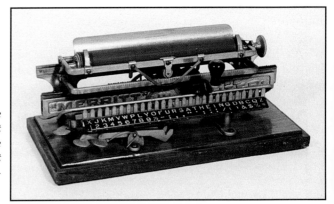

Merritt (linear index): This handsome little index machine is most valuable when all the nickel-plated parts are in the best possible condition, and the letter index is undamaged. The black platen on this example is in good shape, but on most specimens, the platen is badly cracked and distorted. (Dickerson collection)

Mignon

The wonderful Mignon Typewriter is, without doubt, the very best index machine that was ever made. Introduced in 1904, this machine was the first typewriter product of Germany's Allgemeine Elektrizitäts Gesellschaft (better known as "AEG"), the large corporation which still markets Olympia Typewriters today.

On the Mignon, the user manipulated the indicator with the left hand and then pressed a print key with the right hand to bring the type-sleeve to the paper. It was a very effective design, slower than keyboard typewriters, but faster than most other index machines, and certainly more durable and practical.

The Mignon was very successful in Europe with 380,000 manufactured over 28 years. Model 2 was the first Mignon to be produced in quantity. It was smaller than later models, and featured a squarish cover over the inner mechanism. The first of these were produced in a red color and are more desirable than the more common black ones.

Models 3 (1913) and 4 (1924) were more rounded and streamlined. The only major difference between the two was the presence of a backspace key on the No. 4. These machines almost always came in black, although other colors, including white, are occasionally found.

Until recently it was thought that the Model 1 Mignon was never produced, but the discovery of a single example in an East German museum belied that theory.

The Mignon was made under a number of different names around the world. Among the reported variants: *Heady, Typorium, Stella, Stallman, Eclipse, Genia*. Here in the U.S., it was manufactured as the *Yu Ess*. Makes sense doesn't it? However, it's not known if the American name was intended to appeal to patriotic interests. It may have stood for Union Schreibmaschine, the AEG subsidiary that produced the Mignon. A later version of the machine is said to have been named *Olympia Plurotyp*. A similar, but not identical index machine was produced as the *Tip-Tip* in Czechoslovakia.

Mignon machines are quite common among collectors, since they are so easily obtained in Europe. They are seen in the U.S. fairly frequently, but not nearly as much as overseas. Most Mignons have some sort of case, either wooden or tin.

Mignon No.1 . . . .$1,000.00+
Mignon No. 2 (red) $350.00
Mignon No. 2 (black) $200.00
Mignon No. 3, 4 (black) $100.00
Mignon No. 3, 4 (any other color) $200.00

Mignon No. 1 (type-sleeve index): *The only surviving example at this writing is in the Heimatmuseum in Erfurt, part of the former East Germany. The machine was not discovered by collectors until the Berlin Wall fell and travel was freely permitted between East and West. (Heimatmuseum Erfurt collection, photo by Peter Muckermann)*

Mignon No. 2 (type-sleeve index): *Model No. 2 featured a papier maché housing over the mechanical linkage which drove the type-sleeve. This is the earliest model a collector is likely to find. (author's collection, ser. 36026)*

Mignon No. 4 (type-sleeve index): *The sleeker housing was featured on both the Mignon 3 and 4. Note the backspace key located to the right of center on the machine's base. This key is absent on the Mignon 3. Otherwise, the two models are nearly identical. (author's collection, ser. 321215)*

Molle

The Molle Typewriter was a minor oddity introduced around 1918 in Wisconsin. Encased in a pleasing, angular shell, this machine sported an unusual key-to-type-bar linkage. When a key was pressed, it moved a tiny crank which rotated a rod underneath. At the other end was a similar crank, which pulled down on the type-bar link, causing the type-bar to pivot up to the platen. The only other machine to use this idea was the famous double-keyboard Smith Premier upstrike machine (see page 127).

Molles are almost always seen with the Model 3 designation. According to author Paul Lippman, inventor John Molle designed a machine called the Jundt in 1908, and another (presumably unnamed) typewriter in 1914. The Molle, therefore, was his third model. After the Molle company failed in 1922, a Chicago company tried to market the machine as the *Liberty*. Almost all of these machines were black, although we do know that some were made in white.

Molle (black) $75.00
Molle (white) $125.00

Molle No. 3, black (3-row, frontstrike): The Molle was both attractive and innovative. Though the 3-row, frontstrike format is not special, the Molle's keys fall into straight columns as well as rows, a marked difference from other machines on which staggered rows result in offset key columns. (Dickerson collection, ser. 4450)

Molle No. 3, white: A scarce color variation for the Molle machine. Most others were basic black. (Dickerson collection, ser. 6065)

Liberty No. 3 (3-row, frontstrike): A name variation of the Molle. Marketed by Liberty Typewriter Co., Chicago, Illinois. (Milwaukee Public Museum)

Monarch

Most 4-row, frontstrike typewriters are of little interest to typewriter collectors, and the Monarch is no exception. However, this 1904 machine has some historical significance worthy of notice. The Monarch was the first visible typewriter produced by the nefarious "Typewriter Trust," officially known as the Union Typewriter Company.

The Typewriter Trust existed in the era of price-fixing robber barons who conspired to monopolize industries and squeeze out the competition. It consisted of all the industry "Big Boys" of the day: Remington, Smith Premier, Densmore, Yost, Caligraph. The Monarch Typewriter Co. was created to produce a machine to compete with the upstart Underwood as well as the turncoat Smith brothers who left their Smith Premier Typewriter Co. to begin producing visible machines under the "L.C. Smith & Bros." name.

While the Monarch was rolled out, the rest of the Trust companies continued to make upstrike machines and use their advertising to denigrate the visible design, arguing that good typists didn't need to see their work. Is it surprising so many of these firms are long-lost memories today?

The Monarch, then, is collectible mostly for its unusual position in typewriter history. It did have a mechanical detail offering an advantage over other machines of the day. The shift key caused the whole assembly of type-bars (the type-basket) to move, while other machines shifted the carriage. The basket shift later became an industry standard. As a 4-row, frontstrike, however, the Monarch is essentially like 98% of all other typewriters made in the first half of the twentieth century. Once the make was retired, the name "Monarch" was used by Remington on a number of its machines.

Monarch (any model) $30.00

Monarch No. 2 (4-row, frontstrike): Attractive decals aside, there is little to attract collectors to Monarch machines. There were three models in all, differing in the number of characters typed. (Milwaukee Public Museum)

Moon-Hopkins
(see Burroughs)

Morris

The Morris Typewriter was another one of those odd, cheap index machines that burst briefly on the scene, only to quickly disappear. The invention of Robert Morris of Kansas City, Missouri, it was made about 1886 by the Hoggson Manufacturing Co. of New Haven, Connecticut.

Conceptually, the Morris was similar to the Hall, in that it used a square rubber type plate which was moved over the printing point by a handle and then pressed to print. It typed only capital letters, which may help explain why it was not of much use to its owners.

Some Morris Typewriters are found packed in little wooden boxes with sliding lids (at least two different boxes are reported). One other interesting detail: the rubber used for the platen was white.

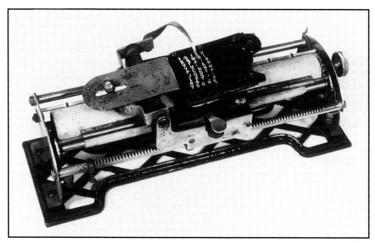

The Morris is quite scarce today, although its rarity has been somewhat exaggerated. Nonetheless, it is a desirable item for any collector.

Morris $1,000.00

Morris (rectangular index): An intriguing little device that proved to be utterly impractical. Notice the white rubber platen and the interesting lattice-work of the base. (Milwaukee Public Museum)

Moya

The Moya Typewriter was invented in 1902 by Hidalgo Moya a Spanish-American who brought the machine to manufacture in Britain. The machine had a 3-row keyboard, and printed through a ribbon with a type-sleeve.

There were two basic models of the Moya. The first was simply labeled "Moya" and was characterized by a stacked pair of ribbon spools directly in front of the type-sleeve. No. 2 of 1905 was called the "Moya Visible No. 2" and was considerably improved. It had a distinctive flat deck of sheet metal concealing most of the works, and the ribbon spools were moved out of the way to the side of the machine.

A model No. 3 Moya Visible has also been reported. Name variants include: *Secretär* (Germany), *Baka I* (France), and *Ideal*.

Moya's company scuttled the machine in 1908 to make room for his next invention, which would prove to be much more successful: the Imperial Typewriter (see page 78).

Moya No. 1 . . . .$500.00
Moya No. 2,3 . . . .$300.00

Moya No. 1 (3-row, type-sleeve): The first version of this machine was awkward at best. Notice the odd placement of ribbon spools and the ribbon path, hiding the work from the user. (Clark collection, ser. 345)

Moya No. 2 (3-row, type-sleeve): The name of the machine is embossed into the flat cover plate behind the keyboard. Notice the change of placement for ribbon spools. The left-hand spool is seen at the bottom of the machine toward the rear. (Pace O'Shea collection, ser. 2600)

Munson

The Munson Typewriter had one of the most intriguing mechanisms of all the single-element typewriters. Patented in 1889 by Samuel John Siefried and James Eugene Munson, it was introduced to the market as a "trust-busting" machine — that is, one to compete head-on with the evil, price-fixing Union Typewriter Co., a consortium of Remington and other major makers also known as the Typewriter Trust.

To type on the Munson, the user first unscrewed a locking knob in the back and slid the rear-striking hammer mechanism out to the left. Upon hitting a key, the type-sleeve (mounted horizontally) first slid left or right, and then rotated a notch up or down to the correct position. The hammer then swung forward to press the paper against the type with the ribbon in between. It was (and still is) a delightful and amazing action to watch.

The Munson was the precursor to the better known *Chicago* Typewriter, which was essentially the same machine with the works enclosed rather than exposed as they were on the Munson. Actually, the enclosed machine was first made under the names Munson No. 2 and then Munson No. 3, with very little difference beweem the two.

Patent and advertising records indicate a very different Munson No. 2, using two type-sleeves (left and right) which were mounted on vertical cranks and pivoted to the platen at each key stroke. No examples are known, and it's uncertain if this machine was ever really produced.

Munson No. 1 . . . .$500.00
Munson No. 2, 3 . . . .$200.00

Munson No. 1, early (3-row, type-sleeve): *A Munson No. 1 is easily identified by its open mechanism, although the nameplate says "Munson" without reference to model number. This early specimen has more nickel-plated bright work than other examples. (author's collection, ser. 1459)*

Munson No. 1, later: *This machine has fewer frills than its predecessor at left. Notice the decrease in nickel-plated parts, including the ribbon spools, which are wooden on this specimen. (Dickerson collection, ser. 1687)*

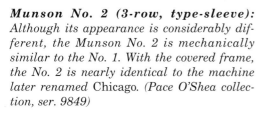

Munson No. 2 (3-row, type-sleeve): *Although its appearance is considerably different, the Munson No. 2 is mechanically similar to the No. 1. With the covered frame, the No. 2 is nearly identical to the machine later renamed* Chicago. *(Pace O'Shea collection, ser. 9849)*

Munson No. 2 (detail): *Decorative nameplate from the front of the Munson No. 2. At least one other style of nameplate (oval in shape) is known. (Pace O'Shea collection)*

Munson No. 3 (3-row, type-sleeve): *Even more similar to the later Chicago, down to the gold ornamentation and the type style used for the logo. Notice that the "Q" key is at the left of the bottom row, instead of the top. This is an odd quirk of all Munsons, Chicagos, and their name-variants. (Dickerson collection)*

National (1889)

The National Typewriter, introduced in 1889, is an attractive collector's piece. Its type-bars were arranged in a half-circle, a configuration which, along with the curved keyboard, gave this machine its overall curved shape. The National also features modular assembly, making it easy to take it apart for cleaning and maintenance. It was one of the few upstrike machines featuring a 3-row keyboard.

The National was the invention of Henry Harmon Unz, a Pennsylvanian who made many design contributions to the typewriter industry, although he seems to have been inspired by one of the patents of Franz Wagner, inventor of the famous Underwood. This machine is a favorite among today's collectors, but be careful not to confuse it with the National portable of 1916. The similarity is in name only.

National (1889) **$500.00**

National-1889, early (3-row, upstrike): *The earliest versions of this diminutive upstrike have a tiny space bar offset to right of center. Notice the word "comma" on the key at the right of the bottom row. Apparently, the manufacturer thought a key marked with "?,." would be confusing. (Rauen collection, ser. 1424)*

National-1889, late: *The full-width space bar identifies this National as a later machine. The advertising record indicates the change on the machine was made at least by mid-1891. (Dickerson collection, ser. 5015)*

National Portable

We designate this machine the "National Portable" to differentiate it from the older and more-interesting curved-keyboard, upstrike typewriter. The National is a rather conventional machine, but has a pleasant appearance when found in very good condition. Many people appreciate the attractive nickel-plated space bar found on some specimens, an unusual feature. In fact, some models of this machine were nickel-plated entirely, making them more desirable to collectors.

The National is often seen under the name *Portex* and other name variants include *Crown, Express,* and *Warner.* A number of different models were offered, with no important differences among them.

National Portable and name variants, black . . .$50.00
National Portable and name variants, nickel . .$150.00

National Portable No. 2 (3-row, frontstrike): a rather ordinary machine, but with good-looking decals. Model shown is labeled No. 2. Other models have few differences. (Milwaukee Public Museum)

National Portable No. 5, nickel (3-row, frontstrike): This National Portable is finished in nickel plate covering the entire machine except the paper table. The decal on the bottom/front edge is worn, but indicates this specimen is a model No. 5. (Williams collection, ser. 20718)

Portex, nickel (3-row, frontstrike): The Portex name variant of the National. Both the Portex and National are usually seen in black, but there is no question that the nickel-plated models are much more desirable. (Russo collection, ser. 22,222)

New American No. 5

The New American No. 5, was a linear index machine with its type on a bar that slid back and forth for letter selection. It was very similar to machines such as the Sun index and the Odell. Although the machine bears a "No. 5" designation, there is no record of models 1 – 4. Another machine, the *International No. 5* appears to have been made by the same manufacturer and is identical to the New American in all but its name.

Most typewriter historians have given 1890 as the date for this machine, but few seem convinced. In fact, the report of an Odell-like machine marked "American No. 5" hints that the New American succeeded the Odell, dating it after 1906. This machine is also usually listed with the *International No. 5* as the primary name and *New American No. 5* as the variation. However, since the machine was made by the New American Manufacturing Co. and since the *New American No. 5* variation is more common, it's listed here under that name.

New American No. 5,
International No. 5 . . . .$175.00

New American No. 5 (linear index): The linear-type slider on this machine was a recurring theme in the early typewriter industry. The same mechanism appeared on the Sun index typewriter as well as the Odell. (author's collection)

New Century Caligraph

The New Century Caligraph, first offered in 1899, was a development of the earlier double-keyboard Caligraph from the same firm, the American Writing Machine Co. The New Century Caligraph is significantly different from

its predecessor. While the Caligraph had its characteristic flat front deck and space bars on the side, the New Century Caligraph was more conventional, with an ordinary frame and the usual space bar placement.

The New Century Caligraph was introduced as the No. 5, succeeding model No. 4 of the old Caligraph line. There was also a No. 6 New Century Caligraph, with more keys than the No. 5.

New Century Caligraph (any model) $75.00

New Century Caligraph (double-keyboard, upstrike): The numeral 6 seen on this machine's front identifies its model number. Specimens of this typewriter may or may not have such markings. The condition of the decal at the top of the machine is important to its value. It is often badly worn. (Rauen collection, ser. 19948)

Niagara

The scarce Niagara typewriter was the only index machine produced by the famous Blickensderfer Typewriter Co. of Stamford, Connecticut. Introduced in 1902, it was made to sell for $15. The Niagara used a number of the same components as other Blickensderfer machines, most notably the type-wheel, ink-roller system, and carriage.

The Niagara typewriter resembles, in many respects, a miniature carnival wheel. It was intended, however, as a serious, if slow typewriter. The same machine was sold as the *Best* typewriter in the Sears & Roebuck catalog. Another name variant is *Stella*.

Niagara $500.00

Niagara (circular index): The Niagara is a rather heavy little machine, despite its appearance. The weight comes from the solid metal casting which serves as base and frame. This specimen types the Polish language. (author's collection, ser. 207)

Noiseless

The Noiseless line of typewriters was developed from the ideas of the great typewriter engineer Wellington Parker Kidder of Boston, and his business partner, C.C. Colby of Stanstead, Quebec, Canada. Kidder was responsible for a number of other ingenious machines. The first was the wonderful curved keyboard Franklin, then came the Wellington (also sold as the Empire and Adler). Finally, there was the Noiseless, first produced around 1912, with full-scale production starting in 1917.

Using the thrust-action mechanism he introduced in the Wellington/Empire/Adler machines, Kidder took it a step further by making the action noiseless, or nearly so. It was done in a wonderfully inventive way. On the back of each thrusting type-bar, Kidder hung a tiny swinging weight. As a key was depressed, the type-bar thrust forward, stopping short of the platen by a small fraction of an inch. At that point, the little weight, having accumulated momentum, swung forward, pushing the type-bar the rest of the way to the platen. The type-bar was thus pressed to the paper instead of striking it.

Only the office-sized Noiseless machines used thrust action. On the Noiseless Portable of 1921, the swinging weight idea was applied to front-striking type-bars.

It's particularly interesting that the platen roller on both the full-size and portable Noiseless machines was made of steel, not rubber as on other typewriters. Many people see this detail and feel there is something wrong with their machines, but not so. Many, but not all Noiseless Typewriters also carried an attractive logo featuring a colorful tiger, something which gives these machines an added appeal.

In 1924, the Noiseless Typewriter Co. was purchased by Remington, which continued for decades making Noiseless machines in both office-size and portable configurations. The same exact machines were also made under license by Underwood. The Remington and Underwood Noiseless machines, while appealing in their own way, have much less collectible value than the original Noiseless Typewriters.

Noiseless (office-size),
Remington Noiseless No. 5 . . . .$75.00
Noiseless Portable $100.00

Remington Noiseless
Underwood Noiseless (any model) $30.00

Noiseless (3-row, thrust-action): The full-size Noiseless machine features the curved front characteristic of most thrust-action machines, on which type-bars were arranged in a fan, radiating from the printing point. The 3-row keyboard, with double shift was unusual for office-sized machines. The first Noiseless with a Remington name (No. 5) appears identical to this machine. (Dickerson collection, ser. 10795)

Noiseless Portable (3-row, frontstrike): *Collectors consider the portable version of the Noiseless line the most desirable model. The steel platen is clearly seen in this photo. It provided a hard surface made necessary by the gentle press of the typeface against the paper. (author's collection, ser. 4082)*

Remington Noiseless No. 6 (4-row, thrust action): *The second model of the Noiseless offered by Remington, and that company's first redesign of the machine. The No. 6 has four characters (two pairs of two) on each type-bar. Each type-bar, then, is controlled by two different keys, with the proper letters brought to the printing point through special linkages. This design persisted on Noiseless machines into the 1960s. (Dickerson collection, ser. XPPAFFO)*

Remington Noiseless No. 8 (4-row, frontstrike): *The most unusual of the several Remington Noiseless portables. This one is heavier than others, and was marketed as a desk model. It features an attractive faceted front, which was also available on the Remington Portable No. 9, a non-noiseless model. A name-variant of the noiseless version is* Smith Premier No. 8. *(author's collection)*

North's

North's Typewriter was a British machine using the backstroke configuration. The type-bars stood erect and swung down to the platen from the rear of the typewriter. Introduced in 1892, the North's machine featured a 4-row keyboard instead of the 3-rows seen on other backstroke machines.

North's Typewriter got its name from the English Lord who financed it. It is seldom seen in the U.S.

North's Typewriter **$1,000.00**

North's (4-row, backstroke): *As with other backstroke typewriters, the North's is dominated not only by its vertical type-bars, but by the elaborate set of rings needed to hold the paper in its awkward path through the machine. (Russo collection, ser. 1094)*

Odell

The Odell typewriter was introduced in 1889, first manufactured in Lake Geneva, Wisconsin, later in Chicago, Illinois, and still later in Momence, Illinois. In additon, at least one specimen indicates a New York origin. The Odell was a linear index machine, consisting of a type-element which slid trombone-style perpendicular to a narrow cylindrical platen. Inking was by roller.

Odell models numbers ran from 1 to 5, but there seem to have been several *different* versions of the No. 1. As they often do, collectors have added letters to the original model numbers to help them tell the different versions apart. Odell No. "1a" had animal-like toes at each corner of its elongated base, and one influential collector has dubbed it the "seal" model. It typed capitals only, and had a nameplate showing "Lake Geneva, WIS.," as its home and a "patent pending" designation. A similar model, with a dogbone-shaped base (without the "feet" detail) was illustrated in an early Odell catalog, but no examples are currently known.

Model "1b" had a redesigned round base and is almost always found in a caps-only version. At least one known specimen, however, types both upper and lower cases. Ornamentation on the base seems to have been inspired by American Indian art, and the design looks as if it were etched into the surface of the mold with a pencil tip. The top surface of the base was painted gold. There were at least three different nameplate variations: the earliest showing "Lake Geneva, WIS." as the place of manufacture, with "patent pending" as on the 1a. Later 1b's included a patent date of 1889, and still later ones showed "Chicago, ILL." as the Odell's home. Some 1b's had bells, some did not.

The Odell No. 2 had a circular base, with an new, elaborate Art Nouveau design. The entire machine was nickel plated, although many have been seen with gold painted trim on the upper casting. The No. 2 (and all later models) typed upper and lower case (although at least one single-case example is known). A bell was included to signal line end. It should also be noted that the nameplate on Odells No. 1 and No. 2 read "Odell's Typewriter," while later models were designated "Odell Typewriter."

Odells No. 3, 4, and 5 were essentially similar to No. 2, but the top casting included a larger, half-moon shaped nameplate, with the model number cast-in. The manufacturer's name was attached on a separate plate.

The Odell was made by several different manufacturers from 1889 to at least 1906 and possibly longer. The rarest model is the 1a. The most common model is the No.4, most often seen with a "Farquar & Albrecht" maker's label. Round-base No. 1's are somewhat rarer than Nos. 2 – 5. Machines came in cases (sometimes plush-lined) or plain wooden boxes. No machine is complete without the sliding type-element (sometimes missing) and the ink roller (often missing).

Odell 1a . . . .$1,000.00+
Odell 1b . . . .$ 250.00
Odell 2–5 . . . .$ 175.00

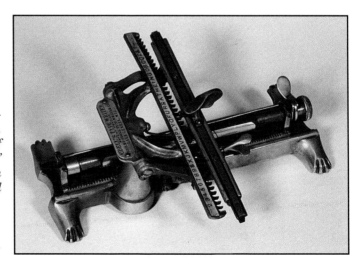

Odell "1a" (linear index): The long base of the earliest Odell is drastically different from later models. Notice the toes on the corners, giving the appearance of animal feet. This machine as been nicknamed the "seal" Odell. The name "Odell's Typewriter" is clearly seen on the nameplate. (Milwaukee Public Museum, no serial number)

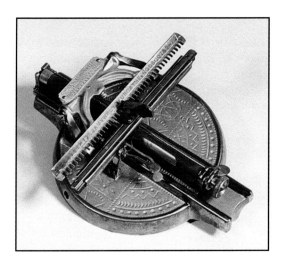

Odell "1b" (linear index): *The round base was a major change for the Odell, setting the pattern for all machines to come. Notice the homemade look of the ornamentation on the base. (Russo collection, no serial number)*

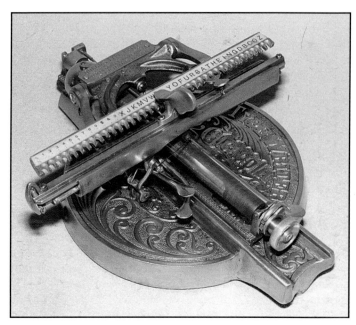

Odell No. 2 (linear index): *The No. 2 model of the Odell types both upper and lower case and had a base decorated in the Art Nouveau style. Notice the little flip-lever on the sliding type-element. The lever was used as a shift key. It is located on the photo just to the right of the finger grip which is at the slider's midpoint. (Schropp Collection, no serial number)*

Odell No. 3 (linear index): *Notice the semicircular casting with the machine's name. This feature is characteristic of all Odells No. 3 and above. (Milwaukee Public Museum, no serial number)*

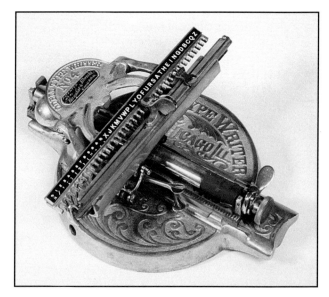

Odell No. 4 (linear index): *The No. 4, sold by Farquar and Albrecht of Chicago is the most often seen of the Odells. It is virtually identical to the No. 3. If you look carefully, however, you'll see the No. 4 has a bell, but the No. 3 doesn't. It's possible, though, that the No. 3's bell is simply missing in the photographed example. (author's collection, no serial number)*

Oliver

If you tell a collector you have an Oliver, there is usually very little else you need to say, since this machine is truly one-of-a-kind and was made in such great numbers that every collector knows exactly what you are talking about. The Oliver was patented in 1894, the invention of the Canadian-born Rev. Thomas Oliver, who is said to have made the prototype out of strips cut from tin cans. Oliver, then a resident of Monticello, Iowa, was eventually able to attract investors who started a company to manufacture his invention, which became one of the most successful typewriters in history.

To call the Oliver simply a downstrike machine does it little justice. It had two banks of type-bars, standing erect at either side of the printing point. These swung down from the sides to hit the platen, whipping through the air in a symphony of motion unlike any other typewriter. The type-bars were U-shaped and actually straddled the carriage. The downstrike configuration was intended to make the writing visible at a time when most typewriters were still of the blind-writing variety.

There is contradictory information on the start of production for the No. 1 Oliver, with various sources dating it at 1894 and 1896. The No. 2, however, was the first Oliver made in commercial quantities, apparently beginning 1896. This was followed over the years by No. 3 (1898), No.5 (1906), No. 7 (1914), No. 9 (1916), and 11 (1922). Corresponding even-numbered models were offered in Europe with foreign keyboards. Even-numbered models were also sold in Mexico, Central America, and South America. Many of these had nickel-plated bases, designed to better withstand the rigors of tropical climates.

Production of Olivers in the U.S. ended in 1926, and the company's assets were sold to a British firm, which continued producing the classic design until 1947, ending with No. 15 and the accompanying No. 16 (with a wide carriage). After that, the Oliver name was applied to a standard frontstrike office model based on a Swedish machine called the *Halda* as well as an attractive 4-row, frontstrike portable. Ironically, Oliver engineers designed a frontstrike machine using U-shaped type-bars in 1922. One prototype was built, but the machine never went into production.

Most Olivers have little value, since they are so very common. The *most* common models are Nos. 5 and 9. There is a premium attached to No. 2 and yet another notch in value for No. 2's made with nickel-plated bases. Most models of the Oliver were painted in an olive color, except for the No. 11, decorated with black paint and handsome pin stripes.

There is one true rarity in the Oliver family, and that is the No. 1, made in very limited quantities. This machine was distinguished from others by having a totally flat base, which was nickel plated. It is difficult to correctly identify an Oliver No. 1, since its model number is not displayed on the machine. The photos and captions give key details differentiating the first Oliver from later models.

Oliver No. 1 . . . .$1,000.00+
Oliver No. 2 (nickel base) $125.00
Oliver No. 2 (olive base) $60.00
Oliver No. 3 . . . .$35.00
Oliver No. 4-16, Oliver portable $20.00

Oliver No.1 (3-row, downstrike): *The rarest of all Olivers, the No. 1 exhibits the same basic characteristics of all its descendants. The differences are in the details. Notice the projecting handles on the base. They are flush with the tabletop, not raised as on later models. Also, the nameplates on the sides show a scalloped forward edge, the ribbon spools are open, and the finish is nickel plate. (Milwaukee Public Museum)*

Oliver No. 2 (3-row, downstrike): *Darker in overall appearance than the No. 1, the Oliver No. 2 is far more common. It is coated with olive paint, the side handles are raised from the tabletop, the ribbon spools are enclosed and the side nameplates have a simple curve on the forward edge. Some, but not all, Oliver No. 2's have the model number on the paper table. (author's collection)*

Oliver No. 2, nickel: *A number of Oliver No. 2's were made with nickel-plated frames, similar to the No. 1. This has prompted some collectors to call them "Oliver 1b," a misnomer. (Rauen collection, ser. 6085)*

Oliver No. 3 (3-row, downstrike): *Very similar to the No. 2, No. 3's are clearly labeled with their model number (as are later models). The No. 3 is a bit more substantial than the No. 2, with a visibly thicker base. (Rauen collection, ser. 95361)*

Oliver No. 5 (3-row, downstrike): *The No. 5 was the first Oliver with a frame enclosing the mechanism, which was exposed in earlier models. Notice the pencil holder, with pencil in position to draw a straight line on the paper by moving the carriage or twirling the platen. (Rauen collection, ser. 425802)*

Oliver No. 9 (3-row, downstrike): *About half of all Olivers you'll see are No. 9's. They differ from the No. 5 in the shape of the frame enclosure. Model No. 7 is nearly identical to the No. 9 and is considered to have been a transitional model. The No. 9 retains the pencil-holder feature found on the No. 5. In this photo, the holder is raised into the position it holds when not in use. (Rauen collection, ser. 753630)*

Oliver No. 11 (3-row, downstrike): *The basic Oliver silhouette remains the same, but the No. 11 has been dressed up a bit. In addition to black paint and pin striping, the odd side handles are gone. In their place are two cutouts on the base at the sides allowing the user to slip fingers under the machine to lift it. (Milwaukee Public Museum)*

Oliver portable (4-row, frontstrike)*: Only the name "Oliver" in the familiar type style identifies this machine as a relative to the earlier 3-row downstrikes. An attractive curiosity, but otherwise unremarkable. (Milwaukee Public Museum)*

Patent Models

Patent model typewriters are precious jewels, each by definition "one of a kind." During the eighteenth and nineteenth centuries, the U.S. Patent Office required inventors to submit models of their devices as part of the application process. However, as the country grew, and as the Industrial Revolution progressed, the Patent Office found itself overloaded with models, and the requirement was dropped.

In 1908, Congress decided to liquidate the 156,000 models then in storage (nearly 100,000 other models had been destroyed in a series of fires that plagued the Bureau of Patents). The Smithsonian Institution was given the opportunity to take them, but chose only 1,061 for its vaults. The rest were put in storage until the 1920s, when they were finally put up for sale.

The models passed through a number of hands, eventually ending up in the possession of a man named O. Rundle Gilbert, who bought most of them in 1941. Two more fires destroyed the bulk of the collection, and Gilbert began selling off the rest in the 1970s. Most of the patent models held by private collectors today come from Gilbert, and patent model collecting is a recognized pursuit in its own right.

The most famous of typewriter patent models, those submitted by Christopher Latham Sholes, are held by the Smithsonian Institution. Models for other machines, however, have made their way to other museums and into the hands of collectors as well.

There is little to guide us in pricing patent models or prototypes. The fact that each is unique is irrelevant, since *all* of them are unique. What can be said is that models with the names of famous typewriter inventors would certainly be worth more than those of the nobodies. Additionally, models of whole machines would be of greater value than models demonstrating just part of a machine. The most valuable of all would be those for historically important machines. In any of these cases, and price aside, typewriter patent models should be treasured and carefully preserved.

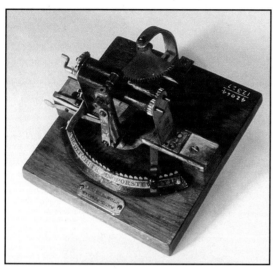

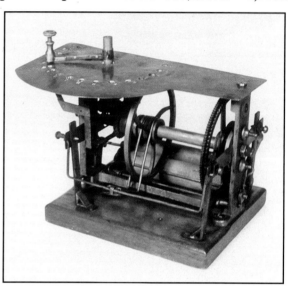

Typewriter patent models   . . .$250.00 – 3,000.00+

Arnold Patent Model: An index machine produced in 1876. Notice that the model includes the alphabet only, with no numerals or punctuation. Patent models were required to demonstrate the invention's principle alone. They did not have to be fully-workable machines. (Milwaukee Public Museum)

Brady-Warner Patent Model: An index machine of 1878. As with many patent models, this one seems to be very nicely made, using rich-colored wood and brass. (Milwaukee Public Museum)

Fred Sholes Patent Model: An 1879 model for a strange backstroke machine invented by Fred Sholes, the son of Christopher Latham Sholes. It's interesting that the three keys on this demonstration model appear to be spare parts taken directly from a Sholes & Glidden. (Casillo collection)

Malling Hansen Patent Model: A tiny model with a single key, meant to demonstrate the basic mechanism of the Skrivekugle invented by Pastor Malling Hansen of Denmark in the 1860s. This is one of three known models submitted by Hansen for his U.S. Patent. (Dickerson collection)

Pearl (1887)

This very rare linear index machine was built from a design patented in 1854 by Robert S. Thomas, who lived in Wilmington, North Carolina. As workable as the design was (several other index machines were later built on related principles), apparently no one came forward to produce it until 1887, when the typewriter market was in full steam and there was demand for low-cost alternatives to standard typewriters.

Author Paul Lippman wrote that this Pearl was manufactured by Enoch Prouty, of Chicago, who also made printing presses. This influence, Lippman said, may have led to the massive size and weight of the production model Pearl. Similar in configuration to the single-case Hammonia, which had a single type-element, the Pearl had characters for upper- and lower-case, numerals, and punctuation on different linear elements. Rotating the handle moved the appropriate element into place, not unlike the cylindrical element of the Sampo.

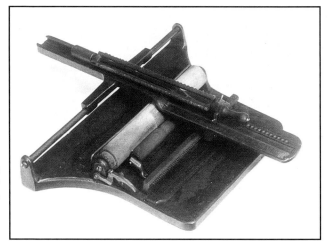

Pearl, 1887 . . . .\$1,000.00+

Pearl, 1887 (linear index): A very primitive index machine manufactured from patents dating back to 1854. Only one example is currently known. (Breker collection)

Pearl (Searing)

The Pearl Typewriter of 1891 was invented by Theodore W. Searing and is known to collectors as the "Searing" Pearl. The reason for this distinction is the existence not only of the earlier Pearl Typewriter (1887), but also of an alleged variant of the Peoples (see page 106) named *Pearl*. It's uncertain whether this People's variant really existed, but an early typewriter historian mentioned it and collectors, therefore, have attached the Pearl name to that machine.

The "Searing" Pearl had a large circular index handsomely printed on a disk of celluloid. The patent date of May 12, 1891, was clearly marked.

Pearl (Searing) \$800.00

Pearl (Searing) - unpainted base (circular index): Even on machines as this, apparently made in very limited numbers, variations are found. Take a look at the unpainted base. See how it extends beyond the ends of the platen, and compare it with the other model. (Clark collection, no serial number)

Pearl (Searing) - painted base (circular index): On this example, the base is not only shaped differently, it is also painted black and decorated with pin striping. It's not clear which of these machines came first. (Clark collection, no serial number)

Peerless

The Peerless Typewriter has a rather spotted history, since it was apparently built to imitate the immensely popular Smith Premier machine. Produced by a subsidiary of the Ithaca Gun Co. in Ithaca, New York, it appeared on the market in 1895. The double-keyboard on the Peerless had keys aligned in straight vertical columns as well as horizontal rows, same as the Smith Premier. On most other typewriters, keys do not line up in columns, but are staggered.

The Peerless actually resembled the Smith Premier in appearance only. Mechanically, it was quite different. Even so, it was taken off the market about 1898 after its makers lost a patent infringement suit brought by Smith Premier.

Peerless **$150.00**

Peerless (double-keyboard, upstrike): Because this machine is visually so close to the Smith Premier, it did not last long. Some examples are painted in a maroon color, and others have no cover plate at the top/front, thereby exposing the type-bar mounting plate, which is nickel plated on such machines. (Milwaukee Public Museum)

Peoples

The Peoples Typewriter, patented in 1891, was a simple machine with a curved index geared to a type-wheel. Early models of this machine were inked by rollers, usually missing on surviving examples. Other models used a ribbon attached to a ring, which fit loosely over the type-wheel. The loose fit allowed the wheel to slip around behind the ribbon, giving a certain randomness to the portion of ribbon the type would contact on each stroke. Pressing the printing key on this machine made the platen rock forward to meet the wheel. A still later version, called the *Champion*, used conventional ribbon on spools.

Some early historical literature reported that the Peoples was also sold as the *Pearl*. This will remain far from certain, however, until some documentation surfaces to confirm it.

Pearl (and name-variants) **$150.00**

Peoples, ribbon (type-wheel index): Note the lid sitting on top of the type-wheel, a feature which appears on many Peoples machines. In this case, someone has attached a ribbon to the lid, since the original ribbon-mount ring appears to be missing. The lid itself is thought by many to have been the ribbon mount. (Dickerson collection)

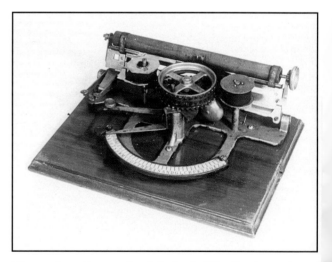

Champion (type-wheel index): The final version of this machine had the same kind of ribbon system used on most other machines. Note that the left spool on this specimen is apparently a homemade replacement for the original, which was lost and could not be replaced. (Milwaukee Public Museum)

Picht

Picht was a line of German index machines first made in 1899. Most were intended to be used by the blind, either for embossing Braille, or for printing regular letters to be read by the sighted.

Most likely to be of interest to typewriter collectors is one of the Picht type-wheel index machines. The model for the blind had both a Braille and a printed index. The same model was later marketed as the *Pioneer* for the sighted alone, without the Braille index.

Picht $250.00

Picht (type-wheel, index): The blind user of this machine could find the letters by feeling for them on the embossed Braille index. A sighted person could use it as well. (Milwaukee Public Museum)

Pittsburg Visible

The Pittsburg Visible Typewriter was a renamed and improved version of the earlier Daugherty Typewriter, the machine which pioneered the 4-row, frontstrike format. Among the chief improvements was the easy removal of the entire keyboard/type-basket assembly.

The Pittsburg dates from 1898. The desirable models are those retaining the odd, foot-shaped profile of the Daugherty. Nearly all of these are model No. 10, although a No. 9 has also been reported.

The Pittsburg No. 11 came out in 1908, followed by the No. 12 in 1911. Each had a much more conventional appearance, although they still had the removable type-basket. These later models were sold under many names here and abroad. Among those reported are: *Americo, American, Broadway Standard, Decker-Beachler, Fort Pitt, Reliance Visible, Reliance Premier, Shilling* and *Wall Street Standard.*

An interesting detail about this machine is the spelling of its name. It dates from the time when the U.S. Post Office forced the city of Pittsburgh to drop the final "h." The city went to court to fight the policy and won, allowing the "h" to reappear. It is not correct, however, to spell the name of the Pittsburg typewriter with a final "h."

Pittsburg Visible (No. 10 & earlier) $200.00
Pittsburg Visible (No. 11 & later) $50.00

Pittsburg Visible No. 12 (4-row, frontstrike): Made to look more like other machines, the Pittsburg No. 12 is thus less desirable to collectors. One appealing feature, however, is the attractive gold ornamentation. (Milwaukee Public Museum)

Pittsburg Visible No. 10 (4-row, front-strike): Although most 4-row, frontstrike machines are hardly collectible, this is the exception to the rule. The elongated shape of the machine makes it distinctly different from others of the same basic format. (Milwaukee Public Museum)

Postal

The Postal Typewriter of 1902 was an engaging machine which used a type-wheel to print through a ribbon. Models 1 through 8 have been reported, but the identifiable machines likely to surface are Nos. 3, 5, and 7.

Models prior to No. 7 were quite similar with only minor differences. The No. 5, for instance had an elevated scale (similar to the Blickensderfer No. 7), while earlier models did not.

The Postal No. 7 was significantly different from earlier models, featuring a substantial solid metal covering over the inner workings of the machine. It is very scarce today, while the earlier models are found with regularity.

The ribbon spools on these machines had special holes to receive hooked levers for reversing the ribbon direction. The spool with the lever engaged was the "take-up" reel, while the other remained a free-turning "feed" reel. If spools are missing on a Postal, they are difficult to replace.

Postal (all except No. 7) $150.00
Postal No. 7 . . . .$750.00

Postal No. 3 (3-row, type-wheel): The Postal is often compared to the Blickensderfer, which it resembles. The operating principle, however, is quite different. This specimen appears to be a No. 3, although, with no model number indicated, we can not be positive. (Milwaukee Public Museum)

Postal No. 5 (3-row, type-wheel): The raised scale is characteristic of the Postal No. 5, as are the two buttons for the shift locks. Other specimens of the No. 5 have the model number stamped into the frame surrounding the nameplate. This one does not, making identification somewhat uncertain. This example includes the wooden base, which should be present for the machine to be considered complete. (Dickerson collection, ser. 27120)

Postal No. 7 (3-row, type-wheel): This machine is obviously different from its predecessors. It features a metal covering hiding most of the works from view. (Auktion Team Köln)

Rapid

While the Wright Brothers were still concentrating on bicycles in Dayton, Ohio, one of their fellow townsfolk was busy designing a typewriter known as the Rapid. Bernard Granville's invention, patented in 1888, was one of the earliest using thrust-action type-bars. Its name, however, might have been something of a misnomer. It certainly was not "rapid" in operation, although it *was* rapid in disappearing from the market place.

Do not confuse this Rapid (which is very rare) with the *Rapid* name-variant of the Fox Visible Typewriter, which, though not exactly common, is very low on the collector's desirability scale.

Rapid . . . .$1,000.00+

Rapid (4-row, thrust-action): Big and boxy, the Rapid gives little hint of its design. Most thrust-action machines have frames echoing the fan of type-bars aimed at the common printing point. The Rapid was a caps-only machine. (Milwaukee Public Museum)

Rem-Sho
Remington-Sholes
(Fay-Sholes, Fay-Sho)

The Rem-Sho is a typewriter that could be called a "machine of many names," a situation which played itself out in the courts as well as the market place. The machine was introduced in 1896 by the Remington-Sholes Typewriter Co., named for its general manager Franklin Remington, and the machine's inventor Zalmon Sholes.

Sholes was the son of C.L. Sholes, who invented the first typewriter. The senior Sholes had been dead for six years and could have had no objection to his name appearing on a new machine. Franklin Remington, however, was a member of the same Remington family that started the world typewriter industry. By this time, the Remington Typewriter Company was no longer connected to the family, and it went to court to keep its name from appearing on a competing machine. So, in 1901 the Remington-Sholes Co. was forced to change to the *Fay*-Sholes Co., using the name of C.N. Fay, the firm's president. All of the typewriters had to be renamed as well.

For a time, the business took on the name of the Arithmograph Company, makers of an adding machine acquired by Fay-Sholes in 1904. Some Fay-Sho typewriters are seen with the Arithmograph device built-in.

The company meanwhile, appealed to the U.S. Supreme Court, which overturned the earlier ruling, allowing Fay-Sholes to return to *Remington*-Sholes as its proud, if imitative, name.

The typewriters produced by this company were called either Remington-Sholes, Rem-Sho, Fay-Sholes or Fay-Sho. The earliest and most desirable of the machines had very attractive bronzed frames, with castings resembling Greek columns. The paper table behind the platen frequently bore the name "Rem-Sho" or "Fay-Sho," with the company's full name appearing elsewhere. Later machines were painted black (sometimes brown) and usually had the longer version of the machine's name on the paper table. The last models, Nos. 10 and 11, were standard 4-row, frontstrike machines.

An interesting mechanical innovation was introduced by the Rem-Sho line. While the shift key on other machines caused the carriage to shift, the Rem-Sho made the entire type-basket shift while the carriage remained stationary. As the industry moved to visible machines, the type-basket shift (later called the "segment" shift) became the standard.

Despite all their legal difficulties, Rem-Sho and Fay-Sho machines must have been quality products. In fact, the early speed typist Charles McGurrin endorsed them by appearing in their advertisements.

The Remington-Sholes firm was eventually sold to a French company, which marketed successor machines (all 4-row, fronstrikes) under the *Japy* name.

Rem-Sho, Fay Sho (upstrike, bronze) $250.00
Remington-Sholes
Fay-Sholes (upstrike, black/brown) $50.00
Remington-Sholes (frontstrike) $50.00

Fay-Sho, bronze (4-row, upstrike): A machine which presents the striking appearance of a bronze Greek temple. At one time collectors were told the early Fay-Sho and Rem-Sho were solid bronze. However, a few clever people armed with magnets showed us the frame was iron, and the bronze was only an attractive plating. (Dickerson Collection, ser. 3248)

Fay-Sholes No. 6 (4-row, upstrike): One of the many later models of the Rem-Sho/Fay-Sho family. This one is painted brown, but most others are black. (Milwaukee Public Museum)

Remington

The history of Remington Typewriters is certainly the history of *the* typewriter, since Remington literally founded the world typewriter industry in 1873. In that year, executives of the gun makers E. Remington & Sons signed a contract to produce the Sholes & Glidden Type-Writer, the machine from which all modern machines are descended. The Sholes & Glidden deserves a chapter all to itself, and you can read about it later. Here, we'll concentrate on machines bearing the Remington brand name.

The first typewriter labeled as a Remington was the No. 2, issued in 1878. The Remington No. 2 was actually the first successful typewriter. Its predecessor, the capitals-only Sholes & Glidden never really took off commercially. The No. 2 was much more reliable and featured both upper and lower case characters, accessed with a shift key. It was called a "shift" key, because it actually shifted the carriage back and forth to align the platen with the correct piece of type on the type-bar.

Along with the No. 2, Remington also made the No. 4, a caps-only machine. The No. 4 was characterized by a large-diameter platen similar to the Sholes & Glidden and unlike the smaller platen on the No 2. Behind the platen on each of these early models was a wooden roller, part of the paper transport system, which also used pulleys and rubber bands. The wooden roller is often missing, but no model No. 2 or 4 is complete without it. The rubber bands are almost never present, but they were replaceable components, and their absence is not a detriment.

There is much to confuse the collector in properly naming the various No. 2's and 4's. They can be called either "Perfected" or "Remington Perfected" or simply "Remington," depending on how they are marked.

When Remington first brought out the two models, they were marketed as the "Perfected Type-Writer." It wasn't until later that "Remington" appeared as the brand name. Collectors will find No. 2 and No. 4 machines both with and without the "Remington" name stenciled on them. Plain, pin-striped machines with no name at all may be designated "Perfected Type-Writer" No. 2 or 4.

As production proceded, Remington changed the markings on the machines. First, stenciled identification with the words "Perfected" and "Remington" appeared above and behind the keyboard. These can be termed "Remington Perfected" machines. Later, the word "Standard" replaced "Perfected." Finally, "Standard" appeared on the bottom front of the frame, below the space bar. Machines showing the name "Standard" are properly called "Remington Standard No. 2" or "No. 4." The "Standard" is usually dropped for brevity in discussing these machines.

Next in the Remington line was the No. 5 (1886), which was quite similar to the No. 2. The chief difference visible to the casual eye is the carriage return bell mounted on the front of the machine. Along with the No. 5 came the No. 3, which was essentially the same machine, but with a wide carriage. We don't know just why Remington saved the No. 3 model designation for the wide-carriage machine.

Quickly succeeding the No. 5 were the No. 6 (1894) and No. 7 (c. 1897), each identical except for the number of keys. The Remington No. 6 had 38 keys, the No. 7 had 42. Few non-collectors can tell the Remington No. 6 or 7 from the No. 2, although there were many differences. Perhaps the most visible change is seen on the carriage. The No. 2 had a large transport wheel placed at center on the front rail of its carriage. The No. 6 (and 7) used a more stable system without the conspicuous wheel.

The Remington Nos. 6 & 7 represented the height of upstrike technology and were extremely popular machines. Additional models in the line offered other features. No. 8 (1897) had a wider, removable carriage, and No. 9 (1902) had 46 keys.

In 1908, after years of resistance, Remington introduced the No. 10, its first visible typewriter. This machine mimicked the Underwood and others by using a 4-row, frontstrike format. Early models of the No. 10 were mechanically similar to the upstrike machines, with individually mounted type-bars, each with its own adjustment screw. Later models of the No. 10 featured blade-shaped type-bars mounted in slots cut into a curved metal block known as the "slotted segment," a feature standard on the Underwood years earlier.

Once the improvements were made to the No. 10, further developments of Remington typewriters were little more than refinements for the next 50 years, taking most succeeding models outside the realm of collectibility.

There are other Remingtons, however, which do interest collectors. One of these is the Remington Electric of 1925. On the Remington Electric, a motor kept a "power-roller" in constant motion. Depression of a key put a drive shoe in contact with the roller, which powered the type-bar toward the platen. It was the principle on which most later electric typewriters were based.

Only 2,500 units of this black, blocky monster of a machine were sold before the project ended. The electrics sold as fast as they could be made, but Remington was unable to come to contract terms with North East Electric Co. of Rochester, New York, maker of its motors and power-rollers. N.E. Electric controlled patents to the system and later applied the power-roller to its own machine. It was called the Electromatic (see page 55), and it eventually became IBM's first electric typewriter.

Many Remington portables are also attractive to today's collectors, who like them for their modest prices. Introduced in 1920, the first of the Remington portables featured type-bars which had to be jacked up into typing position with a lever at the machine's side. Releasing the lever dropped the type-bars back into the flat position, for carrying. Most of these portables were black, but after about 1926, as Dupont's colorful Duco Enamel paint became popular, they were offered in a wide variety of colors which remain very appealing today.

The very first of the Remington portables had only one shift key at the left side of the machine. Such specimens are rare (and little noticed), since the second shift key (at right) was apparently added quickly thereafter. Some collectors consider any side-lever Remington portable with two shift keys to be a No. 2. However, a number of different improvements were made to this machine, and it's unclear just where Remington placed the line between models 1 and 2.

Later models, beginning with the Remington Portable No. 3 (1930) were reworked to eliminate the side lever. During the '30s, Remington introduced numerous portables with a confusing array of configurations, model numbers, and brand names. Among the machines on the Remington roster were the *Remie Scout, Monarch Pioneer, Cadet, Bantam, Remette, Smith Premier,* as well as other numbered models, not necessarily consecutive. One of these is labeled the "*Remington Rand Model 1,*" a source of confusion to collectors who have visions of a Sholes & Glidden when hearing someone say he has a "Remington No. 1."

Among the more interesting Remington portables was the No. 5 of 1933, which came in two versions. One was a rather plain machine, looking a lot like its predecessors, but the other had a very attractive, rounded, streamlined covering representing the ultimate in Art Deco Moderne. On the paper tables of some, the word "Streamliner" appeared in a flashy type style. The Remington No. 5 portable should not be confused with the Remington No. 5 upstrike.

A similar streamlined design appeared on the 1935 Remington 3B, featuring a cost-saving "3½-row" keyboard. On this machine, the numerals were doubled up on four keys at the top of the keyboard (the "half" row). Numbers 2-3-4-5 were typed in the lower case mode, but you needed to shift to get numbers 6-7-8-9.

Remington also offered a variety of *Noiseless* machines in both office-size and portable versions. These are discussed under the section on the Noiseless Typewriter (see page 97).

There are two Remington oddities worthy of mention. One is the Remington Junior, a compact 3-row, frontstrike machine from 1914. Most interesting about the Remington Junior is its ribbon transport, with ribbon spools at the back and the ribbon running through the machine. The other curiosity is the Rem-Blick of 1928, an exact copy of the Blickensderfer No. 5. Remington produced the machine after buying up Blickensderfer's old tools and dies from the bankrupt Roberts Typewriter Co. The machine was also sold as the *Baby-Rem*.

Every collection should have at least one Remington in honor of this company's significance to typewriter history. Most Remingtons were made in very large numbers and are consequently still quite available to collectors today.

Remington No. 2, upstrike	$150.00
Remington No. 3, upstrike	$225.00
Remington No. 4, upstrike	$350.00
Remington No. 5, upstrike	$150.00
Remington No. 6-9, upstrikes	$50.00
Remington No. 10	$20.00
Remington Electric (1925)	$150.00
Remington Portable (any model, black)	$20.00
Remington Portable (colors)	$25.00
Remington Junior	$40.00
Rem-Blick, Baby-Rem	$85.00

Remington No. 2 (4-row, upstrike): The open, black frame of the Remington No. 2 set the pattern for years to come, creating the mold for what most people think of as an "antique typewriter." Notice the large wheel at the center of the carriage. It's a key characteristic for telling the No. 2 from later machines. (author's collection, ser. 50792)

Remington No. 4 (4-row, upstrike, caps only): *Contemporary with the No. 2, the Remington No. 4 has a larger platen and no shift key. Look to the right of the front/left frame post, and you will see no shift spring and lever (as are present on the No. 2). That's a quick way to identify the No. 4 if the model number is not there. (Dickerson collection, ser. 4621)*

Perfected Type-Writer No. 4 (4-row, upstrike, caps only): *Notice the total absence of any name on this machine, distinguishing it from the "Remington No. 4," which is clearly identified. These "Perfected" machines were made early in the production run of model No. 4. (Rauen collection, ser. 33)*

Remington No. 5 (4-row, upstrike): *The No. 5 is characterized by a much "busier" look than its predecessors. The easiest way to identify it is by the bell mounted on the front. The No. 3 is identical, except for a wide carriage. (Schropp collection, ser. 948)*

Remington No. 6 (4-row, upstrike): *Much improved and updated, the No. 6 and its near-twin No. 7 are the most common of the Remington upstrikes. Notice the difference in the front of the carriage as compared to the Remington No. 2. There is no prominent center wheel. (Rauen collection, ser. 156,428)*

Remington No. 8 (4-row, upstrike): *Without the obvious model number, it would be hard to tell the No. 8 from other Remingtons. The slightly wider carriage gives it away. (Rauen collection, ser. 9,150)*

Remington No. 9 (4-row, upstrike): *Another tough model to identify in the absence of a displayed number. In this case, you have to count the keys. The No. 9 had 46. (Rauen collection, ser. 8290)*

Remington No. 10 (4-row, frontstrike): *Remington's first visible typewriter. The U-shape at the front of the frame reflects the changed position of the type-bars, situated to strike from the front. A primitive five-key tabulating system is located above the keyboard. (Rauen collection, ser. RD 40,548)*

Remington Junior (3-row, frontstrike): *A very different looking Remington. Notice the boxy shape and flat surfaces. If the decals are missing, the 3-row keyboard identifies it quickly. (Milwaukee Public Museum)*

Remington Portable No. 1 (4-row, oblique frontstrike, side lever): The first of the Remington portables, featuring the side lever to raise the type-bars into position for typing. This specimen is one of the very earliest, with a shift key at left only. Later No. 1's have shift keys at left and right. The actual dividing line between the Remington Portable No. 1 and No. 2 is unclear. For purposes of this book, a No.1 is identified by the lightweight "cradle" supporting the type-bars. (author's collection, ser. NS12574)

Remington Portable No. 2 (4-row, oblique frontstrike, side lever): Most of these are in basic black, but many are found in attractive color schemes. This particular example is in "Collette and Endowa Blue." Notice the much more substantial cradle behind the type-bars as compared to the No. 1. (author's collection, ser. V119207)

Remington Portable No. 3 (4-row, frontstrike): Similar to the earlier models, this one no longer has a lever to raise the type-bars. Offered in black or colors. This example is painted in "Light and Dark Orchid." (author's collection, ser. V338449)

Remington Portable No. 3B (3½ row, frontstrike): To economize during the Depression, Remington put all eight of the necessary numerals on four keys ("1" was typed with a lowercase "L" and zero by a capital "O"). Collectors often call this layout a "3½-row keyboard." This model was produced for 6 months only in 1935 – 36. (author's collection)

Remington Portable No. 5 "Streamliner" (4-row, frontstrike): *Some examples of this machine have the "Streamliner" decal, others do not. A different version of the No. 5 portable looks very much like the No. 3. The red key the extreme right is an ordinary tab key, but it is labeled "self starter." (author's collection)*

Remington Electric (1925) (4-row, frontstrike): *Collectors refer to this bulky and boxy machine as the Remington Electric of 1925, to differentiate it from electrics made decades later. It is based on the Remington No. 12, a standard 4-row, frontstrike. (Milwaukee Public Museum)*

Rem-Blick (3-row, type-wheel): *A Remington reissue of the classic Blickensderfer No. 5. Offered with the Universal "QWERTY" keyboard instead of Blickensderfer's standard "DHIATENSOR." (Milwaukee Public Museum)*

Remington Noiseless
(see Noiseless)

Rex Visible
(see Harris Visible)

Rofa

The appealing Rofa Typewriter was introduced in Germany in 1921 and apparently enjoyed healthy sales due to pent up demand for typewriters in the wake of World War I. The curved, 3-row keyboard and upright type-bars make the machine quite similar to the British Imperial and the earlier Franklin from the U.S.A. A straight-row model, labeled "No. 4" was introduced in 1923. Earlier models were not numbered.

The Rofa was inked with a roller instead of a ribbon, a feature which figured prominently in marketing the machine. A special handle made it possible to change ink rollers without soiling the fingers.

Not many Rofas made their way to the United States, but they are fairly common in Europe. Name variants include *Correspondent* and *Ma Secretaire*.

Rofa, curved keyboard $125.00
Rofa, straight keyboard $100.00

Rofa, curved (3-row curved keyboard, downstrike): The Rofa came in two basic versions. This is the curved keyboard version. The other is essentially the same, but with a straight keyboard. (Milwaukee Public Museum)

Royal

The Royal Typewriter was invented by E.B. Hess, of New York, and introduced in 1906, beginning a long and distinguished presence in the market place. The Royal Typewriter Co. came to dominate the typewriter industry during the middle decades of the twentieth century. However, because its products were so widely sold, most are of only marginal collector's value today.

Of some interest to collectors are the very early Royals, often called "flatbed" machines (Royal Standard, Royal No. 1, Royal No. 5) because of their relatively flat shape. Apart from that specific peculiarity of form, they were ordinary 4-row, frontstrike machines. At their introduction, some considered them innovative in offering an unobstructed view of the platen (though the feature was not exclusive to Royal). Many other machines had frames with horizontal bars at the upper front which might have been bothersome.

A later machine, the No. 10 (1914), is admired for its lovely beveled glass "windows" on the sides of the frame. Some old typewriter repairmen have called the Royal No. 10 the best manual machine ever made, and indeed, it was a high quality typewriter. However, these machines are so common as to have practically no value today.

Superficially similar to the No. 10 is the rare "Royal Grand." You can identify the Grand by the fact that it has no visible ribbon spool enclosures on the top surface of the machine and no glass windows on the sides. It is thought that the Royal Grand was marketed briefly at the same time as the original flatbed machines, though details of its history are sketchy.

Of subsequent models, Royal portables of the late 1920s have some limited appeal for collectors, since many of them came in attractive colors. Later portables, especially those produced in the 1950s, sometimes came in lovely pastels such as pink and blue.

In the early 1950s Royal offered one of its portables with a special gold plated finish. Gold plating, of course, is so remarkably thin that the actual value of the precious metal on the machine is negligible. However, this typewriter has great visual appeal and is valuable on that account. In 1995, a gold-plated Royal portable belonging to James Bond author Ian Fleming sold at auction for $85,000. It should be stressed, however, that nearly all of its value is attributed to its original owner and very little to the machine itself.

Royal, flatbed (Standard, No.1, No.5) $50.00
Royal Grand $500.00
Royal Portable (gold-plated) $250.00
Royal (all other models) $20.00

Royal No. 5 (4-row, frontstrike): The odd, low profile of this machine makes collectors call it a "flatbed" model, one of several early Royals in this configuration. A Royal No. 5 (1911) also happens to be the first collectible typewriter the author ever purchased — although he bought it to do his correspondence at the time. (Milwaukee Public Museum)

Royal Grand (4-row, frontstrike): *The black boxy outlines of this early Royal can easily be confused with the later, more common Royal No. 10. Notice, however, that this machine has no externally visible ribbon spools. This particular specimen also bears the word "Grand," making identification unmistakable. (Rauen collection, ser. 206)*

Royal No. 10 (4-row, frontstrike): *The beveled glass on this machine's sides is an appealing feature. This example is an early No. 10, which has two windows on each side, later machines have only one. (Rauen collection, ser. X 253171)*

Royal portable (4-row, frontstrike): *Royal portables, such as this model (c. 1928), are very common. They came in many different color schemes including this very attractive red and black. (Russo collection, ser. P59888)*

Royal Portable, gold plated (4-row, frontstrike): *"Quiet De Luxe" was a Royal model name used from the 1930s to 50s. The 1948 version shown here was created by famed industrial designer Henry Dreyfuss. In the 1950s, it was offered in a gold-plated finish for a premium price. (Russo collection, ser. 1903707)*

Salter

The Salter Typewriter was a British machine invented in 1892 and manufactured by a company famous for the penny scales travelers used to weigh themselves in railway stations.

Most of the Salters were 3-row, downstrike machines. The first model was actually the "No. 5," the only Salter with a curved keyboard. The very first of these are said to have had inking by roller, but this was quickly replaced with a ribbon-inking system, and such machines were designated "Improved." Numbered models prior to No. 5 may have been prototypes that never reached market.

In 1900, the Salter No. 6 debuted, featuring a straight keyboard and a pair of interesting looking "pillars" adding extra support to the type-bar frame. The pillars were eliminated in 1907 on the No. 7. The No. 10, very similar to the No. 7, came out in 1908. A model No. 9 of the same year had a wide carriage.

The Salter Visible, made in 1913, was the last machine of this brand name. It was quite different from its predecessors, with a 4-row keyboard and an oblique-frontstrike design.

Name variants reported for the Salter include *Birch, Rapide, Royal-Express,* and *Salter-Perfect.*

The Salter Company may have left the typewriter business long ago, but it returned to its roots and remains alive today, manufacturing bathroom and kitchen scales.

Salter No. 5 . . . .$800.00
Salter No. 6 . . . .$350.00
Salter No. 7, 10 . . . .$200.00
Salter No. 9 (wide carriage) $250.00
Salter Visible $500.00

Salter No. 5, Improved (3-row, curved keyboard, downstrike):
The Salter No. 5 was among the earliest of the curved-keyboard, downstrike machines. Introduced in 1892, shortly after the Franklin, it is quite a different variation on the same theme. (Dickerson collection, ser. 2158)

Salter No. 6 (3-row, downstrike): If a model number is not visible, the No. 6 is identified by the two "pillars" or posts at each side of the frame. (Russo collection, ser. 4663)

Salter No. 7 (3-row, downstrike): Models 7 and onward of the Salter are quite similar, but they seem to be clearly marked. The frame has been beefed up, and the pillars of the No. 6 are eliminated. (Russo collection, ser. 13284)

Salter No. 10 (3-row, downstrike): *Notice the similarity to the No. 7. Changes are in details only and quite subtle. (Dickerson collection, ser. 20414)*

Salter Visible (4-row, oblique frontstrike): *The format was changed to make the typing more visible, and to conform with the more popular 4-row keyboard. This specimen is gray in color. A later version was black with other minor differences as well. (Williams collection, ser. 213)*

Sampo

The Sampo Typewriter, of 1894 was manufactured in Sweden. Its flat-decked appearance was not unlike the earlier Hammonia of Germany.

The Sampo was basically a linear index machine, but since the type-element was cylindrical, it could be called a type-sleeve machine as well. The type-sleeve was rotated for access to capitals and punctuation.

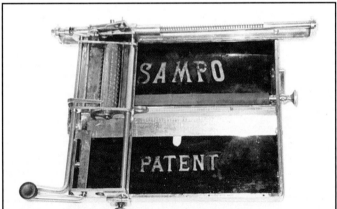

The Sampo was once thought to be exceedingly rare, but a number of specimens have since surfaced to alter that fact. A reported name variant is *Finnland.*

Sampo **$700.00**

Sampo (type-sleeve/linear index): *The large "Sampo/Patent" stencil on this machine's flat deck gives it a distinctive appearance. It is one of the few collectible machines to come from Sweden. (Williams collection, ser. 760)*

Sampson Permagraph

The Sampson Permagraph shows us there are always surprises for us in collecting typewriters. This electric type-sleeve machine was totally unknown to collectors until 1992, when a specimen turned up.

Invented in 1929 (patent granted in 1934) by Charles H. Sampson of Rochester, New York, it was patented not as a typewriter, but as a "printing machine." This explains why no typewriter researcher had ever written about it before. Typewriter historians are well-schooled in the habit of combing through old patent indexes, looking up anything that includes the word "typewriter." They don't, however, look for "printing machines."

The Sampson Permagraph was actually created as an electric *checkwriter* for use in banks. The type-wheel is struck from behind by a grooved hammer, which perforates the paper as well as printing on it. Sampson's descendants say the machine sold well for its purpose.

This machine would be an unwieldy acquisition for any collector. It is very large, measuring 26" wide and weighing 52 pounds.

Sampson Permagraph $250.00

Sampson Permagraph (4-row, type-wheel, electric): This massive machine was a single-element electric typewriter pre-dating IBM's Selectric by three decades. The Sampson, however, was a special-purpose machine for imprinting checks and other documents produced by banks. (Wilhelm collection, ser. L2029)

Saturn

The strange and wonderful Saturn Typewriter was a Swiss product placed on the market in 1899. Its design was a curious hybrid, combining a keyboard with an index.

To type, the user placed one finger in a ring and moved a cable to the proper row on a chart. Another finger was used to press the key for the column where the desired letter was found.

Understandably, not many Saturns were sold, and so they are rare today. A possible name variant is *Stauder*, the name of the company that made the machine.

Saturn . . . .$1,000.00+

Saturn (cable/key index): Although this machine does have keys, it is conceptually an index machine, since two separate actions are needed to type: first, a letter selected in a row on the chart; second, a key depressed to print. (Beck Collection)

Shimer

The Shimer Typewriter of 1898 is a rather conventional 4-row, upstrike machine. The main thing distinguishing it from others is that it is rare. It also has a name that allows for colorful collector disagreements: is it pronounced "shEYE-mur" or "Shimmer?"

Despite their small numbers, we do see variation among existing Shimers. A specimen in the Clark collection (ser. 1090), for instance, has white keytops and ribbon spool cranks. Another, in the Russo collection and shown at left, has black keytops and no cranks (ser. 1024).

Such a hard-to-find machine is a desirable collector's item today.

Shimer $500.00

Shimer (4-row, upstrike): To the untrained eye, the Shimer is little more than an ordinary, old blind-writer. However, it is quite scarce and should not be overlooked. (Russo collection, ser. 1024)

Sholes & Glidden

Just about any collector you talk to wants to own a Sholes & Glidden Type-Writer. The reason is simple. It was the first.

Invented by Christopher Latham Sholes, it dates from 1874. Many other writing machines were invented earlier, but the Sholes & Glidden, manufactured by Remington, marks the true beginning of the world typewriter industry. Details of the history of this important machine are provided in Chapter 3.

The first Sholes & Glidden was a beautiful typewriter, densely decorated with floral decals and golden ornaments. It had the QWERTY keyboard and typed capitals only, using an upstrike mechanism. It was mounted on a table and equipped with a pedal linked to a large pulley on the right side for the carriage return. A table top model was also offered, with a handle at the side for the same purpose.

The Sholes & Glidden remained in production for about five years, during which about 5,000 units were made. The finicky machine was constantly being tweaked, revised, and adjusted so that today it is very difficult to find two examples exactly alike. The importance of this typewriter makes today's collectors interested in every variation.

Among the roughly 5,000 Sholes & Gliddens produced by Remington from 1874 to 78, there were six major variations. These were created when Remington began making a "Perfected" version of the machine in 1877, which included a number of hardware improvements and a plain black paint job. The "Perfected" hardware was also offered as a retrofit on existing machines, so today, we see many different combinations of original and updated hardware.

Here are the six basic Sholes & Glidden variations:

1. **Decorated/Treadle** — all-original, floral-decorated machine, mounted on the original table, with foot pedal carriage return
2. **Decorated/Lever** — all-original, floral-decorated machine with a side lever for carriage return.
3. **Decorated/Remodel** — floral-decorated machine with updated hardware. Machines updated at the factory have an "A" stamped ahead of their serial numbers, which are located on the wooden slat just behind the top row of keys. Machines updated at the dealer level will not have the "A." Updated hardware includes, among other things, a nickel-plated return lever mounted on the carriage, removal of the side wheel and lever, addition of a metal scale at the machine's front and a heavy lid to cover the top. Some or all of these changes may have been made.
4. **Black/Remodel** — machine repainted black in addition to the changes mentioned above. Unless there is an "A" in the serial number, it is very hard to distinguish this machine from a Black "Perfected" varia-

tion. One clue might be presence of a hole (possibly plugged) left after the carriage return pulley was removed.

5. **Black/"Perfected"** — black machine manufactured with the updated hardware as original equipment. Serial numbers are generally above 3600. This machine was originally marketed as the "Perfected Type-Writer No. 1."

6. **Decorated/"Perfected"** — ornamented machine with updated hardware as original equipment. Very few of these seem to have been made, although they are illustrated in contemporary brochures.

One would think that the Sholes & Glidden is an extremely rare item today. However, due to a marketing ploy by Remington, we are fortunate to have many (possibly hundreds) of these machines as survivors heading into the next century. Around the turn of the last century, Remington realized that its first machines would make excellent promotional devices. At that time, Remington began calling them "Remington No. 1," even though they were never given that name in their own time. Remington urged its dealers to save the old junkers and put them in their retail windows for display. Thus, the original typewriters were saved for posterity instead of being destroyed like so many of their successors.

Sholes & Glidden - Decorated/Treadle . . . .$5,000.00+
Sholes & Glidden - Decorated/Lever . . . .$2,500.00+
Sholes & Glidden - Decorated/Remodel . . . . .$2,000.00+
Sholes & Glidden - Black/Remodel $1,000.00
Sholes & Glidden - Black/Perfected $1,000.00
Sholes & Glidden - Decorated/Perfected . . . . .$2,000.00+

Sholes & Glidden, Decorated/Treadle (4-row, upstrike, caps only): The original machine as it was issued from the Remington factory. The typewriter is permanently mounted to the table, and the treadle is connected by a cable to the large pulley wheel at the machine's right. This, in turn, was strung to the carriage for the return function. (Clark collection, photo by Business Technology Associates)

Sholes & Glidden, Decorated on Remington table (4-row, upstrike, caps only): Although this appears to be a complete original treadle model, it is not. This particular example is displayed here on a treadle table for illustration only. The table itself is not an original treadle table. Notice the single crossbar at bottom. This is characteristic of later tables supplied by Remington for any number of its available models. The foot pedal was likely added later for display purposes. The original treadle table had two crossbars at bottom. (Milwaukee Public Museum)

Sholes & Glidden, Decorated/Lever (4-row, upstrike, caps only): A lever at the right side is linked to the pulley for carriage return. The heavier decoration as compared to the treadle machine is of little significance. Decoration differs in detail on almost every Sholes & Glidden. (Milwaukee Public Museum, ser. 2044)

Sholes & Glidden, Decorated/Remodel (4-row, upstrike, caps only): *The newer style return lever and the lid are two obvious features of the Sholes & Glidden's "Perfected" hardware added in a factory remodel. Look carefully, and you may see the mounting hub at right/rear, which shows us that this machine originally had a side lever. No such hub would be there on a remodeled treadle machine. (Milwaukee Public Museum, ser. A814)*

Sholes & Glidden, Black/Remodel (4-row, upstrike, caps only): *This machine is shown ready for use, with its keyboard lid opened. The nickel-plated carriage return lever and scale on the top/front edge are examples of "Perfected" hardware. The serial number, without an "A" indicates this machine was remodeled at the dealer level. (Russo collection, ser. 1576)*

Sholes Visible

Christopher Latham Sholes, creator of the first typewriter, reaped little wealth from his invention. He sold off most of his rights well before they produced any significant royalties, despite urgings from his backer, James Densmore, to retain a greater interest. Nevertheless, Sholes had many other typewriter ideas, and the Sholes Visible was the result of one of them.

Patented in 1891 and introduced in 1901, the machine was a frontstrike of very peculiar design. The type-bars were bunched up in a channel at the machine's center. When a key was depressed, the associated type-bar "jumped" out of its slot and traveled down the channel to the platen. It was thought this system would produce the best alignment.

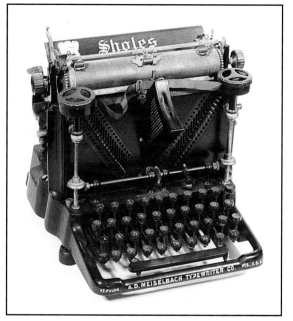

The Sholes Visible was produced first by the Meiselbach Typewriter Co. of Kenosha, Wisconsin, and later, reportedly, by the "C. Latham Sholes Typewriter Co." The name on the machine may read *Sholes Visible* or simply *Sholes.* Some machines are said to have only the *Meiselbach* name on them. A known name variant is *Bonita Ball Bearing.*

Sholes Visible **$400.00**

Sholes Visible (4-row, odd frontstrike): *The projection at the center of the machine houses all the type-bars. Note the Sholes name on the paper table and the Meiselbach Co. name on the lower front of the frame. (Dickerson collection, ser. 2215)*

Bonita Ball Bearing (4-row, odd frontstrike): *Though nearly identical to the Sholes Visible, the Bonita Ball Bearing does differ in details. Notice the carriage return lever at left, not present on the pictured example of the Sholes Visible. This Bonita bears a decal from the Pacific Hardware and Steel Co. of San Francisco, although it's not known if this was the manufacturer, or simply the retailer. (Clark collection, ser. 3084)*

Simplex

The cheap, multicolored, sheet-metal machines with the name "Simplex" are seen everywhere at every flea market and antique show you can find. Most of these have very little value, although some collectors try to see how many of the seemingly endless variations they can accumulate.

The majority of Simplex typewriters are toys and nothing more. However, when this little rubber-type device was first placed on the market around 1891, there were attempts to sell it as a serious, inexpensive writing machine.

These first Simplex typewriters are the ones to look for. They differed from all later models by carrying their paper in a long metal clip which attached to the sheet at one side and traveled through the little machine on a groove in the wooden base. The original Simplex (informally called "No. 1" by collectors) was a caps-only machine. The Improved Simplex, introduced around 1895, typed both capitals and lower case. Several later Simplex machines are labeled "No. 1" but have cylindrical platens. These should not be confused with the original Simplex Typewriters, and none of these Simplexes should be confused with the British machine of the same name, which is a twin to the rare Herrington typewriter (see page 76).

Simplex, Improved Simplex **$75.00**

Simplex "No. 1" (circular index): *The original Simplex is identified by the caps-only configuration and the name on the machine, which reads simply "The Simplex Typewriter." The paper carrying rod is shown at left, mounted on the machine. This piece separates from the typwriter for inserting the paper and can easily be missing. Without it, the machine is not complete. This specimen indicates "pat. applied for" dating it before 1892, when the patent was granted. (Clark collection, no serial number)*

Improved Simplex (circular index)*: This particular example gives modern day collectors a precise date, an "1898" at the center of the type-wheel. The Improved Simplex was advertised as early as 1895, but it's not clear which models may have had such specific years indicated. Notice the absence of colored paint. Later toy simplexes usually were painted red and green. (Clark collection, no serial number)*

Smith Premier

The Smith Premier Typewriter, introduced in 1889, is certainly one of the great success stories in typewriter history. This excellent machine was the brainchild of Alexander T. Brown, an engineer who was working for Lyman C. Smith and his brothers in Syracuse, New York. Smith was manufacturing breech-loading shotguns when Brown proposed an idea for a new typewriter and was given the opportunity to develop it.

The new device was a double-keyboard, upstrike machine with a novel mechanism. Where other typewriters linked their keys to type-bars with ordinary levers, the Smith Premier used a system of cranks. Pressing a key would turn a tiny crank below. The crank's horizontal shaft ran under the machine, turning another crank at the opposite end. The second crank was linked by a pull-rod to a type-bar above. The system made for a quick, easy touch unequaled on other machines of the day.

The Smith Premier also had a built-in type cleaning brush. Each machine came with a separate crank, which was inserted into the type-basket and used to rotate the brush hidden inside. The brush was mounted on a screw, and cranking would raise it, bringing it into contact with the type-heads on the way. Smith Premier made the brush a great advertising point, letting users know they could clean their type easily and quickly, without ever soiling the fingers!

The most important of the Smith Premier models is the No. 1. It is easily identified, since it is the only model with lovely cast-in ornaments on each side of the machine. The No. 1 also differed from later models in having two space bars instead of one. At first, these machines had no knobs for turning the platen, although later, knobs were supplied.

The Smith Premier No. 2 of 1896 is probably the most common of the line. This machine (along with the companion Model 4) may have been as successful in its day as the popular Remington Nos. 6 and 7. Smith Premier Nos. 2 and 4 were much plainer than the No. 1, without the ornamented sides. No. 2 had 76 keys, No. 4 had 84. Models of these machines dating after 1905 or so may have "tri-chrome" ribbon selectors, allowing the operator to use a ribbon with three inks: the usual black and red, plus a third which may have been purple copying ink for use with a letter press or hektograph ink for use in the gelatin duplication process.

Other Smith Premiers of interest are the wide-carriage models: No. 3 (12" carriage), No. 5 (9½" carriage), and No. 6 (16" carriage). Each had 84 keys.

The last of the Smith Premiers qualifying as collectible is the No. 10 of 1908, which was a double-keyboard, frontstrike machine. Unfortunately, the engineering excellence which made the upstrike Smith Premiers so successful did not carry over to the No. 10. It seems flimsier than its predecessors, and it hardly has the same appeal. Still, considering how many No. 10s survive today, this must have been a popular product in its own time.

An interesting member of the Smith Premier family is the *Buckner Lino-Typewriter*, a machine described in the work of author Paul Lippman. The *Lino-Typewriter* was built on the body of a Smith Premier No. 1, but had the keyboard of a standard Linotype typsetting machine. It was made under contract by Smith Premier apparently beginning 1911, and was intended for typesetters who were used to their Linotype keyboards.

The Smith Premier Co. was part of the Union Typewriter Co., a price-fixing trust essentially controlled by Remington. Once the Smith Premier No. 10 passed from the scene, Remington continued using Smith Premier as an alternative name on many of its products.

Every collection should have at least one of the Smith Premier upstrikes. Fortunately, they are common enough to be available to almost anyone.

Smith Premier No. 1 . . . .$125.00
Smith Premier No. 2,4 . . . .$50.00
Smith Premier No. 3,5,6 (wide carriage) $125.00
Smith Premier No. 10 . . . .$50.00

Smith Premier No. 1 (double-keyboard, upstrike): *Distinctive ornamentation makes this machine appealing. Look closely at the side, and you will see an Art Nouveau motif of cattails and flowers, with the "Smith Premier No. 1" name proudly displayed. Also notice the two separate space bars, and absence of platen knobs. (author's collection, ser. 22249)*

Smith Premier No. 2 (double-keyboard, upstrike): *With more of a "basic black" look, the Smith Premier No. 2 is the most common of the line. Notice the little lever on the narrow deck just in front of the carriage. This is the selector for the tri-chrome ribbon. (Dickerson collection, ser. 106735)*

Smith Premier No. 3 (double-keyboard, upstrike): *Otherwise identical to the No. 4, with 84 keys, the No. 3 features a 12" carriage for typing on wide ledger pages. (Milwaukee Public Museum)*

Smith Premier No. 10 (double-keyboard, fronstrike): *The double-keyboard idea applied to visible writing. The No. 10 was not as sturdy as the earlier, upstrike models. (Milwaukee Public Museum)*

L.C. Smith & Bros.

The L.C. Smith & Brothers typewriter is a conventional 4-row, frontstrike machine of interest to collectors mainly for its place in history. The Smiths were major players in the early typewriter industry due to their immense success with the Smith Premier Typewriter, which came out in 1889. In 1893, Smith Premier joined with other major companies including Remington, to form the Union Typewriter Co., popularly known as the "Typewriter Trust."

The Trust did a pretty good job of squeezing the competition, but part of the strategy was an intense effort to denounce the competing technology of visible typewriting. The Trust had enormous resources tied up in the old upstrike blind writing format, and even though it, too, was developing a visible machine (the Monarch), it could not afford to simply junk its factories already producing blind-writers.

Seeing the "typing" on the wall, L.C. Smith and his brothers resigned from the Trust in 1903 to form the L.C. Smith & Bros. Typewriter Co. They apparently saw no reason to stick with blind-writers, and their sights were set exclusively on visibles. The first L.C. Smith machines came out in 1904. A familiar story says the No. 2 was actually introduced a few months before the No.1, but there is some evidence that the No. 1, in fact, came first. The principal difference between the two was the number of characters: No. 1 typed 76, No. 2 typed 84.

L.C. Smith & Bros. merged with the Corona Typewriter Co. in 1926, creating Smith-Corona. The company remained successful for many decades, and remains in business today, having emerged in 1997 from its bankruptcy two years earlier.

L.C. Smith machines of various models are readily available in the flea markets and junk shops of America. They have little monetary value, but they certainly have a place in any collection.

L.C. Smith & Bros. (any model) $20.00

L.C. Smith & Bros. No. 2 (4-row, frontstrike): The 4-row, frontstrike design conformed to the mold that became dominant at the beginning of the twentieth century. Early L.C. Smith machines bear an attractive decal, featuring the typewriter inside a horseshoe, flanked by three horses. (Wild collection)

Standard Folding

The Standard Folding Typewriter, first produced in 1908, was the predecessor of the illustrious folding Corona (see page 41). The machine was the invention of Frank Rose, who received his first patents in 1904 and formed the Rose Typewriter Co. to begin manufacture. A group of investors bought the firm in 1909 and changed its name to the Standard Typewriter Co.

The Standard Folding was an intriguing little machine, built with an all-aluminum frame. Aluminum at the time, was still somewhat novel as an industrial material. The new typewriter was designed so its carriage folded forward over the keyboard, allowing it to fit into a compact case for travel. It became the first truly successful type-bar portable and made its manufacturers the dominant makers of portable typewriters for years to come.

To most eyes, all Standard Folding Typewriters look alike, although there were two models. On the first, the "Caps" shift key was on the left and the "Figs" shift key was on the right. The second model had both shift keys on the left side of the machine.

Almost all Standard Foldings were rather plain, with the brand name in Old English lettering on the front. A few had more elaborate decoration, but it is unclear just why they were made that way.

Smith-Corona Company literature claims a Standard Folding Typewriter was used by President Theodore Roosevelt on his hunting trip to Africa in 1909. However, Smith-Corona simply got it wrong. A letter written in 1910 confirms that the machine indeed traveled on Roosevelt's expedition, but it was used by Associated Press reporter W. Robert Foran. According to the Theodore Roosevelt Association, the former President did not type.

Copies of the Standard Folding were also produced in Europe, apparently under license from the American firm. European versions were sold under a number of names, including *Albus, Atlas, Azed, Emka, Engler, Franconia,* and *Proteus.*

Standard Folding $75.00

Standard Folding No. 1 (3-row, frontstrike, folding): The aluminum frame gives this machine its characteristic look, along with the post-Victorian lines designed with little sense of style. Notice the Caps and Figs shift keys on opposite sides of the keyboard, identifying this as a No. 1 (Dickerson collection, ser. 1031)

Standard Folding No. 2 (3-row, frontstrike, folding): To most people, this machine is identical to the No. 1. However, notice that both shift keys are now located at the left of the keyboard. (Dickerson collection, ser. 5575)

Stenograph

The Stenograph sought by collectors should never be confused with the modern Stenograph, one of today's leading stenographic typewriters, which happens to use the same brand name. The original Stenograph was invented by Miles Bartholomew in 1879 and first produced in 1882. It was a strange looking contraption, indeed.

Today, the Stenograph is often mistaken for something else. An antique dealer in California labeled one as a "telegraph instrument." A columnist in *Yankee* Magazine told readers it was likely a code device from the Civil War. It is certainly hard to tell what it was intended to do just by looking at it.

Using only nine keys, the Stenograph typed a code of dashes onto a thin roll of paper. The user struck keys in a "chord" technique, printing various combinations of dashes, which then had to be "decoded" into letters and numerals. The chief limitation of the Stenograph was its ability to print the code for only one letter or numeral at a stroke. Later steno machines printed a whole word (or at least one syllable) on every stroke.

Stenograph (shorthand typewriter): The nine keys on this little machine printed a code of dashes on a narrow paper tape. The example shown is the second of three models. Other versions differ primarily in the shape of the base casting. (author's collection, ser. 3528)

Despite its drawbacks, the Stenograph had a moderate success, and it is not as scarce as you'd expect. At least three different models were made, each with subtle differences in the frame and mechanical linkages.

Stenograph $125.00

Sterling

The Sterling Typewriter was a single-element machine using a swinging-sector element and a rear-striking hammer. Its first model was very similar, though not identical, to the Eagle and Defi Typewriters (see page 52) of 1905 and may date from that year as well.

The Eagle and Defi look as if they were designed specifically to be mounted on wooden bases. The Sterling, however, seems well able stand on its own frame, although a base may have been offered as well. A redesign of the Sterling was offered in 1911 with rounded edges and a smoother look.

Sterling $500.00

Sterling, early (3-row, swinging-sector): The flat deck and sharp angles give the early Sterling an appearance much like the Eagle and Defi machines. The Sterling has a frame surrounding the keyboard, while the other two do not. (Clark collection, ser. 1734)

Sterling, late (3-row, swinging-sector): Similar to the earlier version. Among the differences observed are Figs and Caps shifts on opposite sides of the keyboard and prominent rings at the rear, apparently used to hold the paper as it fed through the machine for typing. (Milwaukee Public Museum)

Sun

The Sun Typewriter Company of New York manufactured a number of machines interesting to today's collectors. Some are index machines, others have keyboards.

Around 1885, the company introduced a linear index typewriter similar in principle to the frequently found Odell. There were two basic models of the Sun index machine. The first was mounted on a simple, rectangular wood base. The second had a

Sun index, wood base, early (linear index): This very early specimen of the Sun index has no space key. Instead, the indicator is moved to a "dead" spot and pressed so that the carriage will advance without printing a character. Ink rollers are clamped to the underside of the linear type element. (author's collection, ser. 591)

dog bone shaped metal base, decorated with gold ornaments. A version of the wooden base machine was sold in Britain as *The Invincible*, apparently made under license from the American patent holders.

In 1901, the company introduced a 3-row keyboard machine using a novel inking system. Before hitting the paper each type-bar brushed past a small ink roller. This ink roller was also in contact with a larger roller which acted as an ink reservoir. There were a number of similar models, the most common being the Sun No. 2. A 4-row version was offered beginning in 1907.

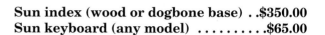

Sun index (wood or dogbone base) . .$350.00
Sun keyboard (any model) $65.00

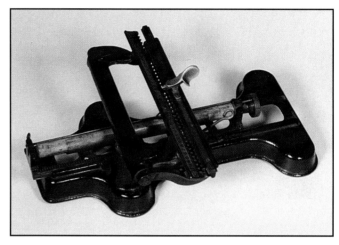

Sun index, wood base, late (linear index): *Later models of this machine show some changes. Notice the character lay-out reversing the position of the letters and numerals as com-pared to the earlier model. This example also has a space key (one of the two levers with loops at center) and a single ink roller mounted on a spring under the type element. The actual type on this machine is made of rubber, as compared to metal on the earlier version. (Rauen collection, ser. 2533)*

Sun index, metal dog-bone base (linear index): *This improved model of the Sun index came out around 1888. The metal base in the dog-bone shape makes it easy to identify. The base was decorated with gold sunburst ornaments, which are badly faded on this specimen. (Milwaukee Public Museum)*

Sun No. 2 (3-row, frontstrike, ink roller): *This is the Sun typewriter most likely to be found in the field. The attractive decals make it a real eye-catcher. Notice the nickel-plated cylinder at the center of the platen. This houses the large reservoir roller of the inking system. (author's collection)*

Sun No. 3 (3-row, frontstrike, ink roller): *A larger, more substantial version of the Sun design. The ink roller assemblies are often missing from Sun machines, as is the case with this specimen. (Dickerson collection)*

Taurus

The little Italian machine known as the Taurus brought portability to new extremes. Dating from 1908, it was made in the shape and size of a pocket watch! The user dialed each letter and pressed the stem to print. The machine printed on a narrow paper tape which was fed out of the case as needed.

Taurus . . . .$1,000.00+

Taurus (circular index): Only 2½" in diameter, the Taurus was made to fit in your pocket. It printed letters on paper tape, making it more similar to today's label-makers than to typewriters. (Russo collection, no serial number)

Travis

The Travis Typewriter was the invention of Byron Brooks, the famous typewriter engineer who designed the shift mechanism which allowed typewriters to type both upper and lower case. Brooks sold his invention to the Philadelphia Typewriter Co. which had plans to market the machine around 1889 (as the "Champion Typewriter") together with a steam-powered tricycle under an umbrella firm called the Moto-Cycle Manufacturing Co.

Plans for the tricycle fell through, and the typewriter was apparently placed on the market for a brief time beginning in 1895. The name Travis came from W. H. Travis, the president of the Philadelphia Typewriter Co.

The Travis had a 4-row keyboard, with a typewheel printing through a narrow ribbon. The paper was rolled up inside a cylindrical basket on the carriage and fed out as typing was done, similar to the Hammond. Reports say this machine was also offered under the name *Philadelphia*.

Travis . . . .$1,000.00+

Travis (4-row, type-wheel): A handsome color scheme for a typewriter from 1905, when basic black was the vogue. Even the ribbon spools are painted on this machine. (Milwaukee Public Museum)

Underwood

Few groups of people must endure the kind of rejection experienced by owners of old Underwood typewriters when they try to sell them to collectors. Due to its tremendous success, this immensely important machine is so common today that it's hard to *give* one to a collector, much less sell one.

Essentially, the Underwood was the first modern typewriter, bringing commercial success to the 4-row, frontstrike format so familiar to all typewriter users. A few machines beat Underwood to the punch, most notably the Daugherty of 1893. However, the Underwood was such a well-engineered product that it left all competition in the dust.

Design of the machine is credited to German immigrant Franz Wager, although a Herman L. Wagner is also listed on at least one patent (relation unknown, if any). The Wagner design was purchased by John Underwood, son of John T. Underwood, a prominent typewriter ribbon maker who had significant business with Remington. It's said the younger Underwood was paying a sales visit to Remington when he was unexpectedly told the typewriter company would be making its own ribbons and no longer needed Underwood. In a flash of anger, Underwood apparently exclaimed, "Well, then, we don't need Remington. We'll make our own typewriters."

Whether or not this colorful story is true, Underwood's financial backing of the Wagner machine proved to be one of the greatest typewriter investments in history. The 4-row, frontstrike design made typing visible in a world where all standard office machines were blind, requiring users to lift the carriage to see their work. Little more than a decade after its introduction, Underwood had a slew of imitators and was forcing the rest of the industry to abandon blind-writers for the new technology. Before long, the company dominated the typewriter business, taking up fully 50 percent of the market and leaving dozens of other firms to divide the rest.

There were many models of Underwood, but the most common was the No. 5, introduced in 1901 and produced for at least 30 years. Millions were made. Other models varied only slightly, with different numbers of keys or wider carriages. The differences aren't really all that important. A few Underwoods were given all-brass frames, making them interesting collectors' pieces. It's thought they were made for use on Naval vessels.

Also of some interest to collectors are the very first models of the Underwood, many of which were labeled "Wagner Typewriter Co." on the back. Others were marked "Underwood Typewriter Co." The No. 1 can be distinguished from later machines by the little lip around the machine's base and the convex frame corners at the upper-front (as opposed to concave corners on later machines). The No. 2 Underwood was identical to the No. 1 except for having 42 keys. The No. 1 had only 39.

Underwood, of course, later produced a full line of office machines and portables. The company made duplicates of Remington's Noiseless machines under license from that firm. There are also charming little 3-row Underwood portables from the 1920s which some collectors like. The later, 4-row portables are less desirable. Many people will get bug-eyed at the spectacular wide-carriage Underwoods made for typing on big ledger pages. However, these are quite common, and their size makes them cumbersome and of little interest to collectors.

Underwood No. 1 (4-row, frontstrike): *With no model number on the machine, certain characteristics identify this as a No. 1. Look at the top/front corner of the frame and see how it curves outward. Then, see the ridge running around the entire frame at the very bottom. Both features are different on later models (Milwaukee Public Museum)*

Underwood No. 5 (4-row, frontstrike): *The Underwood No. 5 is ubiquitous. See how it differs from the No. 1: no ridge around the bottom of the frame, and the top/front corners curve inward instead of out. The "No. 5" decal, of course, makes this easy to identify. The little decal of the seated dog at left was applied by the St. Paul Typewriter Exchange, which at some point refurbished this specimen. (author's collection, ser. 1757275-5)*

Underwoods were terrific typewriters. Apart from offering visible writing, they were engineered with a unique linkage giving them a touch snappier than any of their competitors. They were also so durable that many still work perfectly, up to 100 or more years after they were made. Despite their low monetary value today, Underwood typewriters are certainly pieces of history worthy of at least a little attention.

Underwood (most models) $10.00
Underwood No. 1, 2 ....$50.00
Underwood (brass) $75.00
Underwood portable (3-row) $15.00

Velograph

Dating from 1886, the Velograph was the first typewriter made in Switzerland. This circular index machine apparently came in several models. The first included two knobs on the circular index, one for upper, the other for lower case. A later model substituted a single knob in the center. A third model is reported, using a linear type-element and was also sold as the *Commerciale*.

Velograph $1,000.00

Velograph (circular index): This early Swiss machine is dominated by its large circular index. This specimen was apparently sold in England. Notice the two arrows of the indicator, labeled "smalls" and "caps." (Williams collection, ser. 364)

Victor index

The Victor Typewriter of 1890 has the distinction of being the industry's first daisy wheel typewriter. The daisy wheel was mounted on a machine with a semi-circular index and an indicator directly geared to the type-element.

The daisy wheel was made of metal but was studded with rubber type, which brushed against two ink pads as the wheel rotated. The Victor was made in Boston, Massachusetts, and originally sold for $15. It is a collector's favorite today.

Victor index $500.00

Victor index (daisy-wheel index): The daisy wheel in the center was geared to rotate as the indicator arm pivoted along the semi-circular letter index. A spring-loaded hammer pressed the type to the paper, not unlike today's electronic daisy wheel machines. (author's collection, ser. 2896)

Victor (keyboard)

All keyboard typewriters with the Victor brand name are frontstrike machines. Few are very interesting, but there are a couple which have modest collector appeal. One is a full-size machine, the other is a portable.

The Victor No. 1 of 1907 was a rather conventional office-size, 4-row, frontstrike machine, but it had a couple of unusual features. Each type-bar was mounted on a fork, consisting of two prongs spaced about an inch apart, designed to give stability and sure alignment. Also, the ribbon path zig-zagged at the printing point so that it actually ran vertically where the letters struck but horizontally to and from the spools. Models No. 2 and 3 are also documented, with apparently few differences. A later model No. 10 dates from 1919 and had a conventional, straight ribbon path. It has been mistakenly called the "No. 10½," because a large "10½" appears on the machine's frame, denoting the length of the typed line. A name-variant is *Harry A. Smith*, named for the entrepreneur who made a habit of buying up inventories of failed machines and reselling them under his own brand name.

Even as an ordinary fronstrike, the Victor has an historical pedigree. The Victor Typewriter Co. of New York was reportedly successor to the Franklin Typewriter Co. of Boston, makers of the Franklin (see page 62), surely one of the industry's most interesting machines.

The Victor portable typewriter is a scarce machine dating from 1927. It was manufactured by the Victor Adding Machine Co., which by then had purchased the Victor Typewriter Co. with the intention of marketing a portable writing machine. The company bought rights to a portable called the *Venus*, said to have been produced in 1925 by the Venus Typewriter Co. The Venus was designed by Max Garbell (inventor of the Garbell, see page 64) and had type-bars with a geared linkage to the keyboard (as did the Franklin, coincidentally). The Victor was based on the same design and was a near twin to the Venus. The Victor portable's conventional appearance makes it less desirable to collectors than its rarity might otherwise indicate.

Victor (Nos. 1-3) $50.00
Victor No. 10 . . . .$30.00
Victor or Venus portable $50.00

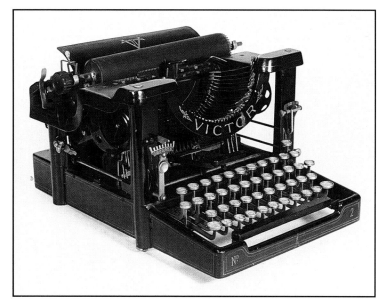

Victor No. 2 (4-row, frontstrike): The lines of the Victor reflect the very standard look of early frontstrike machines. This model features the angled ribbon path that set it slightly apart from its competitors. (Milwaukee Public Museum)

Victor Portable: (4-row, frontstrike): As ordinary as it looks, this is a rare machine. Even so, few collectors find it desirable. A very similar machine was named Venus. *(Russo collection, ser. 10,002)*

Virotyp

This little index machine was a French product dating from 1914. The round typing mechanism traveled along a stationary carriage and could be removed from the base for operation while being held freely in the hand. No desk or table was needed. It was offered for use by people who were "on the move."

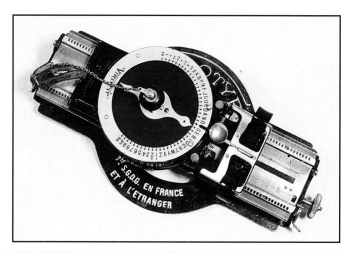

Virotyp (circular index): An index machine with a circular dial for selecting letters. Tiny type slugs in the circle rubbed against ink pads before pressing against the paper to print. (Russo collection, ser. 7562)

Virotyp $200.00

Virotyp (circular index): *A slightly later version of the Virotyp machine. This one has a rectangular base and a rather heavy metal lid. (author's collection, ser. 8467)*

Volksschreibmaschine

Autos have their *Volkswagens* and typewriters have their *Volksschreibmaschines* (*Schreibmaschine* is German for *typewriter*). However, the typewriter version of the familiar name achieved nothing of the success earned by its automotive counterpart.

This German index machine was introduced around 1898. The round letter index was set at right angles to the circular type-wheel, which had rubber type along its edge. An improved model was marketed as the *Diskret*.

Volksschreibmaschine $1,000.00

Volksschreibmaschine (circular index): *This lightweight German index machine is almost as hard to find as its name is to pronounce. (Milwaukee Public Museum)*

Wellington
(Empire)

The Wellington Typewriter gets its name from the innovative inventor Wellington Parker Kidder, a resident of Boston, Massachusetts. His design for a thrust-action machine was the first step in his long-held dream of producing a typewriter with nearly silent action (see Noiseless, page 97) The Wellington was originally introduced in 1892. Kidder soon after teamed up with Canadian businessman C. C. Colby to set up a manufacturing and distribution network in countries outside the U.S., where the machine would be sold under the "Empire" name.

The firm contracted to actually produce the machines was the Williams Mfg. Co., which had facilities both in Canada and the U.S. The Canadian factory made Empires, the U.S. factory made Wellingtons. A machine bearing a "Williams Mfg. Co." decal should not be confused with the Williams Typewriter, which was made by the Williams *Typewriter* Co. of Derby, Connecticut.

Colby also arranged to license the machine to a German firm, which produced the Adler line of typewriters. Early Adlers were nearly identical to early Wellingtons (see Adler, page 19). The machines under all three names were very popular and sold in numbers great enough that many survive today.

The variations among Wellingtons and Empires are subtle. The earliest Wellingtons may have square-shaped keys, as indicated in an advertisement announcing introduction of the machine. The vast majority of known specimens, however, have round keys.

Two manufacturing operations, taking place in two different factories, serving two different marketing networks, resulted in slightly divergent development of the Wellington and Empire. The Empire line exhibited improvements in design and function, while the Wellington line stayed basically the same. For instance, the machines designated Wellington and Wellington No. 2 were very similar, while the *Empire* No. 2 was quite different by being much bulkier than the original Empire. The firm distributing the Empire also remained in business much longer than the Wellington Typewriter Co.

One of the more observable differences among Wellingtons and Empires is the shape of the space bar: either T-shaped or straight. The two different shapes are seen on both Wellingtons and Empires, and the T-shape is apparently the earlier of the two. The variation in this line of machines is a subject which has yet to be explored in depth among collectors. Until it is, the information we have will remain vague.

Reported Wellington/Empire name variants include *British Empire, Kanadische Empire, Davis,* and *Lindeteves.* The most likely name variant to be found in the U.S. is *Wanamaker*, which was sold by the John Wanamaker department store in Philadelphia, PA. The name *"Wanamaker"* will appear on these machines with or without the name "Wellington."

Wellington (square keys) $150.00
Wellington, Empire (any other model) $75.00

Wellington No. 2 (3-row, thrust-action): *This very well designed machine is often found in fully functional condition. Typing on one may be a problem, however, since it requires a ⅞" ribbon, a difficult width to find. (author's collection, ser. 3372)*

Empire (3-row, thrust-action): *Nearly identical to the Wellington No. 2 shown above, this Empire has a few minor differences. Notice the straight (versus T-shaped) space bar and the keys for the shift as opposed to the nickel-plated rocker switch on the Wellington. (author's collection, ser. 39087)*

Empire No. 2 (3-row, thrust-action): *Clearly built on the same principles as its predecessor, the No. 2 is a bulkier, more substantial machine. (Dickerson collection, ser. 136002)*

Williams

The Williams Typewriter of 1891 is a favorite of nearly all typewriter collectors. Its type-bars were arranged in two symmetrical fans in front of and behind the platen. The typefaces rested in ink pads, and the type-bars "hopped" forward to the platen in what is called a "grasshopper" action. One writer from the early days of typewriters described the moving type-bars on a Williams as something like a flock of chickens pecking for corn! He wasn't far off.

The paper on a Williams followed a strange path. It was first fed into an internal paper basket in front of the platen (and under the type-bars). It then unrolled, passing over the upper surface of the platen, to be collected in another paper basket behind the platen. As a result only a line or two of typing was actually visible at any time, something disappointing on a machine marketed for offering writing "in sight."

As strange as all this sounds, the Williams was reasonably successful, with a number of different models produced over a period of about 15 years. The differences in these models are important to collectors and are often difficult to ascertain.

The very first Williams had a 3-row, curved keyboard and was decorated with gold scrollwork. The curved keyboard and the ornamentation were soon dropped in favor of a straight keyboard and a plain black frame. Both of these machines, however, were designated "No. 1." Today, a collector who is told of a Williams No. 1 will be anxious to hear whether it is a No. 1 curved or No. 1 straight.

The Williams No. 2 also had a straight, 3-row keyboard and was essentially similar to the No. 1. The differences included the shape of the nameplate and the guides for the type-bars (see photos). The No. 2 frequently was not marked with its model number, so knowing these differences can be important.

No. 3 was the designation given to early wide-carriage machines made by Williams. However, there were No. 3's built on No. 1 bases and No. 3's built on No. 2 bases. Some wide-carriage Williams machines had the word "Academy" stenciled on the frame, and it is said that they were made concurrently with the later 4-row models.

Williams models No. 4 (1900) and No. 6 (1904) are easy to identify, because they were almost always marked. These two very similar machines had four rows of keys instead of three as on earlier models.

At the time the No. 6 was being sold, Williams offered a "Junior" model, which was practically the same as the earlier No. 2. Another name, *Englewood*, appears on one example of this style of machine.

There have also been reports of a "half" Williams, based on the 4-row models, with only one fan of type-bars. This machine apparently typed capitals-only for use in telegraph offices.

Although all Williams Typewriters are desirable to collectors, the top machine of the line is the curved No. 1. This model was so quickly refitted to the straight version that few were made, and fewer survive.

Williams No. 1-curved ....$1,000.00+
Williams No. 1-straight, No. 2 ....$200.00
Williams No. 3, Academy $300.00
Williams No. 4, 6 ....$175.00
Williams Junior $200.00

Williams No. 1-curved (3-row, grasshopper action, curved keyboard): There is little problem in identifying the first Williams, since it was the only one with a curved keyboard. Notice the gold scrollwork on the frame, the only Williams with such decoration. (Milwaukee Public Museum)

Williams No. 1-straight (3-row, grasshopper action): *Since there is no model number shown on a No. 1, you identify it by its features. Notice the nameplate. It laps over the top / front edge of the frame. Now, look at the type-bars. They rest between little guides which protrude above them. The space bar on this specimen is shown in its folded-inward position, required for the machine to fit in its case. (Dickerson collection, ser. 3941)*

Williams No. 2 (3-row, grasshopper action): *Not all No. 2's are marked as this one is. However, they are not hard to identify. The nameplate on this model is flush with the top / front surface of the frame. Also, the protruding type-bar guides of the No. 1 are no longer present. (Rauen collection, ser. 12218)*

Williams No. 3 (3-row, grasshopper action, wide carriage): *The No. 3 designation is given to any early 3-row Williams with a wide carriage. On this example, the wide carriage is fitted to a No. 2 frame. (Dickerson collection, ser. 1648)*

Williams No. 4 (4-row, grasshopper action): *The No. 4 is a much bulkier machine than earlier models. Collectors find the 4-row Williams models marginally less desirable than the 3-row models. (author's collection, ser. 25995)*

Williams Academy (3-row, grasshopper action): This wide-carriage 3-row model is superficially similar to the No. 3. However it also has some features in common with the No. 4 (such as nickel-rimmed keytops; wide, non-folding space bar), supporting the suggestion that it was made concurrently with that model. The word "Academy" appears on the upper/rear edge of the machine. (Pace O'Shea collection, ser. 07241)

World

The World Typewriter was a simple index machine, using a semi-circular type-element manipulated by a simple swing handle, which also selected letters on a curved strip. Inking was via two ink pads, and the type was rubber (almost always missing today). The World was the invention of Boston's John Becker, who marketed the machine himself beginning as early as 1885, although he didn't receive his first patent until Oct. 12, 1886.

Becker was not content to stand still and developed a business relationship with the Pope Manufacturing Co. of Boston, maker of Columbia Bicycles. Pope geared up production of the little machine, stamping out units like cookies and flooding the market with them. Most of the Worlds you will see were made by Pope. However, the cycle maker apparently had only a few years' patience for the enterprise, and the machine was handed off to another firm once Pope washed its hands of it.

The World has been the subject of much research in the past few years, resulting in a great deal of information on the minutiae of its variations. Collectors divide World Typewriters into two categories, which they informally call "No. 1" and "No. 2."

A World "No. 1" is a single-case machine, typing capitals only. A "No. 2" is a double-case machine, typing capitals as well as lowercase. Not all No. 1's are earlier than No. 2's, since both machines were largely offered concurrently. Actually, the World was not sold officially as "No. 1" or "No. 2." Virtually all advertisements list them as either "single-case" or "double-case" with no model number mentioned.

There is more to it, however, than just No. 1 and No. 2. The earliest World machines had what has been termed a "graceful" framework when compared to later and more common examples. This graceful World was apparently offered only as a single-case model before the double-case was introduced in 1887. The graceful World had 42 characters, while later single-case models had 44.

Most single-case Worlds had an index assembly with two spokes located in the 4-o'clock and 8-o'clock positions — a clear distinction from the curved spokes seen on the graceful model. A few Worlds had an open type-head (the swiveling part), accommodating a paper name tag. The majority, however, were solid, with the brand name and patent date (Oct. 16, 1886) cast into the metal.

The total production of single-case Worlds seems to break down in to three divisions that we'll call *earliest, early* and *late*. The earliest is the graceful World described above. Early and late are identified by the "comb" of spring steel fingers used to keep the paper in place. Early single-case Worlds had 35 fingers in the comb, late machines had 21 fingers.

There was also some early/late variation among double-case Worlds. The preponderance of these machines were made by Pope Manufacturing and had a large, attractive Pope nameplate underneath the type assembly. Early double-case machines had the same 4-o'clock/8-o'clock spokes as the single-case machines and printed 72 characters. Late double-case machines had a sheet metal (not cast) printing assembly, with a curved opening to allow viewing of the scale beneath it. These machines printed 77 characters.

Some machines post-date those made by Pope Manufacturing and were labeled "The New World," although we're not sure just what was so new about them. They were marketed by the "Type-Writer Improvement Co."

The World Typewriter remained on sale until about 1893, when lower-priced machines apparently drove it off the market. Late advertisements claimed "100,000" of them in use, and given the number that have survived, it's possible that figure is not terribly exaggerated. Most World machines are close to each other in value, with a premium attached to the graceful World, which appears to be the earliest of them all. The World was often offered in an attractive walnut case, some examples of which were plush-lined. Presence of the case adds value to the machine.

The World is reported to have been sold in Europe as the *Boston* Typewriter, although no such name variants have been found. One other known alternate name is *Machine Express*.

World ("graceful"), single-case, 42 characters $250.00
World (all other models) . .$125.00

World, single-case, graceful (semi-circular index): If you closely examine the index assembly, you'll see the graceful curves of the spokes holding the index (letter chart) to the rest of the assembly. This, in addition to the 42 characters, identifies this machine, thought to be the earliest of the Worlds. The name appears on a plate mounted on the machine base, unlike later machines. (Schindler collection, no serial number)

Machine Express (semi-circular index): This is a single-case World sold under an alternate name. Note the 4-o'clock and 8-o'clock spokes on the index carrier, the usual configuration for single-case models. This machine is an example of one with an open type-head. In this case, a paper name label is attached. The 35 fingers in the paper comb identify this as an early single-case machine. (Auktion Team Köln, no serial number)

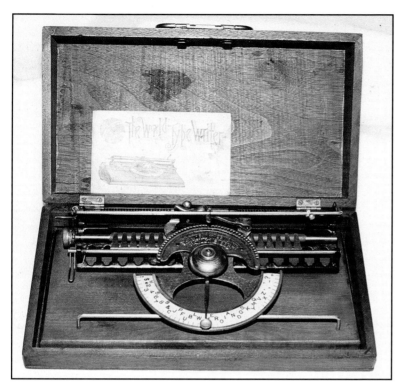

World, single-case, late (semi-circular index): *This example of a late single-case World is shown in its walnut case and with its instruction booklet. It has the 4-o'clock and 8-o'clock spokes, and the name/patent date is cast into the type-head. It has 21 fingers on the paper comb, the main identifying clue for late single-case machines. (Wilhelm collection, no serial number)*

World, double-case, early (semi-circular index): *The 72 characters and the 4-o'clock/8-o'clock spokes identifies this as an early version of the double-case World. The ivory-colored name plate mounted on the base below the typing unit is from the Pope Manufacturing Co., which made most of the World machines. The name and patent date are cast into the type-head. (Schropp collection, no serial number)*

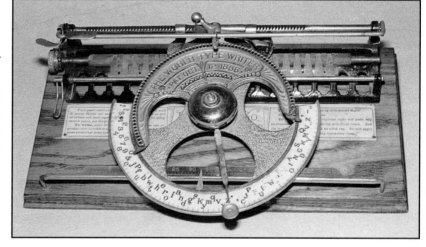

World, double-case, late (semi-circular index): *The index carrier of this late machine differs in shape from the early and is the most common of the double-case variations. Note the curved hole for viewing the scale. This machine prints 77 characters. (Milwaukee Public Museum, no serial number)*

Yetman Transmitting Typewriter

Although this appears to be little more than a heavy, 4-row, frontstrike machine, the Yetman was an innovative early teletype machine. It included a Morse Code conversion device which translated any keystroke into the appropriate dots and dashes for conventional telegraph transmission. The keyboard could be used to send a telegraph signal, or to type a letter, or both.

Yetman Transmitting Typewriter $150.00

Yetman Transmitting Typewriter (4-row, frontstrike, telegraphic): This large heavy machine was both a typewriter and a telegraph instrument. The carriage return lever was in the form of a pull-crank, not unlike those on adding machines. (Milwaukee Public Museum)

Yost

The Yost Typewriter made its debut in 1887, bearing the name of one of the industry's great salesmen, George Washington Newton Yost. Yost joined James Densmore in 1873 to sell the original Sholes & Glidden Type-Writer to E. Remington & Sons. It is said that the rough-hewn Densmore would not have stood a chance alone, and it was the smooth-talking Yost who actually secured the deal.

Yost did not remain with Densmore in the sales end of the first typewriter enterprise. He soon struck out on his own to form the American Writing Machine Co., makers of the Caligraph (see page 35). The restless promoter then left that company to produce the machine with his name on the front.

The Yost Typewriter was a double-keyboard, upstrike of a very novel design. Its upstrike type-bars actually performed a "grasshopper" movement. They rested in an ink pad on the perimeter of the type circle and jumped to the center for printing, landing in a tiny square-shaped type guide. The direct inking produced an exceptionally clear impression when compared to conventional ribbon-inked machines.

The Yost was very successful and was produced in many different models over many years. Earliest was the No. 1 machine, which has a rather flat base, and is identified by two round medallions inlaid into the base at the back corners.

Two succeeding models were called The New Yost (1889) and the Yost No. 4 (1895) They are nearly identical and are the most common of the Yosts to be found. Author Paul Lippman wrote of successive models with carriages for wider paper: No. 5 (9½"), No. 6 (12"), No. 7 (12½") and No. 8 (16").

Next in the Yost model sequence was the No. 10 of 1902. This was a slightly larger, more enclosed machine, with a heavier base.

The Yost No. 15 of 1908 was a 4-row, frontstrike, but with the same "grasshopper" action for the pad inking system, and a platen shift mechanism. Model No. 15 was apparently also sold as the "Model A." Another 4-row, frontstrike, No. 20, appeared in 1912, substituting a type-basket shift for the platen shift.

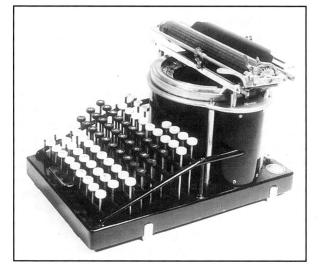

Yost No. 1 ....$250.00
Yost No. 4-10, New Yost $100.00
Yost No. 15, No. 20, Model A (visible) $75.00

Yost No. 1 (double-keyboard, upstrike, "grasshopper" action): The first of this make shows no model number. It is identified by its squarish base and the two "coins" imbedded into each corner the base at the rear. The coin on the right side is visible in this photo. The No. 1 also has no buttress supports at the rear as on later models. (Dickerson collection, ser. 3952)

New Yost (double-keyboard, upstrike, "grasshopper" action): Distinguished from the No. 1 by its rounder lines. The name and model are clearly marked. (Rauen collection, ser. 20778)

Yost No. 4 (double-keyboard, upstrike, "grasshopper" action): Nearly a twin to the New Yost, but clearly marked as a No. 4 on the paper table. Notice the buttress support visible at the right / rear of the machine. This support is also present on the New Yost, but not on the No. 1. (Dickerson collection, ser. 29171)

Yost No. 10 (double-keyboard, upstrike "grasshopper" action): A heavier and more squared-off appearance sets this Yost apart from earlier models. The celluloid covered keytops on the No. 10 are often deteriorated and are especially difficult to restore. They appear to be in good condition on this specimen. (Russo collection, ser. 73761)

Yost No. 20 (4-row, frontstrike "grasshopper" action): One of two essentially similar visible versions of the Yost. Though conventional in appearance, it's fascinating to watch the "grasshopper" mechanism at work, something not possible while typing on the blind-writing models. (Dickerson collection, ser. KS65964)

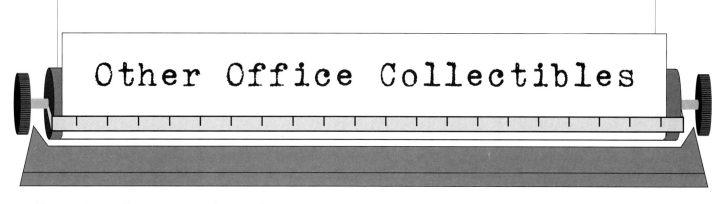

Other Office Collectibles

Typewriter collectors very often seek many other objects from the early office. Some of the major categories include ribbon tins, calculators, check protectors, and typewriter "ephemera," meaning all of the advertisements, trade catalogs, letterheads, and other items picturing or accompanying writing machines.

Ribbon Tins

Typewriter ribbon tins are the most popular of the related items accumulated by typewriter collectors. Tins came in a fabulous variety, with thousands of different brands, sizes, and designs available. There is so much variety that collectors can gather up hundreds of different tins without fearing that they've "collected them all," and there will be no more to find.

Ribbons were packaged in tin containers at least as early as 1892 and probably earlier. The tins remained on the market into the 1960s, giving us a good seven decades or more of products to choose from.

The great majority of ribbon tins were made to hold standard ribbons, ½" in width. Most of these tins are square or round and between 2" and 2½" across. Earlier typewriters used ribbons about 1½" wide which were packed in box-shaped or cylindrical containers that collectors now call "tall" tins. Certain early "flat" tins were also made to hold wide ribbons, but without spools. These tins measure about ¼" x 1½" x 4".

There is usually little or no premium attached to tins which have ribbons and/or spools inside. In many cases, these ribbons are used — placed there for disposal after the new ribbon from the tin had been installed on the typewriter. At other times, however, the original ribbon, wrapped in cellophane or foil is still present. If the wrapping is decorated, this may add value to the tin. On certain tall tins, the spool inside is decorated, something that will certainly add value to the tin.

The major national ribbon brands, with the largest number of different tins include Carter's, Kee-Lox, Miller-Bryant-Pierce, Mittag & Volger, Panama, and Webster. There are many additional brands frequently found, some national, some regional, and some local. Examples include M.B. Cook (Chicago), Little's (Rochester, New York), Columbia Carbon & Ribbon (Glen Cove, New York), Columbia Carbon Co. (Dayton, Ohio), Codo (Chicago), Stenno (Portland, Oregon), Old Town (Brooklyn, New York), and many others. Other brands came from typewriter companies themselves. Underwood, Remington, and Smith-Corona are the most often found, but many other typewriter makers offered their own ribbons as well.

Collectors will also be interested in the manufacturer of the tin itself, if known. Decorated Metal, of Brooklyn, New York, was the largest of the typewriter ribbon tin makers, and its name is often seen in very small print on the upper edge of a tin's bottom half. Another major maker was J.L. Clark of Rockford, Illinois. Its logo looks like an inverted letter "T" inside the letter "C". When found, the tiny logo is usually seen on the extreme edge of a tin's bottom surface. Collectors sometimes place a slight premium on tins made by early tin companies such as Somers Bros., Mersereau, Colonial Can, Hudson, Tindeco, and American Stopper.

Pricing on ribbon tins is largely arbitrary, since the market is so highly specialized. Although there are exceptions, many dealers will base their prices only on the beauty of the artwork and condition of the tin. Dealers often have little or no knowledge at all of a tin's rarity or importance, so common tins with attractive graphics tend to be overpriced. Some examples are the common Panama tins, Webster's Battleship, Columbia's "Clean & Good" twins and the various colorful Beaver tins of M.B. Cook.

Recognizing that aligning relative rarity and attractiveness is difficult, values in typewriter tins need to be painted with a broad brush. These very general categories are suggested, with considerable overlapping:

Type I: common tins with plain decoration, $2.00 – 5.00
Type II: common tins with attractive decoration; uncommon tins with plain decoration, $3.00 – 8.00
Type III: uncommon tins with attractive decoration; scarce tins with plain decoration, $5.00 – 12.00
Type IV: scarce tins with attractive decoration; rare tins with plain decoration, $8.00 – 20.00
Type V: rare tins with attractive decoration; rarest tins with plain decoration, $15.00 – $25.00
Type VI: rarest tins with attractive decoration, $20.00 – $35.00+

The photos of tins presented here are in general alphabetical order. A few tins, which became available late in the photo session, are shown outside alphabetical order at the end. Each tin is given its value designation in parentheses beside its name.

ROW 1: Anonymous or no-name tins: anony-mous / antelope (II), anonymous / generic radial(I), anonymous / generic "vines"(I), anonymous / horse & rider (III), anonymous / pendant (II)
ROW 2: anonymous / seagull (II), anonymous / sail-boat, abstract (III), A&W (II), Addressograph, women on four sides, dark background (IV), Addressograph, woman on two sides, light back-ground (IV)
ROW 3: Addressograph Duro-Clear (III), Advocate (III), Allied, seagull (II), Allied Flagship, sailboat (II), American Brand, tall (VI)
ROW 4: American Brand (IV), Amneco (III), Art (III), Atlas (III), Aulta (II)

ROW 1: Badger Brand, yellow (V), Badger Brand, blue (IV), Bates Wire Stapler (III), Battleship Brand, old style (III), Battleship Brand, deco style (II)
ROW 2: Bay State (V), Bell (II), Belmont (III), Blur Less (IV), Blur Less Platinum (IV)
ROW 3: Bucki D&D (III), Bucki Supreme (III), Bundy (IV), Cardinal (III), Carnation (II)
ROW 4: Carrib (III), Carter's Five O'Clock (II), Carter's Cavalier (II), Carter's Golden Arrow (IV), Carter's Guardian (III)

ROW 1: *Carter's Guardian (II), Carter's Ideal, round logo (III), Carter's Ideal, oval logo (III), Carter's Ideal, flowers (II), Carter's Ideal, orchid (II)*

ROW 2: *Carter's Ideal, cyclamen (II), Carter's Ideal, lotus (II), Carters Ideal, bird of paradise (II), Carter's midnight, shooting stars (II), Carter's Midnight (II)*

ROW 3: *Carter's Nylon Electric (III), Carter's Silk (III), Carter's Super Nylon (II), Carter's Valiant (II), Carter's Typewriter Ribbon, tall (V)*

ROW 4: *Century (II), Chicago Super, city scene (III), Codo, silkmoth & tree (II), Codo Keen-Rite (III), Colonial Quality Ribbon (III)*

ROW 1: *Columbia, tall (IV), Columbia, twins, red (III), Columbia, twins, orange (II), Columbia, twins, blue (II), Commercial (III)*

ROW 2: *Conquest (IV), Copy-Right Brand, Indian chief (III), Cotton King (IV), Crown (III), Crystal, beaver (III)*

ROW 3: *Dandy Line (VI), Distinctive Silk (II), Ditto, deco (III), Ditto, lace (III), Durite (IV)*

ROW 4: *Duro Clear (III), Elliott-Fisher (III), Ellwood, with typewriter (III), Ellwood, blue (III), Ellwood, deco with typewriter (III)*

ROW 1: *Emerald (III), Empress (III), Eureka (IV), Everlasting (IV), Flax (III)*

ROW 2: *Fox (IV), Frye Mfg. Co (III), Geo. S, Miller (III), Gibraltar (IV), Globe (III)*

ROW 3: *Gold Medal (III), Golden Gate (IV), Golden Poppy (III), Grand Prize, blue & white (III), Grand Prize, multicolor (IV)*

ROW 4: *GuhalBro (III), Herald Square (II), Highlander (II), Hub (II), Imco (IV)*

ROW 1: *Imperial Mfg. Co., tall (IV), Imperial Write Master (III), International (III), International Business Machines, silver and blue (III), International Business Machines, gold and blue (III)*

ROW 2: *Ivory Brand (I), Ivory Brand, tall (IV), Kee-Lox Brand (I), Kee Lox, tall, deco (III), Kee Lox SilKeeLox (II)*

ROW 3: *Kee Lox, geisha (II), Kee Lox, tulips (II), Klean Write (III), Kreko, square (III), Kreko, round (III)*

ROW 4: *Langham (III), Liberty Brand, tall (IV), Liberty Brand, red/white/blue (IV), Little's Indeliba (III), M&M (III)*

ROW 1: *Madame Butterfly (III), Burroughs mainline (II), Manhattan (IV), MS (III), Master Copy, with secretary (III)*

ROW 2: *Miller Line Kopy-Rite (IV), Miller Line, tall (III), Mitzpah (III), Monarch (IV), Monogram, Underwood (II)*

ROW 3: *National Standard Ink Ribbon (IV), Ne-To Erasing Shield (IV), For use on Noiseless, John Underwood Co. (III), Norta type cleaner (III), Old Reliable, beaver (III)*

ROW 4: *Old Town, with Brooklyn Bridge (III), Old Town, with seal (III), Old Town Dawn (IV), Old Town Hermetic, key open (III), Old Town Nylon +AF, key open (III)*

ROW 1: *Panama, round, navy and gold (II), Panama, square, navy and gold (II), Panama, round, blue, red, and green (II), Panama Bronze (III), Panama Commercial Brand (III)*

ROW 2: *Panama Ink Control (IV), Panama Popular Brand (III), Panama Standard (III), Paragon, with offset seal (III), Paragon, with center seal (III)*

ROW 3: *Paramount (III), Perm-o-Rite (III), Philco (III), Pigeon, black (III), Pigeon adder ribbon, red (III)*

Row 4: *Pigeon, large (IV), Pinnacle, square (III), Pinnacle, round, purple and pink (III), Pinnacle, round, purple and black (III), Preferred (I)*

ROW 1: *Princess Brand, yellow and brown (III), Princess Brand, red and white (III), Quality (III), Queen (III), Rainbow (II)*

ROW 2: *Red Star (III), Regal Remtico, tall (IV), For use on Remington, John Underwood & Co. (III), Ribbons, compass (IV), Rite-Rite (III)*

ROW 3: *For use on Royal, John Underwood Co. (III), Roytype, with typewriter (III), Roytype Park Avenue, with hunter & dog (IV), Sanitary, tall (V), Satin Finish Brilliant, black boy (IV)*

ROW 4: *Satin Finish Executive, black boy (V), Secretarial, square, silver (III), Secretarial, round, silver (III), Secretarial, round, gold (III), Silhouette (III)*

ROW 1: *Silver Brand (I), Spartan (III), Stafford's Immaculate (III), Stafford's Ser-vuS (III), Stenotype, dark green (II)*

ROW 2: *Stenotype, light green (II), Stormtex (IV), Success (III), Super-Superb, beaver (IV), Superb, beaver (III)*

ROW 3: *Supreme (III), Tagger, brown and black (III), Tagger, maroon and gold (III), Tagger, stripes (III), Thorobred (II)*

ROW 4: *True-Mark, hunter and gazelle (III), Typ-O-Typ (III), The Original Underwood (III), Underwood Corporation Sundstrand Ribbon (III), Underwood Elliot Fisher Co. (II)*

ROW 1: *Uni-Sun (IV), U.S. Brand (III), Viking, yellow and blue (IV), Viking, orange and blue (III), Vivid (III)*

ROW 2: *Webster Star Brand, deco, tall (IV), Webster Star Brand, deco (III), Wonder Brand, lady and mirror (II), Write-Right (III), Milo (III)*

ROW 3: *Aurora (III), Elk (II), Elk Brand (IV), Monogram, Nedich Process, tall (IV), American Flag, upside down flag/German (V)*

ROW 4: *Two Flags, Austrian (IV), Celesta, German (IV), Osma, German (III), Mascotte Ribbon, Scottish (IV), Colibri, Italian (IV)*

Paragon tins: *The flat Remington Paragon tin (left), made by Mersereau, is an example of a tin made for a ribbon without a spool. All such tins are desirable (V). The tall Paragon (right), made by Decorated Metal, is attractive, but much more frequently found (III).*

Underwood's: *This tall (1⅝" x 1⅝" x 1⅞") tin dates from the early 1890s, before Underwood got into the typewriter business. Highly ornate, no two sides are alike. Even the ribbon spool inside is decorated. The tin maker is Mersereau (VI).*

Calculators

Many typewriter collectors are equally interested in old mechanical calculators, which came in a wide variety of sizes and styles. Prices range from $1 to $1,000 and more.

There is no one way to classify old calculators, so the route we'll follow here is simply descriptive. Collectible calculators can be divided up into three major classes: keyboard calculators, slide-set calculators, and small, hand-held calculators.

Keyboard calculators

As with typewriters, there are many variations. They may have small 10-key keyboards (the modern configuration), or they may have long columns of 9 keys for each numerical place. To drive the mechanism, a machine may have either a crank or pull-lever... or neither. Those without levers or cranks are often called "key-set" machines. They register numbers immediately as the keys are pushed. Some keyboard calculators may have a movable carriage, which is used to accomplish multiplication or division. Electric calculators use motors to power the mechanism and are distinguished from electronic calculators, which use tubes, transistors, or integrated circuits instead of machinery and are outside the scope of this book. Familiar names like Burroughs, Monroe, Victor, and Dalton have little value.

Slide-set calculators

Slide-set calculators have tabs or buttons which the user slides back and forth to set numbers. Many of these are roughly cylindrical in shape and include a crank and movable carriage. These are collectively called Baldwin or Ohdner-type calculators for the inventors who pioneered the designs. They were extremely popular in Europe and most are quite common today.

Other slide-set calculators are rectangular, usually set into wooden boxes. They include a movable carriage and a crank, which is often mounted on the upper surface (not the side). These rectangular machines may be called Thomas-type machines, for Thomas de Colmar's Arithmometre, the first of their kind. Many of these are also designated "stepped-drum" machines, because that describes the inner mechanism.

Small, hand-held calculators

This last major division of collectible calculators has a huge variety of machines. Many of them are designed to be operated with a stylus. The stylus could have been used to pull down chains, racks, or rods. On others, a stylus was used to rotate dials (either concentric or side-by-side). Some of these were well-made, expensive devices, others were tinny and cheap. Most often seen are the thin, sheet metal adders on which you need to take the stylus "up and over" when you want to carry. These are collectively called "Troncet" adders (for the Frenchman who invented the first), and they sell for 50¢ to $5 everywhere.

Calculator or Adder?

According to some, the terms *calculator* and *adding machine* or even *adder* should not be used interchangeably. Calculator applies to those machines capable of doing all four arithmetical operations. Adding machines are those which add and subtract only and carry from one column to another automatically. Adders are machines on which the user has to do something extra to carry the tens (such as the "up-and-over" movement on Troncet adders).

The abbreviated list of values here is meant to demonstrate the range in the field. It is far from comprehensive.

Add-o-Meter (stylus, rotary) $10.00
Arithma (Troncet) $5.00
Baby Calculator (Troncet) $5.00
Baldwin (any model) ....$1,000.00+
Brunsviga (Ohdner type) $50.00
Burroughs (keyboard, pull handle) $20.00
Comptometer, wood (key-set) $150.00
Curta (peppermill shape) $150.00
Dalton (10-key, pull-handle) $20.00
Gem, Golden Gem (stylus, pull-chains) $20.00
Gem, wood case (stylus, pull-chains) $75.00
Grant (any model, slide-set) ....$1,000.00+
Grossbeck's (stylus, rotary) $500.00

Lightning adder (stylus, rotary) $10.00
Magic Brain (Troncet) $5.00
Marchant (Ohdner type) $50.00
Marchant (keyboard, crank) $20.00
Millionaire (slide set, crank) $350.00
Monroe (keyboard, crank) $25.00
Ohdner $50.00
Rapid Computer (stylus, sliding racks) $50.00
Spalding (primitive rotary) $1,000.00
Sundstrand (10-key) $10.00
Thomas Arithmometre . . . .$1,000.00+
Victor (keyboard, pull-handle) $10.00

Comptometer, wood (keyboard calculator): One of the most successful calculators of all times, the very common Comptometer can be found at every flea market for $25 or less. A wood-sided Comptometer is different, however, representing the earliest of these devices. They are less common and more desirable. (Dickerson collection)

Curta (hand-held, slide-set): This is a relatively modern machine, introduced in 1948. A fine instrument, it was the smallest mechanical calculator capable of performing all four arithmetic functions. The example shown is a Type II, with 11 columns. Type I had only nine columns. (author's collection, ser. 532352)

Improved Gem Adding Machine (stylus, pull-chain): The user of this machine used a pencil or stylus to pull chains down in the channels representing each column. The sum appeared in little windows, and the number wheels were reset by turning the knob at bottom / right. The version shown, encased in wood is more desirable than the more common model, encased in metal. The names of these machines can be confusing. A collector would understand you if you described this one as a "Gem with a wood case." (Russo collection, ser. 30411)

Gem Adding Machine (stylus, pull-chain): *Mechanically identical to the Improved Gem Adding Machine (page 153), this is a smaller, more portable model. Sold in great numbers during the early part of the century, this adder is easily found today. Many are called "Golden Gem." (Russo collection, ser. 15,590)*

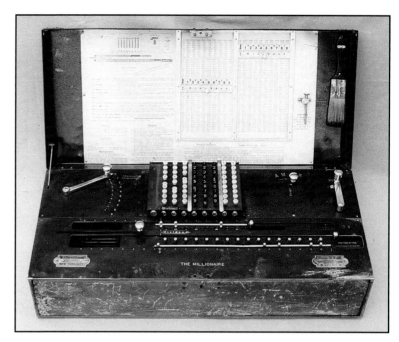

Millionaire (key-set, direct multiplier): *This massive 70-lb. machine resembles Thomas-type devices with its rectangular, box-shaped configuration. The Millionaire was one of the few direct multiplying machines. Other calculators multiplied via compound addition. Earlier models of the Millionaire were slide-set, the earliest models had wooden sides, and some later versions were electrically powered. (author's collection)*

Check Protectors

Check protectors were introduced in the nineteenth century to guard against alteration of checks. The most basic are simple stamps which corrugate the surface of the check. More elaborate machines may either print or punch the value of the check. Most common are machines made by Todd, including the long, black streamlined device that looks something like an Art Deco railroad locomotive. Prices are hard to define, because the number of check protector collectors is quite small.

Values . . . .$20.00 – 100.00

Check Protectors *(L-to-R): J. B. Parks Nat'l. Saftety Check Punch, S&P, Chicago Check Perforator, Abbott Check Punch (Russo collection)*

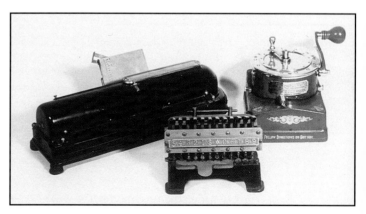

Check Protectors *(L-to-R): Todd, Climax, Beebe Indelible Check Protector (Russo collection)*

Pencil Sharpeners

To have anything but marginal value, a pencil sharpener should look different and operate with something other than the standard planetary gears familiar to so many of us. Look for mechanisms of rotating knives, grindstones, and other odd configurations.

Values . . . .$30.00 – 100.00

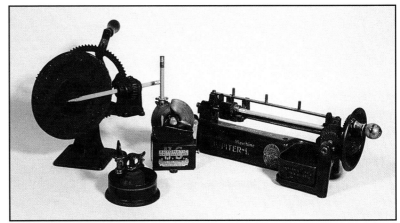

Pencil Sharpeners (L-to-R): Gem, President, U.S. Automatic Pencil Sharpener, Jupiter No. 1. (Russo collection)

Other Office Machines

There is a wide universe of other office machines attractive to typewriter collectors. This can include duplicating machines, addressing machines, stencil printers, typewriter-type "printing presses" (Multigraphs), envelope sealers, dictating machines, and more.

Dictating machines is a special category, since this includes the earliest commercial phonographs, which were intended for business use. For information on this area, you should consult reference books on phonograph collecting.

With the exception of the early phonographs, there is virtually no defined market for these miscellaneous office devices. Prices are strictly "whatever you can get."

Ephemera

Ephemera is a catch-all category for anything else related to typewriters and old office equipment. Some examples:
Old trade magazines: *Phonographic World, Typewriter Topics, System, Business Man's Monthly, Frank Harrison's Shorthand Reporter, Browne's Phonographic Monthly,* and many others. Note that the word "phonographic" refers to shorthand, not record players. Phonography was a nineteenth century term applied to stenography. Values $5.00 – 10.00.
Trade Catalogs: for office equipment, office furniture, stationery, supplies, etc. Those pre-dating 1900 are the most desirable. Values $5.00 – 75.00.
Advertising/Promotion items: mirrors, paperweights, blotters, eraser shields, tape measures, letter openers, posters, poster stamps, match covers, trade cards, post cards, brochures, flyers, letterheads, etc. Values $2.00 – 50.00.
Lapel pins: typewriter company awards, speed typing awards, etc. Values $10.00 – 20.00.
Magazine ads: dating 1875 – 1930 from popular magazines such as *Harper's, Munsey's, Century, Scientific American, Cosmopolitan, Frank Leslie's Popular Monthly, Saturday Evening Post,* and many others. Values 50¢ – $5.00 per ad.
Typewritten letters: Any typewritten letter written entirely in capitals and dated 1874 – 78 will probably have been written on a Sholes & Glidden Type Writer. As such it is automatically collectible. Values $10.00 – $25.00.

In this area, it's quite obvious that anything goes. If it's typewriter or office-related, it's collectible and has some value.

Appendix A
Rating Typewriter Condition

As with any collectible, condition is probably the most important factor in assessing the value of an old typewriter. It's good, therefore, for you to be able to understand the "language" in which most collectors describe condition.

At present, the most uniformly recognized condition rating system is the one which originated in Europe. In this system, condition is expressed on a six-point scale, "1" being highest. Two numbers are used, one for appearance, the other for mechanical function. So, for example, if a machine is rated as "1/3" the "1" would represent appearance and the "3" represents mechanical function.

The exact meaning of the numbers is somewhat subjective, but they have been described this way:
  1 — very good, as new, works perfectly
  2 — good, only slight traces of use
  3 — traces of considerable use, perhaps some paint chips or slight rust
  4 — strong traces of use, minor parts missing
  5 — significant rust or deterioration, major parts missing or broken
  6 — totally defective, useful for parts only

Many collectors find the descriptions of these rating levels difficult to use, so it may be better to simply imagine 1 as the best a machine could possibly be, 6 as the worst, and try to place your machine on a relative level in between.

There has been some effort to develop a 10-point scale (10 being best) in the United States, since Americans seem to have a preference for it. A value of 6 on this scale is the reference point for the prices listed in this book. In *ETCetera*, the magazine of the Early Typewriter Collectors Association, we've suggested the following descriptive words to go with each level:

  10 — Near Mint
   9 — Excellent
   8 — Very Good
   7 — Good
   6 — Decent
   5 — Fair
   4 — Rough
   3 — Poor
   2 — Parts
   1 — Wrecked

Actually, there is little substitute for a clear photo in showing a collector the condition of your machine. However, the more information you can give, the better. On the following page is a handy form you can fill out to describe your machine in detail. Make a copy of this, send it to a collector, and it'll really be appreciated!

Typewriter Condition Questionnaire

Please take some time to answer the following questions about your typewriter. You will find the experience interesting and will get to know the machine better simply by considering each of the following points. Thank you.

1. Name of machine _____

2. Model number if shown: _____

3. Serial number:_____

4. General condition:
    - a. very dirty
    - b. moderately dirty
    - c. slightly dirty
    - d. clean
    - e. brilliant

5. If there is any rust:
    - a. heavy rust
    - b. moderate rust
    - c. slight rust
    - d. no rust

6. Color of paint: _____

7. Condition of paint:
    - a. very worn or chipped
    - b. moderately worn or chipped
    - c. slightly worn or chipped
    - d. no wear or chips visible
    - e. clouded
    - f. somewhat glossy
    - g. brilliantly glossy

8. Condition of decals/logos:
    - a. very worn
    - b. moderately worn
    - c. slightly worn
    - d. no wear

9. Condition of bright metal parts:
    - a. mirror bright
    - b. dull bright
    - c. yellowed
    - d. slightly worn
    - e. worn
    - f. very worn
    - g. peeling

    If corroded:
    - h. slight
    - i. moderate
    - j. heavy

10. Condition of rubber rollers:
    - a. clean/smooth
    - b. slightly rough
    - c. rough
    - d. chipped/damaged
    - e. flat spots

11. Obvious missing parts:
    - a. keys
    - b. paper table
    - c. type bars or elements
    - d. roller knobs
    - e. ribbon spools or covers
    - f. ribbon
    - g. other _____

12. How well does the machine work: how easily can you type a sentence on it?
    - a. easily
    - b. with slight difficulty
    - c. with great difficulty
    - d. not at all

13. If machine does not function, please try to try to describe what is wrong:

    _____

    _____

    _____

14. Type of case and/or base:
    - a. wood box
    - b. leatherette covered box
    - c. leather case
    - d. base with metal cover
    - e. base with wooden cover
    - f. other _____

15. Condition of case and/or base:
    - a. very good
    - b. worn
    - c. very worn
    - d. a mess
    - e. has base, cover missing
    - f. has cover, base missing

16. What do the different logos and decals say?

    _____

    _____

    _____

17. If there are tools, instructions, and/or accessories, please describe:

    _____

    _____

    _____

18. Comments:
    _____

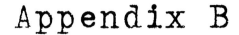

Appendix B
Shipping Old Typewriters

Sending an old typewriter to a distant place safely does not have to scare you. It's really a fairly simple matter that has more to do with the materials you select than anything else.

The object of packing a machine is to make it so secure, that neither it nor any of its parts can move during shipment. That means padding it effectively with a combination of crumpled or shredded paper (newspaper is fine) and styrofoam peanuts, and using a sturdy cardboard box which allows space for 4" of padding all around the machine in its case. That means top, bottom, and all four sides.

Specific instructions are given here in two sets of diagrams. The first shows you what to do with a machine that has its own case. The second shows you what to do if the machine does not have its case.

Packing a typewriter properly takes about 20 minutes, that's all. It takes no special skills or tools, and there's no reason why any machine should not reach its destination safely.

PACKING A TYPEWRITER
FOR SHIPMENT

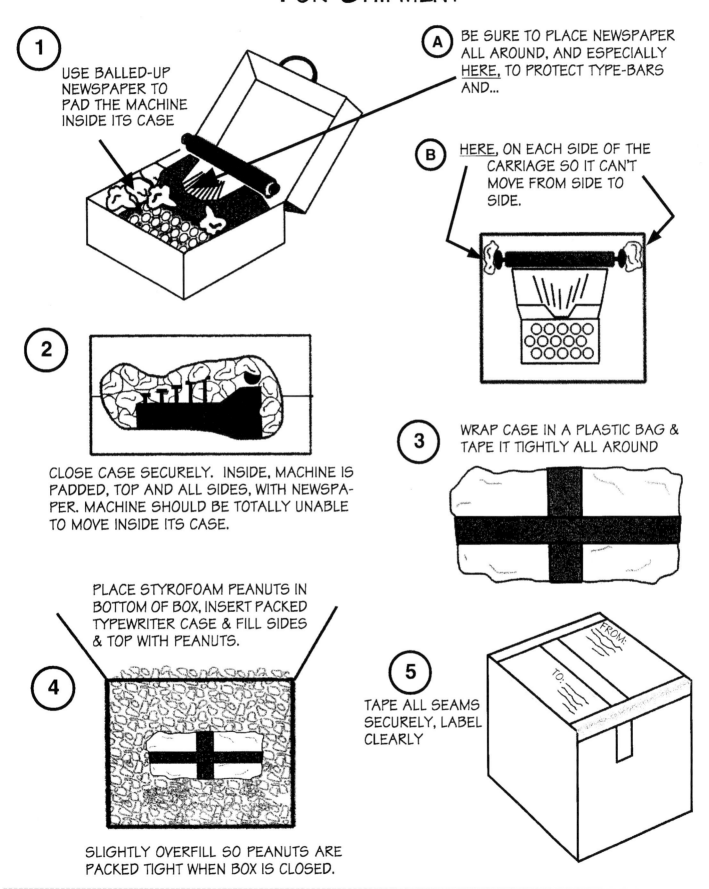

1 USE BALLED-UP NEWSPAPER TO PAD THE MACHINE INSIDE ITS CASE

A BE SURE TO PLACE NEWSPAPER ALL AROUND, AND ESPECIALLY HERE, TO PROTECT TYPE-BARS AND...

B HERE, ON EACH SIDE OF THE CARRIAGE SO IT CAN'T MOVE FROM SIDE TO SIDE.

2 CLOSE CASE SECURELY. INSIDE, MACHINE IS PADDED, TOP AND ALL SIDES, WITH NEWSPAPER. MACHINE SHOULD BE TOTALLY UNABLE TO MOVE INSIDE ITS CASE.

3 WRAP CASE IN A PLASTIC BAG & TAPE IT TIGHTLY ALL AROUND

4 PLACE STYROFOAM PEANUTS IN BOTTOM OF BOX, INSERT PACKED TYPEWRITER CASE & FILL SIDES & TOP WITH PEANUTS.

SLIGHTLY OVERFILL SO PEANUTS ARE PACKED TIGHT WHEN BOX IS CLOSED.

5 TAPE ALL SEAMS SECURELY, LABEL CLEARLY

IF A TYPEWRITER HAS NO CASE, MAKE IT A CARDBOARD SHELL

1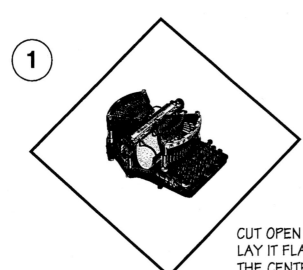

CUT OPEN A CARDBOARD BOX AND LAY IT FLAT. PUT THE MACHINE IN THE CENTER.

2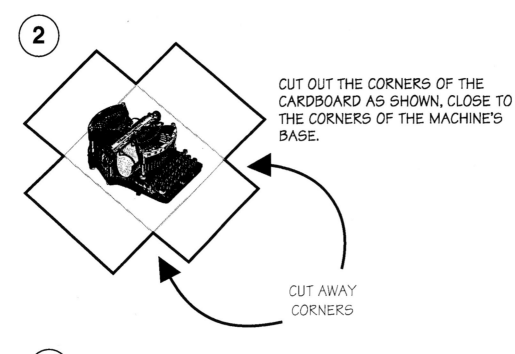

CUT OUT THE CORNERS OF THE CARDBOARD AS SHOWN, CLOSE TO THE CORNERS OF THE MACHINE'S BASE.

CUT AWAY CORNERS

3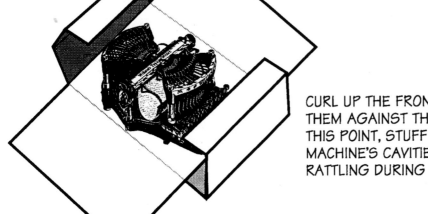

CURL UP THE FRONT AND REAR FLAPS, FOLDING THEM AGAINST THE MACHINE'S SURFACE. AT THIS POINT, STUFF NEWSPAPER BALLS INTO THE MACHINE'S CAVITIES TO KEEP PARTS FROM RATTLING DURING SHIPMENT

PRESS FRONT AND REAR FLAPS CLOSED, AND
SECURELY WRAP TAPE ALL THE WAY AROUND
THE FOLDED FRONT AND BACK FLAPS AND THE
PACKAGE BOTTOM. THEN, STUFF SOME MORE
NEWSPAPER IN FROM THE SIDES TO ADD EXTRA
CUSHIONING BETWEEN THE CARDBOARD AND
THE MACHINE.

FOLD THE TWO SIDE FLAPS UPWARD. THEY
SHOULD TOUCH THE SIDES OF THE MACHINE
AND/OR NEWSPAPER PADDING. KEEP IT TIGHT.

FOLD CORNERS OF THE SIDE FLAPS FLUSH
AGAINST THE SURFACE OF THE PACKAGE. YOU
MAY BE WORKING AGAINST THE GRAIN OF THE
CARDBOARD CORRUGATIONS, BUT FORCE IT SO
THE PACKAGE IS TIGHT AGAINST THE MACHINE
SURFACES OR PADDING. TAPE THE SIDE FLAPS
SECURELY ALL THE WAY AROUND THE PACKAGE.
IT DOESN'T HAVE TO LOOK PRETTY, IT JUST
NEEDS TO BE SECURE.

PACK THE SHELL INSIDE A LARGER BOX WITH
STYROFOAM PEANUTS, FOLLOWING THE SAME
INSTRUCTIONS GIVEN FOR SHIPPING A TYPE-
WRITER THAT IS INSIDE ITS OWN CASE.

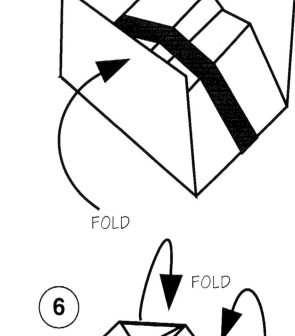

Appendix C
Restoring Old Typewriters

For most people, restoring old typewriters is strictly a do-it-yourself affair. It is usually too expensive to have true professional work done on most machines, even if you can find someone qualified to do it. So, if you're not a typewriter technician, here are some ideas to try.

Tools

As a first step, gather yourself a good set of tools — the more the merrier. You won't necessarily need specialized typewriter repair tools (some of these are so weird, you'd never guess what to use them for anyway). Here's what you do need:

electric rotary tool: important all-around cleaning/polishing device. Also, wire brushes, felt buffs, metal polishing rouge (white or yellow — check jewelry supply stores or well stocked hardware stores), rubberized abrasive discs like Cratex.
screwdrivers: all sizes, especially small ones and some with skinny blades to handle fine-slotted machine screws. Also, an offset screwdriver and Phillips-head.
brushes: toothbrushes, round brushes, etc. for cleaning in hard-to-reach places
pipe cleaners: for cleaning in even harder to reach spaces; cotton swabs, too.
scouring pads: great all-purpose scrubbers
needle-nose pliers
long-handled tweezers
dental picks: for scraping away crud in tiny crevices, also good for installing and removing springs
small metal files

That'll pretty much get you started. Next, you'll need a supply of cleaners and lubricants. Don't use WD-40, as it leaves a residue that can seize up the works after time passes. Check your local machinist supply, auto, and electronic stores. They stock spray machine oil, mixtures of oil & solvent, solvent alone, etc. You'll need to experiment with several of these to see how you like them in different situations. When you're in the hardware store and see a cleaner or solvent that may look good, buy it and try it. You will rely on these supplies to clean up your typewriter's parts as you take it apart.

Your Workbench

Next, set up a convenient place to work. An out of the way table in the garage is best. Some of us can't leave our junk lying out all the time and must set up a workplace so things can be put away after each session. Try keeping your tools in plastic tool-carriers. You can keep them in a storage cabinet and just set them down on your work table each time you set up for work.

A suggestion for your work surface: cover it with a couple thicknesses of plastic drop cloth. You can replace this easily when things get impossibly dirty. It also forms a wrinkled surface that you will appreciate the first time you drop a tiny screw and see that it doesn't roll off onto the floor (where you'll never find it).

Tackling the Job

Now, you should be ready to go to work.

If this is your first time, choose a machine that isn't worth a fortune, so you don't have to worry if you make a mess of it. A Blickensderfer or Oliver is an excellent choice.

The basic strategy for restoration is:
1. Take things apart.
2. Clean and/or polish them.
3. Put them back together.

It sounds simple, but if you try to do the whole machine at once, you're dead. Instead, disassemble part of the machine a little at a time — no more, say, than takes about half an hour. You'll need another half hour to put it back together. It's not a bad idea to take it apart, then put it right back together and do it a couple of times until you have it down. When you're sure, then you can do the cleaning that needs doing. In any case, if you can help it, never leave something unassembled overnight. You're bound to forget how to put it back together.

To be even more thorough, keep a notebook and draw pictures. When you take apart the right-hand side of a Blickensderfer carriage, for instance, you'll find notes invaluable. That particular assembly has about six layers of parts, each of which has to fit in a correct position. By keeping notes, you can get them back together with no trouble.

Be careful when you take things apart. Be sure to eyeball everything well so you don't remove one screw and find it held together a dozen different parts which have just collapsed in your hands. You'll almost never have technical manuals at hand, so remember, it's up to you to figure it out.

Cleaning in Place

If there are parts of the machine that you can't get apart (such as those assembled with rivets), just leave them assembled. You can generally clean them in place, and they'll be fine.

In fact, some situations call for leaving everything assembled and cleaning it all in place. One collector has successfully soaked machines in kerosene, and another has used a 1:1 mixture of kerosene and diesel fuel. If you decide to try this, you should test the mixture on your machine's decals before you start so you can be sure you won't destroy them.

The basic procedure here is to fill a tub with the cleaner, put in the machine (after removing all rubber parts) and let it sit for a few hours. When done, hose it off with the nozzle of your garden hose. Once rinsed, it has to be lubricated. If using kero and diesel, just put it back in that (unless the bath has become too dirty). If using kero, you'll need to dump it in a tub of machine oil. The oil should displace the water and prevent any rust. Wiping away the excess oil on the machine is a real job, but it's more tedious than difficult.

Which Cleaning Method?

Whether assembled or together, you must decide what kind of cleaning is needed for each part of the machine.

Generally, you should do whatever is least intrusive. You don't want to start grinding away with abrasives when a simple brush with solvent will do.

If a part is crusted with loose dirt and/or grease, solvent with a stiff brush may take it all off. Be careful not to get solvent on painted parts. The paint may dissolve.

If the dirt and grease is very old, it may be hardened and need more drastic action. That's time for the rotary tool. On plated parts, first try buffing with the felt buff and jeweler's rouge. You may find this will immediately give you a brilliant shine. Be generous with the rouge, and re-apply it to your buff frequently. It will turn black on you from the heat, but don't worry, it's working. When you're finished, remove the residue by hand with a rag and solvent (alcohol is good for this).

If parts are not plated, try whizzing them with your rotary tool's wire brush. These little brushes are expensive, they don't last long, and they throw off the most irritating splinters in existence, but that's the way they are. Otherwise, they're terrific for removing gunk, especially in hard to reach places.

If you find that you have rust or other corrosion to deal with, it's time to call in the Cratex. This is an abrasive imbedded in rubber, formed into wheels, rods, and bullets for use on the rotary tool. It comes in four grades, from coarse to extra fine. Cratex will gently grind away corrosion and also part of the metal surface. On plated parts, it will remove the plating, but that's OK if the plating is flaking or corroded. Who needs flaked or corroded plating? To do it right, start with coarse grade, and re-grind the surface with each successively finer grade. After using Cratex, the surface will be bright but dull, so follow it up with jeweler's rouge. This will give you a mirror bright surface, depending on your patience. This is an acceptable end result, but you may wish to go further and do some re-plating. You can have this done professionally, or experiment with home-brew systems. Note that most bright plating on typewriters is nickel, not chrome. If you opt for the polished base metal, be sure to give it a wipe with oil or coating of wax to protect it from rusting.

If you are working with long, narrow parts like pull rods or carriage rails, try cleaning off the crud by dry scouring them with a scouring pad, with or without solvent. It'll go a lot faster than working your way down the length with a rotary tool.

Cleaning Painted Surfaces

Painted surfaces require a whole different strategy. Solvents are often harmful to paint, but not always. Test an inconspicuous spot before you proceed.

One of the best harmless treatments for painted surfaces is to clean them with shop hand cleaner. This is the greasy stuff used to get horrible auto-shop-type grime off your hands. It does a very nice job on typewriters, too. Just rub it on, scrub gently with an old toothbrush, and then wipe it off. Wiping it off may take some doing, since it gets into all the crevices; but between your rags, cotton swabs, and pipe-cleaners, you should be able to get it all. This stuff leaves behind a thin, shiny, oily coating which should act to protect your machine. If the toothbrush doesn't give you enough scrubbing power, use hand cleaner with the scouring pad, but be very gentle. One caution here: don't use cleaner that has ammonia in it. It will cloud any varnish layer that happens to be on your machine, and it can remove decals.

If you have abrasions or dull spots in your paint, use auto polishing compound to rub it into shininess. This takes a lot of work, but it is effective. Polishing compound will also remove decals, so you may need to carefully work around them.

When you are finished working on a machine's painted surface, a coat of high-quality paste wax will give you a nice shine.

To Restore or Not?

There is no one way to restore a collectible typewriter. Besides, you many not always want to restore. Very rare machines should seldom be subjected to this treatment. Their "as found" condition speaks to their individual histories and most collectors agree they should be gently cleaned, and that's it. Some dealers currently go so far as to strip old machines down to the bare metal, and then re-paint, re-plate, and apply new reproduction decals (or hand paint to simulate old decals). This makes for nice-looking (and expensive) decorator pieces, but for serious collectors, these machines have lost much of their historical value. Such overhauls might also confuse collectors of the future, who may observe repro decals, for instance, and assume they are different versions issued by the original manufacturer.

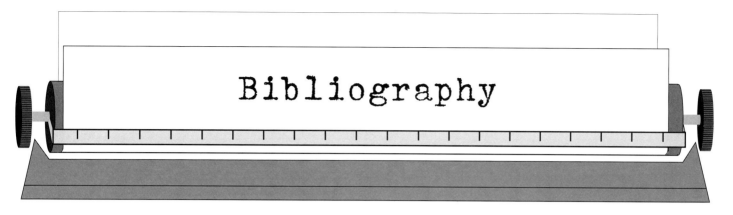

Bibliography

In writing this book the author has relied upon his observations of existing machines, interviews with other collectors, plus his considerable archive of original advertisements, documents, photos, and other materials. In addition, he has consulted the following books and publications, many considered standard references in the field. For those interested in additional reading, a number of these books can be obtained directly from your local library, or through an inter-library loan.

Adler, Michael, *The Writing Machine*. George Allen & Unwin, Ltd., London, 1973.

Beeching, Wilfred A., *Century of the Typewriter*. William Heinemenn Ltd., London, 1974.

Bliven, Bruce, Jr., *The Wonderful Writing Machine*. Random House, New York, 1954.

Current, Richard N., *The Typewriter and the Men Who Made It*, second edition. Post-Era Books, Arcadia, CA, 1988.

Dingwerth, Leonhard, *Marken, Namen und Modelle*. Historisches Schreibmaschinen-Archiv, Verle, Germany, 1995.

ETCetera, Magazine of the Early Typewriter Collectors Association.

HbW Aktuell, magazine.

Historische Bürowelt, magazine.

kwbl / Dutch Q, magazine.

Leertaste, magazine.

Lippman, Paul, *American Typewriters, A Collector's Encyclopedia*. Original & Copy, Hoboken, NJ, 1992.

Mares, G. C., *The History of the Typewriter, Successor to the Pen*, 1985 edition. Post-Era Books, Arcadia, CA, 1985.

Martin, Ernst (pseud. Johannes Meyer), *Die Schreibmaschine*, facsimile edition. Verlag Basten GmBH, Aachen, Germany, 1981.

Masi, Frank T., ed., *The Typewriter Legend*. Matsushita Electric Corporation of America, 1985.

McCarthy, James M., *The American Digest of Business Machines*. American Exchange Service, Chicago, 1924.

Muckermann, Peter, *Die Geschichte der Lambert*. Rheda-Wiedenbrück, Germany, 1992.

Müller, Freidrich, *Schreibmaschinen von 1900*, facsimile edition. Verlag TH. Shäfer, Hanover, Germany, 1986.

Post, Dan, ed., *A Collector's Guide to Antique Typewriters*, Post-Era Books, Arcadia, CA, 1981.

Type Writer Times, magazine.

Type-Writer, The, magazine.

Typenkorb & Typenhebel, magazine.

Typewriter Exchange, The, magazine.

Annotated Index

This index offers not only page references, but also notes and values on machines not covered in the main body of this book. Some of the information here is based on resources that are less complete than in the other sections of the book and is therefore more susceptible to innacuracy. Names of typewriters are shown in *italics*.

Schade - an 1896 plunger machine from Germany that imitated the design of Denmark's *Skrivekugle*. Rare. ($1,000+)

Skrivekugle - radial-strike plunger design invented by Malling Hansen of Denmark. An extremely desirable machine due to the fine quality of its manufacture, but even more for its historical importance as history's first typewriter to be successfully mass produced (even if production number may have barely exceeded 1,000). Forgeries of this machine have been reported, and collectors who can afford this rarity must proceed with caution. ($10,000+)

Secor - a 4-row, frontstrike of 1911 sold not only as a typewriter but a billing machine. Innovative technically, it did not succeed in the marketplace. ($20)

Sphinx - a curvaceous 4-row, frontstrike portable dating from 1913 in Germany. It featured two attractive decals of sphinxes on the front. ($75)

Stearns - a conventional 4-row, frontstrike machine of 1908. Not common, but not desirable. ($20)

Stoewer - 4-row, frontstrike typewriter from Germany introduced c. 1903. Also known as *Stoewer Record*. Sold in England as the *Swift*. ($30)

Thürey - a highly unusual German type-bar machine, dating from 1908. The keys are arranged in six vertical rows at the center of what appears to be a rather complex mechanism. ($1,000+)

Torpedo - a German line of 4-row fronstrike machines. Includes frequently found modern portables. ($20)

Triumph Visible - 4-row, oblique frontstrike machine marked in 1907 by the Visible Typewriter Co. of Kenosha, WI. Also sold as *Triumph Perfect Visible*, *Imperial*, and *Imperial Visible*. It was the predecessor to the *Burnett* (see page 33), and looks similar to that machine, except with exposed type-bars. ($300)

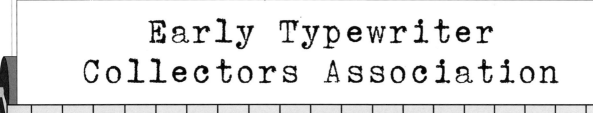

Early Typewriter Collectors Association

Your Connection to the Nationwide Collectors Network

The Early Typewriter Collectors Association (ETC) has been serving collectors since 1987. It is the country's only organization devoted to the collecting of typewriters, other office machines, and their ephemera. *ETCetera*, its quarterly magazine, is the only regularly-published journal in the U.S. directed especially to typewriter collectors.

ETCetera offers interesting articles, restoration and collecting tips, numerous photographs (both in black & white *and* color) of machines, ribbon tins, and other ephemera, news of the collecting network, buy/sell/trade ads, and more.

Membership in ETC costs $20/year ($25 outside North America). ETC is also an ideal contact point for people who do not collect, but wish to sell one or more machines they own.

As a member of ETC, and still an active collector, the author invites offers of machines for sale. In this arena, you will see that old typewriters are treated with importance. Elsewhere, as you may have found, they are treated as so much junk.

For information or an ETC membership application, please send a self-addressed-stamped envelope to Darryl Rehr, PO Box 641824 L.A., CA 90064-1824. Those with machines to sell are advised to send a photo. E-mail at dcrehr@earthlink.net

COLLECTOR BOOKS

Informing Today's Collector

For over two decades we have been keeping collectors informed on trends and values in all fields of antiques and collectibles.

DOLLS, FIGURES & TEDDY BEARS

4707	A Decade of **Barbie** Dolls & Collectibles, 1981–1991, Summers	$19.95
4631	**Barbie** Doll Boom, 1986–1995, Augustyniak	$18.95
2079	**Barbie** Doll Fashions, Volume I, Eames	$24.95
3957	**Barbie** Exclusives, Rana	$18.95
4632	**Barbie** Exclusives, Book II, Rana	$18.95
4557	**Barbie,** The First 30 Years, Deutsch	$24.95
4657	**Barbie** Years, 1959–1995, Olds	$16.95
3310	**Black Dolls,** 1820–1991, Perkins	$17.95
3873	**Black Dolls,** Book II, Perkins	$17.95
1529	Collector's Encyclopedia of **Barbie** Dolls, DeWein	$19.95
4506	Collector's Guide to **Dolls in Uniform,** Bourgeois	$18.95
3727	Collector's Guide to **Ideal Dolls,** Izen	$18.95
3728	Collector's Guide to Miniature **Teddy Bears,** Powell	$17.95
3967	Collector's Guide to **Trolls,** Peterson	$19.95
4571	**Liddle Kiddles,** Identification & Value Guide, Langford	$18.95
4645	**Madame Alexander** Dolls Price Guide #21, Smith	$9.95
3733	**Modern Collector's** Dolls, Sixth Series, Smith	$24.95
3991	**Modern Collector's** Dolls, Seventh Series, Smith	$24.95
4647	**Modern Collector's** Dolls, Eighth Series, Smith	$24.95
4640	Patricia Smith's **Doll Values,** Antique to Modern, 12th Edition	$12.95
3826	Story of **Barbie,** Westenhouser	$19.95
1513	**Teddy Bears & Steiff** Animals, Mandel	$9.95
1817	**Teddy Bears & Steiff** Animals, 2nd Series, Mandel	$19.95
2084	**Teddy Bears, Annalee's & Steiff** Animals, 3rd Series, Mandel	$19.95
1808	Wonder of **Barbie,** Manos	$9.95
1430	World of **Barbie** Dolls, Manos	$9.95

FURNITURE

1457	American **Oak** Furniture, McNerney	$9.95
3716	American **Oak** Furniture, Book II, McNerney	$12.95
1118	Antique **Oak** Furniture, Hill	$7.95
2132	Collector's Encyclopedia of **American** Furniture, Vol. I, Swedberg	$24.95
2271	Collector's Encyclopedia of **American** Furniture, Vol. II, Swedberg	$24.95
3720	Collector's Encyclopedia of **American** Furniture, Vol. III, Swedberg	$24.95
3878	Collector's Guide to **Oak** Furniture, George	$12.95
1755	Furniture of the **Depression Era,** Swedberg	$19.95
3906	**Heywood-Wakefield** Modern Furniture, Rouland	$18.95
1885	**Victorian** Furniture, Our American Heritage, McNerney	$9.95
3829	**Victorian** Furniture, Our American Heritage, Book II, McNerney	$9.95
3869	**Victorian** Furniture books, 2 volume set, McNerney	$19.90

JEWELRY, HATPINS, WATCHES & PURSES

1712	Antique & Collector's **Thimbles** & Accessories, Mathis	$19.95
1748	Antique **Purses,** Revised Second Ed., Holiner	$19.95
1278	Art Nouveau & Art Deco **Jewelry,** Baker	$9.95
4558	**Christmas Pins,** Past and Present, Gallina	$18.95
3875	Collecting Antique **Stickpins,** Kerins	$16.95
3722	Collector's Ency. of **Compacts, Carryalls & Face Powder Boxes,** Mueller	$24.95
4655	Complete Price Guide to **Watches,** #16, Shugart	$26.95
1716	Fifty Years of Collectible **Fashion Jewelry,** 1925-1975, Baker	$19.95
1424	**Hatpins** & Hatpin Holders, Baker	$9.95
4570	Ladies' **Compacts,** Gerson	$24.95
1181	100 Years of Collectible **Jewelry,** 1850-1950, Baker	$9.95
2348	20th Century Fashionable Plastic **Jewelry,** Baker	$19.95
3830	Vintage **Vanity Bags & Purses,** Gerson	$24.95

TOYS, MARBLES & CHRISTMAS COLLECTIBLES

3427	**Advertising Character** Collectibles, Dotz	$17.95
2333	Antique & Collector's **Marbles,** 3rd Ed., Grist	$9.95
3827	Antique & Collector's **Toys,** 1870–1950, Longest	$24.95
3956	Baby Boomer **Games,** Identification & Value Guide, Polizzi	$24.95
3717	**Christmas** Collectibles, 2nd Edition, Whitmyer	$24.95
1752	**Christmas** Ornaments, Lights & Decorations, Johnson	$19.95
4649	Classic Plastic **Model Kits,** Polizzi	$24.95

4559	Collectible **Action Figures,** 2nd Ed., Manos	$17.95
3874	Collectible Coca-Cola Toy **Trucks,** deCourtivron	$24.95
2338	Collector's Encyclopedia of **Disneyana,** Longest, Stern	$24.95
4639	Collector's Guide to **Diecast Toys & Scale Models,** Johnson	$19.95
4651	Collector's Guide to **Tinker Toys,** Strange	$18.95
4566	Collector's Guide to **Tootsietoys,** 2nd Ed., Richter	$19.95
3436	Grist's Big Book of **Marbles**	$19.95
3970	Grist's Machine-Made & Contemporary **Marbles,** 2nd Ed.	$9.95
4569	**Howdy Doody,** Collector's Reference and Trivia Guide, Koch	$16.95
4723	**Matchbox®** Toys, 1948 to 1993, Johnson, 2nd Ed.	$18.95
3823	**Mego** Toys, An Illustrated Value Guide, Chrouch	15.95
1540	**Modern Toys** 1930–1980, Baker	$19.95
3888	**Motorcycle** Toys, Antique & Contemporary, Gentry/Downs	$18.95
4728	Schroeder's Collectible **Toys,** Antique to Modern Price Guide, 3rd Ed.	$17.95
1886	Stern's Guide to **Disney** Collectibles	$14.95
2139	Stern's Guide to **Disney** Collectibles, 2nd Series	$14.95
3975	Stern's Guide to **Disney** Collectibles, 3rd Series	$18.95
2028	**Toys,** Antique & Collectible, Longest	$14.95
3979	**Zany Characters** of the Ad World, Lamphier	$16.95

INDIANS, GUNS, KNIVES, TOOLS, PRIMITIVES

1868	Antique **Tools,** Our American Heritage, McNerney	$9.95
2015	Archaic **Indian** Points & Knives, Edler	$14.95
1426	**Arrowheads** & Projectile Points, Hothem	$7.95
4633	**Big Little Books,** Jacobs	$18.95
2279	**Indian** Artifacts of the Midwest, Hothem	$14.95
3885	**Indian** Artifacts of the Midwest, Book II, Hothem	$16.95
1964	**Indian** Axes & Related Stone Artifacts, Hothem	$14.95
2023	**Keen Kutter** Collectibles, Heuring	$14.95
4724	Modern **Guns,** Identification & Values, 11th Ed., Quertermous	$12.95
4505	Standard Guide to **Razors,** Ritchie & Stewart	$9.95
4730	Standard **Knife** Collector's Guide, 3rd Ed., Ritchie & Stewart	$12.95

PAPER COLLECTIBLES & BOOKS

4633	**Big Little Books,** Jacobs	$18.95
1441	Collector's Guide to **Post Cards,** Wood	$9.95
2081	Guide to Collecting **Cookbooks,** Allen	$14.95
4648	Huxford's **Old Book** Value Guide, 8th Ed.	$19.95
2080	Price Guide to **Cookbooks & Recipe Leaflets,** Dickinson	$9.95
2346	**Sheet Music** Reference & Price Guide, 2nd Ed., Pafik & Guiheen	$18.95
4654	**Victorian Trading Cards,** Historical Reference & Value Guide, Cheadle	$19.95

GLASSWARE

1006	**Cambridge Glass** Reprint 1930–1934	$14.95
1007	**Cambridge Glass** Reprint 1949–1953	$14.95
4561	Collectible **Drinking Glasses,** Chase & Kelly	$17.95
4642	Collectible **Glass Shoes,** Wheatley	$19.95
4553	Coll. **Glassware** from the 40's, 50's & 60's, 3rd Ed., Florence	$19.95
2352	Collector's Encyclopedia of **Akro Agate Glassware,** Florence	$14.95
1810	Collector's Encyclopedia of **American Art Glass,** Shuman	$29.95
3312	Collector's Encyclopedia of **Children's Dishes,** Whitmyer	$19.95
4552	Collector's Encyclopedia of **Depression Glass,** 12th Ed., Florence	$19.95
1664	Collector's Encyclopedia of **Heisey Glass,** 1925–1938, Bredehoft	$24.95
3905	Collector's Encyclopedia of **Milk Glass,** Newbound	$24.95
1523	Colors In **Cambridge Glass,** National Cambridge Society	$19.95
4564	**Crackle Glass,** Weitman	$19.9
2275	**Czechoslovakian Glass** and Collectibles, Barta/Rose	$16.95
4714	**Czechoslovakian Glass** and Collectibles, Book II, Barta/Rose	$16.95
4716	**Elegant Glassware** of the Depression Era, 7th Ed., Florence	$19.95
1380	Encylopedia of **Pattern Glass,** McClain	$12.95
3981	Ever's Standard **Cut Glass** Value Guide	$12.95
4659	**Fenton** Art Glass, 1907–1939, Whitmyer	$24.95
3725	**Fostoria,** Pressed, Blown & Hand Molded Shapes, Kerr	$24.95
3883	**Fostoria Stemware,** The Crystal for America, Long & Seate	$24.95
3318	**Glass Animals** of the Depression Era, Garmon & Spencer	$19.95
4644	**Imperial Carnival Glass,** Burns	$18.95

COLLECTOR BOOKS
Informing Today's Collector

3886	**Kitchen Glassware** of the Depression Years, 5th Ed., Florence	$19.95
2394	**Oil Lamps II**, Glass Kerosene Lamps, Thuro	$24.95
4725	Pocket Guide to **Depression Glass**, 10th Ed., Florence	$9.95
4634	Standard Encyclopedia of **Carnival Glass**, 5th Ed., Edwards	$24.95
4635	Standard **Carnival Glass** Price Guide, 10th Ed.	$9.95
3974	Standard Encyclopedia of **Opalescent Glass**, Edwards	$19.95
4731	**Stemware Identification**, Featuring Cordials with Values, Florence	$24.95
3326	**Very Rare Glassware** of the Depression Years, 3rd Series, Florence	$24.95
3909	**Very Rare Glassware** of the Depression Years, 4th Series, Florence	$24.95
4732	**Very Rare Glassware** of the Depression Years, 5th Series, Florence	$24.95
4656	**Westmoreland Glass**, Wilson	$24.95
2224	World of **Salt Shakers**, 2nd Ed., Lechner	$24.95

POTTERY

4630	**American Limoges**, Limoges	$24.95
1312	**Blue & White Stoneware**, McNerney	$9.95
1958	So. Potteries **Blue Ridge Dinnerware**, 3rd Ed., Newbound	$14.95
1959	**Blue Willow**, 2nd Ed., Gaston	$14.95
3816	Collectible **Vernon Kilns**, Nelson	$24.95
3311	Collecting **Yellow Ware** – Id. & Value Guide, McAllister	$16.95
1373	Collector's Encyclopedia of **American Dinnerware**, Cunningham	$24.95
3815	Collector's Encyclopedia of **Blue Ridge Dinnerware**, Newbound	$19.95
4658	Collector's Encyclopedia of **Brush-McCoy Pottery**, Huxford	$24.95
2272	Collector's Encyclopedia of **California Pottery**, Chipman	$24.95
3811	Collector's Encyclopedia of **Colorado Pottery**, Carlton	$24.95
2133	Collector's Encyclopedia of **Cookie Jars**, Roerig	$24.95
3723	Collector's Encyclopedia of **Cookie Jars**, Volume II, Roerig	$24.95
3429	Collector's Encyclopedia of **Cowan Pottery**, Saloff	$24.95
4638	Collector's Encyclopedia of **Dakota Potteries**, Dommel	$24.95
2209	Collector's Encyclopedia of **Fiesta**, 7th Ed., Huxford	$19.95
4718	Collector's Encyclopedia of **Figural Planters & Vases**, Newbound	$19.95
3961	Collector's Encyclopedia of **Early Noritake**, Alden	$24.95
1439	Collector's Encyclopedia of **Flow Blue China**, Gaston	$19.95
3812	Collector's Encyclopedia of **Flow Blue China**, 2nd Ed., Gaston	$24.95
3813	Collector's Encyclopedia of **Hall China**, 2nd Ed., Whitmyer	$24.95
3431	Collector's Encyclopedia of **Homer Laughlin China**, Jasper	$24.95
1276	Collector's Encyclopedia of **Hull Pottery**, Roberts	$19.95
4573	Collector's Encyclopedia of **Knowles, Taylor & Knowles**, Gaston	$24.95
3962	Collector's Encyclopedia of **Lefton China**, DeLozier	$19.95
2210	Collector's Encyclopedia of **Limoges Porcelain**, 2nd Ed., Gaston	$24.95
2334	Collector's Encyclopedia of **Majolica Pottery**, Katz-Marks	$19.95
1358	Collector's Encyclopedia of **McCoy Pottery**, Huxford	$19.95
3963	Collector's Encyclopedia of **Metlox Potteries**, Gibbs Jr.	$24.95
3313	Collector's Encyclopedia of **Niloak**, Gifford	$19.95
3837	Collector's Encyclopedia of **Nippon Porcelain I**, Van Patten	$24.95
2089	Collector's Ency. of **Nippon Porcelain**, 2nd Series, Van Patten	$24.95
1665	Collector's Ency. of **Nippon Porcelain**, 3rd Series, Van Patten	$24.95
3836	**Nippon Porcelain** Price Guide, Van Patten	$9.95
1447	Collector's Encyclopedia of **Noritake**, Van Patten	$19.95
3432	Collector's Encyclopedia of **Noritake**, 2nd Series, Van Patten	$24.95
1037	Collector's Encyclopedia of **Occupied Japan**, Vol. I, Florence	$14.95
1038	Collector's Encyclopedia of **Occupied Japan**, Vol. II, Florence	$14.95
2088	Collector's Encyclopedia of **Occupied Japan**, Vol. III, Florence	$14.95
2019	Collector's Encyclopedia of **Occupied Japan**, Vol. IV, Florence	$14.95
2335	Collector's Encyclopedia of **Occupied Japan**, Vol. V, Florence	$14.95
3964	Collector's Encyclopedia of **Pickard China**, Reed	$24.95
1311	Collector's Encyclopedia of **R.S. Prussia**, 1st Series, Gaston	$24.95
1715	Collector's Encyclopedia of **R.S. Prussia**, 2nd Series, Gaston	$24.95
3726	Collector's Encyclopedia of **R.S. Prussia**, 3rd Series, Gaston	$24.95
3877	Collector's Encyclopedia of **R.S. Prussia**, 4th Series, Gaston	$24.95
1034	Collector's Encyclopedia of **Roseville Pottery**, Huxford	$19.95
1035	Collector's Encyclopedia of **Roseville Pottery**, 2nd Ed., Huxford	$19.95
3357	**Roseville** Price Guide No. 10	$9.95
3965	Collector's Encyclopedia of **Sascha Brastoff**, Conti, Bethany & Seay	$24.95
4314	Collector's Encyclopedia of **Van Briggle** Art Pottery, Sasicki	$24.95
1563	Collector's Encyclopedia of **Wall Pockets**, Newbound	$19.95
2111	Collector's Encyclopedia of **Weller Pottery**, Huxford	$29.95
3452	Coll. Guide to **Country Stoneware & Pottery**, Raycraft	$11.95
2077	Coll. Guide to **Country Stoneware & Pottery**, 2nd Series, Raycraft	$14.95
3434	Coll. Guide to **Hull Pottery**, The Dinnerware Line, Gick-Burke	$16.95

3876	Collector's Guide to **Lu-Ray Pastels**, Meehan	$18.95
3814	Collector's Guide to **Made in Japan** Ceramics, White	$18.95
4646	Collector's Guide to **Made in Japan** Ceramics, Book II, White	$18.95
4565	Collector's Guide to **Rockingham**, The Enduring Ware, Brewer	$14.95
2339	Collector's Guide to **Shawnee Pottery**, Vanderbilt	$19.95
1425	**Cookie Jars**, Westfall	$9.95
3440	**Cookie Jars**, Book II, Westfall	$19.95
3435	Debolt's Dictionary of **American Pottery Marks**	$17.95
2379	Lehner's Ency. of **U.S. Marks** on Pottery, Porcelain & China	$24.95
4722	**McCoy Pottery**, Collector's Reference & Value Guide, Hanson/Nissen	$19.95
3825	**Puritan Pottery**, Morris	$24.95
4726	**Red Wing Art Pottery**, 1920s–1960s, Dollen	$19.95
1670	**Red Wing Collectibles**, DePasquale	$9.95
1440	**Red Wing Stoneware**, DePasquale	$9.95
3738	**Shawnee Pottery**, Mangus	$24.95
4629	Turn of the Century **American Dinnerware**, 1880s–1920s, Jasper	$24.95
4572	**Wall Pockets** of the Past, Perkins	$17.95
3327	**Watt Pottery** – Identification & Value Guide, Morris	$19.95

OTHER COLLECTIBLES

4704	Antique & Collectible **Buttons**, Wisniewski	$19.95
2269	Antique **Brass & Copper** Collectibles, Gaston	$16.95
1880	Antique **Iron**, McNerney	$9.95
3872	Antique **Tins**, Dodge	$24.95
1714	**Black** Collectibles, Gibbs	$19.95
1128	**Bottle** Pricing Guide, 3rd Ed., Cleveland	$7.95
4636	**Celluloid Collectibles**, Dunn	$14.95
3959	**Cereal Box** Bonanza, The 1950's, Bruce	$19.95
3718	Collectible **Aluminum**, Grist	$16.95
3445	Collectible **Cats**, An Identification & Value Guide, Fyke	$18.95
4560	Collectible **Cats**, An Identification & Value Guide, Book II, Fyke	$19.95
1634	Collector's Ency. of **Figural & Novelty Salt & Pepper Shakers**, Davern	$19.95
2020	Collector's Ency. of Figural & Novelty **Salt & Pepper Shakers**, Vol. II, Davern	$19.95
2018	Collector's Encyclopedia of **Granite Ware**, Greguire	$24.95
3430	Collector's Encyclopedia of **Granite Ware**, Book II, Greguire	$24.95
4705	Collector's Guide to **Antique Radios**, 4th Ed., Bunis	$18.95
1916	Collector's Guide to **Art Deco**, Gaston	$14.95
3880	Collector's Guide to **Cigarette Lighters**, Flanagan	$17.95
4637	Collector's Guide to **Cigarette Lighters**, Book II, Flanagan	$17.95
1537	Collector's Guide to **Country Baskets**, Raycraft	$9.95
3966	Collector's Guide to **Inkwells**, Identification & Values, Badders	$18.95
3881	Collector's Guide to **Novelty Radios**, Bunis/Breed	$18.95
4652	Collector's Guide to **Transistor Radios**, 2nd Ed., Bunis	$16.95
4653	Collector's Guide to **TV Memorabilia**, 1960s–1970s, Davis/Morgan	$24.95
2276	**Decoys**, Kangas	$24.95
1629	**Doorstops**, Identification & Values, Bertoia	$9.95
4567	Figural **Napkin Rings**, Gottschalk & Whitson	$18.95
3968	**Fishing Lure** Collectibles, Murphy/Edmisten	$24.95
3817	**Flea Market Trader**, 10th Ed., Huxford	$12.95
3976	Foremost Guide to **Uncle Sam** Collectibles, Czulewicz	$24.95
4641	**Garage Sale & Flea Market Annual**, 4th Ed.	$19.95
3819	**General Store Collectibles**, Wilson	$24.95
4643	**Great American West** Collectibles, Wilson	$24.95
2215	Goldstein's **Coca-Cola** Collectibles	$16.95
3884	Huxford's Collectible **Advertising**, 2nd Ed.	$24.95
2216	**Kitchen Antiques**, 1790–1940, McNerney	$14.95
3321	Ornamental & Figural **Nutcrackers**, Rittenhouse	$16.95
2026	**Railroad** Collectibles, 4th Ed., Baker	$14.95
1632	**Salt & Pepper Shakers**, Guarnaccia	$9.95
1888	**Salt & Pepper Shakers** II, Identification & Value Guide, Book II, Guarnaccia	$14.95
2220	**Salt & Pepper Shakers** III, Guarnaccia	$14.95
3443	**Salt & Pepper Shakers** IV, Guarnaccia	$18.95
4555	**Schroeder's Antiques Price Guide**, 14th Ed., Huxford	$12.95
2096	**Silverplated Flatware**, Revised 4th Edition, Hagan	$14.95
1922	Standard **Old Bottle** Price Guide, Sellari	$14.95
4708	**Summers' Guide to Coca-Cola**	$19.95
3892	**Toy & Miniature Sewing Machines**, Thomas	$24.95
3828	Value Guide to **Advertising Memorabilia**, Summers	$18.95
3977	Value Guide to **Gas Station** Memorabilia, Summers & Priddy	$24.95
3444	**Wanted to Buy**, 5th Edition	$9.95

This is only a partial listing of the books on antiques that are available from Collector Books. All books are well illustrated and contain current values. Most of these books are available from your local bookseller, antique dealer, or public library. If you are unable to locate certain titles in your area, you may order by mail from COLLECTOR BOOKS, P.O. Box 3009, Paducah, KY 42002-3009. Customers with Visa or MasterCard may phone in orders from 7:00–5:00 CST, Monday–Friday, Toll Free 1-800-626-5420. Add $2.00 for postage for the first book ordered and $0.30 for each additional book. Include item number, title, and price when ordering. Allow 14 to 21 days for delivery.

Schroeder's
ANTIQUES
Price Guide

. . . is the #1 best-selling antiques & collectibles value guide on the market today, and here's why . . .

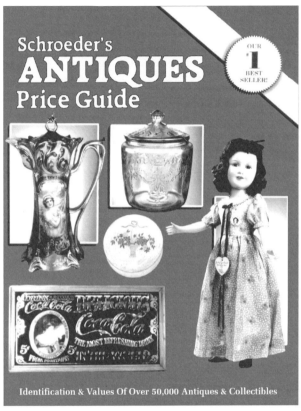

Schroeder's ANTIQUES Price Guide

OUR #1 BEST SELLER!

Identification & Values Of Over 50,000 Antiques & Collectibles

8½ x 11, 608 Pages, $12.95

• *More than 300 advisors, well-known dealers, and top-notch collectors work together with our editors to bring you accurate information regarding pricing and identification.*

• *More than 45,000 items in almost 500 categories are listed along with hundreds of sharp original photos that illustrate not only the rare and unusual, but the common, popular collectibles as well.*

• *Each large close-up shot shows important details clearly. Every subject is represented with histories and background information, a feature not found in any of our competitors' publications.*

• *Our editors keep abreast of newly developing trends, often adding several new categories a year as the need arises.*

If it merits the interest of today's collector, you'll find it in *Schroeder's*. And you can feel confident that the information we publish is up to date and accurate. Our advisors thoroughly check each category to spot inconsistencies, listings that may not be entirely reflective of market dealings, and lines too vague to be of merit. Only the best of the lot remains for publication.

Without doubt, you'll find
SCHROEDER'S ANTIQUES PRICE GUIDE
the only one to buy for
reliable information and values.

COLLECTOR BOOKS
A Division of Schroeder Publishing Co., Inc.